Threads of Time

Threads of Time

A Global History 400–1750

Sheena Coupe and Barbara Scanlan

Longman
New York

Threads of Time

Copyright © 1993 by Longman Publishing Group.
All rights reserved.
No part of this publication may be reproduced,
stored in a retrieval system, or transmitted
in any form or by any means, electronic, mechanical,
photocopying, recording, or otherwise,
without the prior permission of the publisher.

Longman, 10 Bank Street, White Plains, N.Y. 10606

Associated companies:
Longman Group Ltd., London
Longman Cheshire Pty., Melbourne
Longman Paul Pty., Auckland
Copp Clark Pitman, Toronto

Designed by R T J Klinkhamer
Illustrations by Alan Jane

History Begins   ISBN 0-8013-1044-X
                   ISBN 0-8013-1040-7 (pbk)
Threads of Time   ISBN 0-8013-1045-8
                   ISBN 0-8013-1041-5 (pbk)

1 2 3 4 5 6 7 8 9 10-VH-9695949392

Contents

1 The breakdown of empires   1

2 Anglo-Saxon England 19

3 The Middle Ages 36

4 China: a world apart 58

5 Japan: the 'walled garden' 77

6 Islam: religion and empire 95

7 East meets west: the crusades 113

8 The Renaissance 130

9 Venturing into unknown seas 143

10 The Spanish conquistadors in the New World 162

11 The Reformation 178

12 Two ruling families 190

13 Problems for the Stuarts 216

14 Colonisation of the New World 235

Acknowledgements 252
Index 254

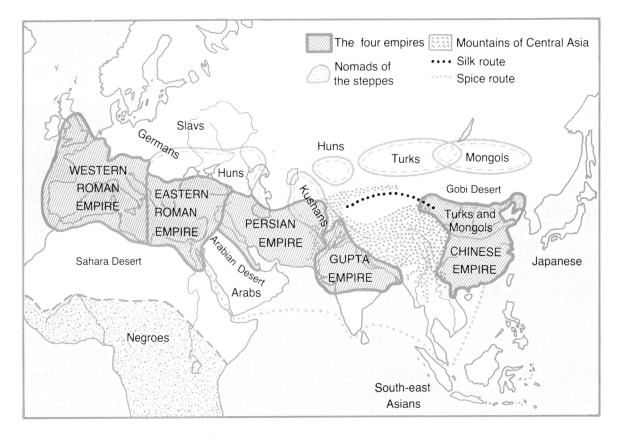

Fig. 1.1 The known world in 400 AD.

1

The breakdown of empires

IN THE YEAR 400 AD—that is, four hundred years after the birth of Christ—there were probably about 200 million people in the world. Today the world's population is around 4000 million. Of the 200 million people alive in the year 400, about 160 million lived in the shaded area shown in the map in Fig. 1.1. This was a belt of agricultural land which stretched from Europe across to China. The other 40 million people were scattered across different parts of the world—there were Indians in America, Aboriginal people in Australia, African tribes in the continent of Africa, and so on. Yet those who lived in the lands of the 'known world', as the area shown on the map in Fig. 1.1 was called, were often quite unaware of the existence of these other people. Instead, they believed tales of strange monsters and demons, gruesome sea-creatures and half-men, half-animals who were supposed to live in these faraway lands.

The map in Fig. 1.1 is an important one for you to study and understand, for it shows how the known world looked at the beginning of the period we shall be examining in this book.

From the map you can see that much of the known world in the year 400 was taken up by four large empires. Three of them—the Roman empire, the Persian empire and the Chinese empire—were at least 600 years old. The other, the Gupta empire in India, was very new, being founded only in 320. The people of these empires made up what they thought was the 'civilised' world. Each empire contained cities, towns and villages, farms, shops, schools, temples and churches. Their people wrote books, painted, sculpted, and designed and built fine buildings. They knew something of science, engineering and mathematics. They had governments and armies, laws and taxes, and accepted the rules and principles of organised religions.

Outside these four empires were people who lived quite different lives. The wildest and fiercest were the nomads, who moved with their herds from place to place in search of food and pasture. These tribes roamed the land known as the *steppes*, or grasslands, to the north of the four empires. There were Huns in the west, Turks in the centre and Mongols to the east, but because all the nomadic tribes were constantly on the move, they ranged throughout each other's territories, fighting for food and land when necessary. In the year 400 there were about four million nomads outside the four empires. Compared with the organised, settled lives of the people inside the empires, the lives of the nomads were bloodthirsty, disorganised and brutal.

To the north of the Roman empire lived another group of people, hemmed in by nomads like the Huns on one side and the border of the Roman empire on the other. These were the German tribes. When they were pushed by the Huns, who

Fig. 1.2 The home of a Hun family. Because the Huns were nomads, they lived in wagons like this which could be dragged from place to place by horses.

moved into their territory, they themselves pushed into the Roman empire. As a result of movements of people like the Huns and the Germans, the map of the known world in 500 looked very different from the map shown in Fig. 1.1.

This chapter examines two of the four empires—the Roman empire and the Gupta empire in India—to see what happened to each one in the century between 400 and 500. It looks, too, at the people who destroyed these empires and what they built in their place.

Rome and the barbarians

The Roman empire

The Roman empire, which began as a small city-state in the sixth century BC, was at its greatest two centuries after the birth of Christ. By then it controlled over 9 million square kilometres of land and contained more than 80 million people. You can see from the map in Fig. 1.3 that

the empire was shaped like a long hollow oval around the Mediterranean Sea.

Defending the empire was no easy task. Even the strong and well-disciplined army of the early empire had to fight hard to keep it intact. Because of its shape, the empire had long and sometimes isolated frontiers which were constantly threatened by raids from people outside the empire. The Roman emperors found that it was impossible for one ruler to defend the empire properly, so they began sharing power with their strongest military general. Attacks on the empire became more frequent after the year 200, and to make defence easier, the emperor Diocletian divided the empire into two sections. He ruled the eastern part from his capital at Nicomedia

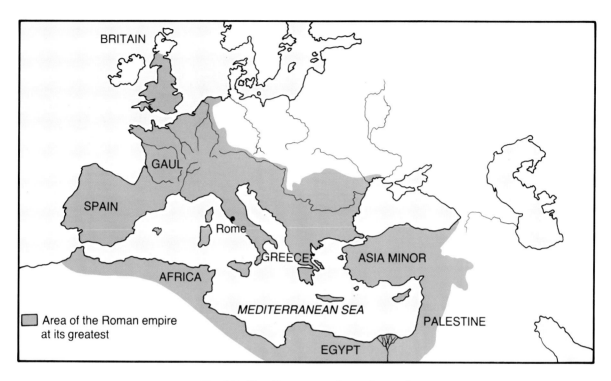

Fig. 1.3 The Roman empire at its peak.

Fig. 1.4 Hadrian's Wall was built on the orders of the emperor Hadrian between 122 and 130 AD. It was designed to keep the barbarian Scots out of Roman Britain. The wall ran for 160 kilometres from east to west. It was made of stone and earth and was over six metres high in some places. Along its length were a series of forts like the one on the left.

(now the city of Izmit in Turkey), while another emperor, Maximian, ruled the western empire from Milan in northern Italy. In 324 the emperor Constantine moved the capital of the eastern empire to an ancient city called Byzantium, which he renamed Constantinople, and reunited the empire for another forty years. However, it was no longer strong enough to survive as a single, united force and in 395 was permanently divided into western and eastern empires. The map in Fig. 1.1 shows how the division was made.

By the fourth century, the western Roman empire was almost 700 years old. It was running down. The emperors were no longer the strong, determined men who had built the empire. Their authority was not accepted—increasingly, army generals murdered emperors and seized power for themselves. Between 211 and 284 there were twenty-three Roman emperors, of whom twenty were murdered by their enemies!

While their rulers were fighting each other, the people of the empire found it more and more difficult to earn a living. Taxes were so high that many farmers were forced to leave their land. Trade declined, and as people became poorer, they could not afford to buy as many goods. Businessmen and merchants went bankrupt. Plague swept through parts of the empire, killing thousands of people. The rich lived in idle luxury and the poor were entertained by degrading spectacles in which men killed each other or were killed by wild animals.

The Roman army, once the strongest and most feared in the world, was becoming weaker. Generals, as we have seen, were more interested in grabbing power for themselves than in serving the empire well. Many citizens became soldiers only because they could find no other work, but even so, not enough Romans were willing to serve in the army. To fill the ranks, the Romans brought in men from outside the empire—'barbarians'—to defend the long frontiers. As they fought in the Roman army, these soldiers learned important military skills—skills that many would later use against their former masters.

Time to understand

The following account of a gladiatorial contest was written by a Roman philosopher called Seneca. Read it carefully and answer the questions below.

> I happened to go to one of these shows at the time of the lunch-hour interlude, expecting there to be some light and witty entertainment then, some respite for the purpose of affording people's eyes a rest from human blood. Far from it. All the earlier contests were charity in comparison. The nonsense is dispensed with now: what we have now is murder pure and simple. The combatants have nothing to protect them; their whole bodies are exposed to the blows; every thrust they launch gets home. A great many spectators prefer this to the ordinary matches and even to the special, popular demand ones. And quite naturally. There are no helmets and no shields repelling the weapons. What is the point of armour? Or of skill? All that sort of thing just makes the death slower in coming. In the morning men are thrown to the lions and the bears: but it is the spectators they are thrown to in the lunch hour. The spectators insist that each on killing his man shall be thrown against another to be killed in his turn; and the eventual victor is reserved by them for some other form of butchery; the only exit for the contestants is death.

1 Why did Seneca go to the show at lunchtime?
2 What did he mean by saying that 'all the earlier contests were charity' compared to the one he saw?
3 Why was this contest more brutal than other contests?
4 Why do you think the crowd preferred this kind of contest?
5 What did Seneca mean by saying that 'the only exit for the contestants is death'?
6 Do you think contests like this are a sign of an unhealthy society? Why?
7 Are there any spectacles like this in our society?

The barbarians

The word 'barbarian', which we still use to mean someone who is ignorant and destructive, was first used by the Greeks. It originally meant 'foreigner' but, because the Greeks and later the Romans did not approve of foreigners, the word 'barbarian' soon came to be applied to all those foreigners outside the Roman empire who, in the Roman view, were ignorant and savage.

According to the Romans, there were many barbarian peoples. In Africa were the dark-skinned Moors; in western Asia were the Arabs and Persians; on the steppes were the Huns, Bulgars, Turks and Mongols. Closer to home were the Germans, some of whom lived in the land just across the frontier, the Celts of Ireland and the Slavs of eastern Europe. Of all these peoples, the Germans were the closest and most important, for it was they who finally broke through and destroyed the Roman empire.

The German tribes

Most of what we know about the German tribes comes from a pamphlet written by a Roman historian called Tacitus at the end of the first century AD. At that time the Germans were changing from being nomadic herders and were becoming settled farmers. Although some of their land was cleared and sown with grain, much of it, according to Tacitus, was still 'covered with forests and filthy swamps'. There were no large cities, although small villages were scattered about, in which up to a hundred families might live. The people of several villages formed a *folk*. The diagram in Fig. 1.5 shows how the people in each *folk* were organised, from the nobles at the top of the social ladder to the slaves at the bottom.

Unlike the Romans, the Germans did not have an elaborate political system. There was no emperor to control all the people. Instead, each *folk* arranged meetings in which all freemen listened to the suggestions of their leaders and either agreed by clashing their spears against their shields or disagreed by hooting and shouting. At first the German leaders were chosen because of their skill in warfare. As time passed, however, leaders were selected only from certain noble families and some tribes were ruled by kings whose sons automatically became kings after them.

This was a man's world. When a couple married, the man gave his wife gifts of oxen, horses, swords, spears and shields. In return, the woman presented weapons to her husband. This showed that she was prepared to share his life of work and danger, in peace and in war. Some women served as priestesses, but most spent their days tending farms, cattle or pigs, weaving linen or wool, making pots from clay and caring for children.

Despite their different customs and societies, the Germans and Romans generally lived quite peacefully as neighbours. They sometimes warred against each other, but they often inter-married, too. One Roman emperor, for instance, married the daughter of a German tribal king. The sons of German kings were sometimes educated in Roman schools and, as we have seen, many Germans volunteered as soldiers in the Roman army in return for regular pay or some land on which to farm. The Germans were not interested in overthrowing the Roman empire and the Romans did not see them as a serious threat, despite the occasional raiding parties which attacked Roman forts along the frontiers. If trouble did break out, the Roman legions along the border were strong enough to stamp it out before it got out of hand.

By the fourth century, however, this situation had changed. The Roman empire was becoming weaker and its army was no longer all-powerful. The traditional methods of German farming were not producing enough food. Hungry tribesmen seized the land of their weaker neighbours, only to have their own land taken by stronger tribes. At the same time, the Huns and other nomadic tribes were moving westward, also searching for new land. The Germans were squeezed between the advancing Huns on one side and the borders of the Roman empire on the other. Something had to give.

Nobles

These families were renowned for skill in battle. Often the nobles gathered a band of supporters called *comitatus*, who served them loyally in peace and war.

Free men and women

Most tribespeople were free. Men were able to take part in assemblies and to judge at courts. They could own land and slaves.

Former slaves

These people had been freed by their masters. They were not allowed to take part in assemblies or courts and had very low standing in the village.

Slaves

These were prisoners of war, men who had lost their freedom by gambling, the children of slaves, debtors and slaves bought from other tribes. Although they had no land of their own, they often worked on their master's land, paying him with food, clothes or animals.

Fig. 1.5 Social ladder of the German tribes.

Time to understand

The diagram in Fig. 1.6 shows the plan of a Roman signal station in Yorkshire, England. Here is some more information about this fort:
—The wall was 1.25 metres thick.
—The watchtower was nearly fifteen metres square, with walls 1.5 metres thick at the base.
—The watchtower was about thirty metres high.
1 From the plan and the information on p. 7, try to draw a picture of this Roman signal station. What would it have been used for?
2 Why do you think a well, hearth and hand mill were built inside the wall?
3 How useful do you think the ditch would have been in stopping invaders?
4 Animal bones and pottery have been found inside the walled section of this fort. These suggest that the guards on duty there lived at the fort. What sort of life do you think they

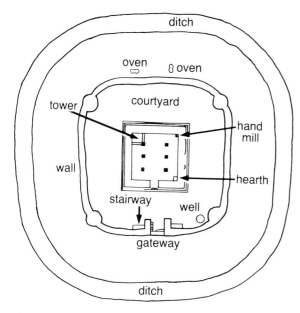

Fig. 1.6 Plan of a Roman signal station in Yorkshire, England.

would have led? How would they have filled in their days? What would have been their main jobs?

5 The ruins of this fort were discovered in 1918. Read how one of the excavators described a particularly gruesome find:

In the south-east corner, we made discoveries which can only be described as sensational. A short, thick-set man had fallen across the smouldering fire of an open hearth, probably after having been stabbed in the back. His skeleton lay face downwards . . . Another skeleton, that of a taller man, lay also face downwards, near the feet of the first, his head pointing south-west. Beneath him was the skeleton of a large, powerful dog, its head against the man's throat, its paws across his shoulders—surely a grim record of a thrilling drama, perhaps the dog one of the defenders, the man an intruder.

An examination of the skull of the man lying across the fire showed that he had been hit several times across the head by a sword and then speared by a sword or spear. Four other skulls were found in the signal station: one on the floor of the tower and three inside the well.

Use all this information to write a story about

what might have happened to explain these violent events.

The barbarian assault and the fall of Rome

We have seen that by the year 400 the Roman empire was weak and disorganised. It may have struggled along for many more years had it not been for the raids and attacks of the tribes who lived outside its borders.

The barbarian raids and invasions which resulted in the fall of the Roman empire were complicated and confused. At the time, people were unaware of the significance of particular events and attacks, although it was obvious to all that the times were changing. Looking back, however, we can see that some tribes, some leaders and some events were more important than others. The series of maps on the next page shows the movements of these more important tribes and what happened to them as, wave after wave, they attacked the western Roman empire.

Time to understand

1 One way we can make events clearer is by drawing a time-line, on which the events can be listed in the right *chronological order*, that is, the order in which they happened.

Under the heading, 'Barbarians attack the Roman empire', draw a time-line. On it, record the most important dates in the series of maps in Figs 1.7–1.10. Next to each date, write briefly what happened in that year. The first one has been done for you below.

Barbarians attack the Roman empire

374 ▮ Huns begin moving into Europe
375

2 What does the word 'vandal' mean today? How do you think this word came to be used

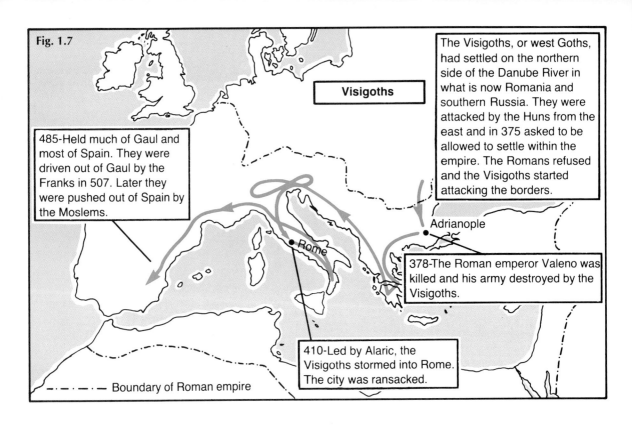

Fig. 1.7

Visigoths

The Visigoths, or west Goths, had settled on the northern side of the Danube River in what is now Romania and southern Russia. They were attacked by the Huns from the east and in 375 asked to be allowed to settle within the empire. The Romans refused and the Visigoths started attacking the borders.

485-Held much of Gaul and most of Spain. They were driven out of Gaul by the Franks in 507. Later they were pushed out of Spain by the Moslems.

Adrianople

378-The Roman emperor Valeno was killed and his army destroyed by the Visigoths.

410-Led by Alaric, the Visigoths stormed into Rome. The city was ransacked.

Rome

— · — · — Boundary of Roman empire

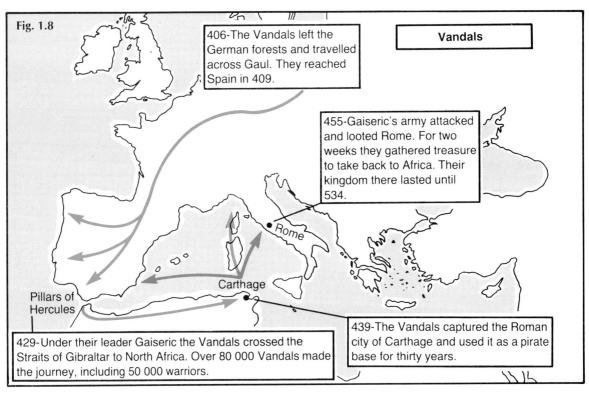

Fig. 1.8

Vandals

406-The Vandals left the German forests and travelled across Gaul. They reached Spain in 409.

455-Gaiseric's army attacked and looted Rome. For two weeks they gathered treasure to take back to Africa. Their kingdom there lasted until 534.

Rome

Carthage

Pillars of Hercules

429-Under their leader Gaiseric the Vandals crossed the Straits of Gibraltar to North Africa. Over 80 000 Vandals made the journey, including 50 000 warriors.

439-The Vandals captured the Roman city of Carthage and used it as a pirate base for thirty years.

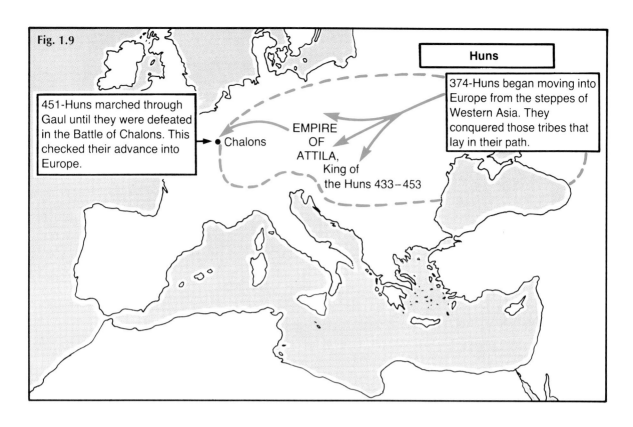

Fig. 1.9

Huns

374-Huns began moving into Europe from the steppes of Western Asia. They conquered those tribes that lay in their path.

451-Huns marched through Gaul until they were defeated in the Battle of Chalons. This checked their advance into Europe.

Chalons

EMPIRE
OF
ATTILA,
King of
the Huns 433–453

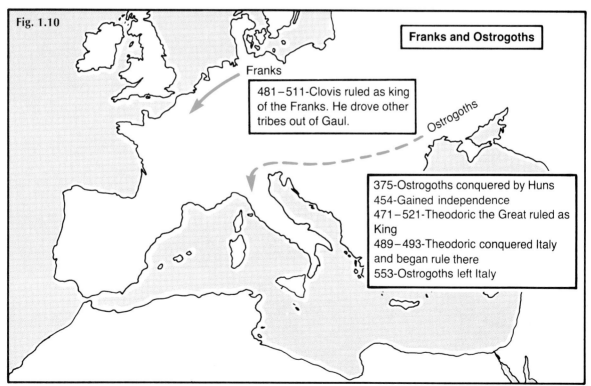

Fig. 1.10

Franks and Ostrogoths

Franks

Ostrogoths

481–511-Clovis ruled as king of the Franks. He drove other tribes out of Gaul.

375-Ostrogoths conquered by Huns
454-Gained independence
471–521-Theodoric the Great ruled as King
489–493-Theodoric conquered Italy and began rule there
553-Ostrogoths left Italy

9

in its present meaning? Does this give you any clues about the behaviour of the Vandal tribe?

3 After their two-week looting of Rome in 455, the Vandals sailed back to Africa with the treasures they had stolen. On the way one of their ships sank with its precious cargo. It has never been discovered. Imagine that a modern diving team had just found evidence of the ship and its cargo. Write a newspaper article about the discovery. What kinds of things might be found?

The new kingdoms

The map in Fig. 1.11 shows Europe at the end of the invasion period. Compare it with the map in Fig. 1.1 at the beginning of this chapter. You can see that instead of one large western Roman empire, the land was now divided into a number of smaller kingdoms, each controlled and settled by a barbarian tribe. The Huns remained nomads and never formed a lasting kingdom. Today, Europe is divided into several countries—Spain, France, Italy, Germany, Russia and others. The borders of these countries were being established by the fifth century, according to the amount of land claimed and settled by different barbarian tribes. 'Frankland', for example, became France, while the land occupied by the Visigoths is today's Spain.

The old world had died. It may have died anyway, even if the Roman empire had not been invaded by its neighbours. But not everything from the past was destroyed. The Christian Church, which grew steadily during the later part of the Roman empire and throughout the invasion period, survived. Many barbarians had been converted to Christianity and in their kingdoms some of the old learning and art were preserved

Fig. 1.11 Europe in 500 AD.

10

if they were linked with the teachings of the Church. Alaric, the leader of the Visigoths, was a Christian, and Clovis, the Frankish king, was converted in 496. 'Worship that which you have burned; burn that which you have worshipped', he was advised upon his baptism.

Time to understand

Although very few barbarians could read or write, they were fine craftspeople, and we can get some idea of their cultures by looking carefully at the things they made. Many of these things were buried in graves or in treasure hoards which were designed to be used by dead kings or nobles in the afterlife.

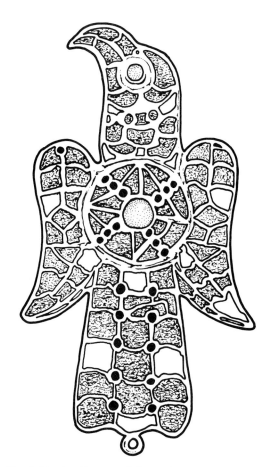

Fig. 1.12 An Ostrogoth brooch.

Fig. 1.12 shows an ornamental brooch that was used to pin a cloak together. It was made by an Ostrogoth in the fifth century. The brooch is made of gold and it once had precious stones all over it.
1 What animal does the brooch represent?
2 Is it a realistic picture of this animal?
3 This brooch was made of gold and jewels. What skills would the maker have needed in order to make the brooch?
4 Use another living creature as a model and try to design a brooch that resembles that in Fig. 1.12.

The eastern Roman empire

You will remember that by the year 395 the Roman empire had been divided into an eastern and a western part. The western empire, as we have seen, had been destroyed by the beginning of the fifth century. What, then, was happening in the eastern empire?

Like the west, the eastern empire was threatened and attacked by barbarian tribes. Unlike the west, however, it was able to withstand these onslaughts.

Constantinople, the capital of the eastern empire, was well protected by sea and built like a fort. While Rome grew weaker, Constantinople became stronger. It was a prosperous trading centre where goods from Asia were as common as those from Europe. In art and architecture, too, ideas from east and west joined to create a distinctive new style. This was called 'Byzantine' after the original name of Constantinople—Byzantium. The empire itself, as time passed, came to be known as the Byzantine empire.

The strongest early ruler of this eastern empire was the emperor Justinian, who held power from 527 to 565. Justinian dreamed of regaining all the land which had once belonged to Rome. His armies conquered most of north Africa, southern Italy and part of Spain. Within the next hundred years, however, this land was again lost.

Justinian was a strong and respected emperor. He was a great builder and during his reign new public buildings and churches were built

Fig. 1.13 Constantinople, an impression by a sixteenth century artist.

throughout the empire. His most lasting monument is the church of Santa Sophia in Constantinople, in which the architectural styles of Europe and Asia are blended to create a magnificent building. Justinian's other great achievement was his summary of Roman law which, before his time, was written down in hundreds of different manuscripts. Justinian needed this summary in order to make new laws for his empire, but its importance is greater than that. The Roman law was fair and thorough. When written down by Justinian's scribes, it provided a ready-made system of law for newly developing societies. It was used right throughout Europe and remains an important part of our legal system today.

Justinian died in 565, but his empire lived on, at times strong and powerful, at times weak and threatened. It was attacked often and by many different groups. Much of its land was lost in battle. There were good emperors and bad, civil wars and changing fortunes. Despite all this, the Byzantine empire managed to survive until 1453 when Constantinople was attacked and overrun by Turkish invaders. It had lasted a thousand years longer than the Roman empire in the west and had contributed a distinctive style of art and architecture to our civilisation.

Time to understand

Look again at the painting of Constantinople in Fig. 1.13.
1 Can you find the church of Santa Sophia? How important do you think this building was in the lives of the people of Constantinople?
2 Where is the Hippodrome, or sporting arena? Can you suggest what it was used for? Why do you think the tall towers were built there?
3 How many other churches can you find?
4 How would you describe the houses shown in the map? Do you think all the houses in Constantinople looked like this?

5 As you can see from the map, Constantinople was surrounded by a wall. Can you suggest why? How effective do you think this would have been in keeping out invaders?

6 Why do you think some parts of the map are drawn sideways?

7 Think about your town or suburb. Try to draw a map of part of it in the style of the map of Constantinople.

8 Why was this city's name changed from Byzantium to Constantinople? Today the city has another name. Can you find out what it is? Of which country is it the capital?

Fig. 1.14 The church of Santa Sophia, which was completed in 537, is Justinian's finest memorial. The central dome is thirty-two metres across. This Byzantine style of architecture was copied and adapted in churches in Italy and eastern Europe.

The Gupta empire in India

You will remember from the map in Fig. 1.1 at the beginning of this chapter that in 400 AD northern India was controlled by a ruling family, or *dynasty*, called the Guptas.

India today is a united, single country ruled from its capital at Delhi. However, for most of its history, India was divided into small kingdoms, each with its own ruler or prince. For thousands of years, invaders—including the nomadic Huns and Mongols from the steppes—attacked from the north-west plains across what is now the country of Pakistan. Empires rose, became strong, expanded their control, then fell to a more powerful group of invaders. Within India, kingdoms warred against each other, seized each other's land and forced weak rulers to accept the rule of the strong.

The Guptas were just one of the ruling dynasties that came to power during India's long history. Their empire spread over northern India from 320 until about 640 but their influence spread more widely over the rest of India and parts of Asia. During the Gupta reign, India enjoyed what could be called a 'golden age' of civilisation.

The Gupta rulers

The founder of the Gupta dynasty was Chandra, an unimportant prince from the Ganges River area in northern India. In 320 Chandra married a princess from a rich and powerful family—a move which increased his own power enor-

13

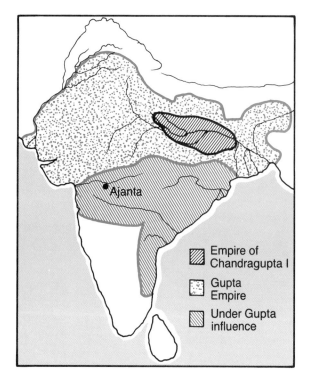

Fig. 1.15 Gupta control in India.

were at their height. This was the golden age of Indian civilisation at exactly the same time as the barbarian tribes were hammering at the door of the decadent and run-down Roman empire.

Life in Gupta times

There were several large towns in Gupta India, but most people lived in small villages, as most Indians do today. During the Gupta period the number of villages grew. Iron axes made it much easier to chop down trees and build houses, so farms were started on land which had previously been unused forest. Farmers used teams of oxen to plough their land and then planted crops of wheat, barley, rice and vegetables. They rotated their crops and left some of the land unplanted each year to make sure that the soil did not lose all its richness. Sometimes they irrigated their land by digging channels and ditches to carry water from rivers.

Craftspeople and merchants lived in the cities and towns. Ports were dotted along India's coast and from them Indian ships sailed to Africa, the Persian Gulf, South-east Asia and China, carrying spices, perfume, ivory and precious stones. In return, ships from Greece and Rome, Persia, Arabia and China called at the Indian ports, bringing goods that were then taken overland to the rest of the country. One import was slaves from Africa, bought by the Indians from Arab traders to work in the villages and towns.

The golden age

During the reign of Chandragupta II, when government was stable and those ruled by the Guptas felt secure, art, literature, music and science flourished. Most people, of course, did not concern themselves with such things, being far too busy earning a living. But for those who were able and willing to turn their attention to science or the arts, the Guptas were encouraging and helpful rulers. Chandragupta II, for example, supported artists and writers in his palace and encouraged other noblemen to do likewise.

mously. He strengthened control over his own land and began attacking and claiming the land of neighbouring rulers. At this time, Chandra took on the name of *gupta* or 'protected one'.

Chandragupta lived for ten years after establishing his dynasty. The task of keeping and expanding the family's power was left to his son, Samudragupta, who ruled for more than forty years. Princes who would not accept his authority were attacked and defeated in battle. Many were allowed to keep their land in exchange for regular payments, or *tributes*, to Samudragupta. These gifts of gold, silver, silk, jewels and precious metals helped to make the Guptas very wealthy.

Chandragupta II, the third Gupta emperor, ruled from about 375 until about 415. A strong and powerful ruler, Chandragupta expanded the empire until it stretched from coast to coast across northern India. He also arranged marriages between members of his family and princes and princesses from other ruling families, to strengthen Gupta power further. It was during Chandragupta's reign that Indian art and culture

The greatest writer of Gupta times was Kalidasa, who has been called 'the Shakespeare of India'. He helped to restore Sanskrit, the ancient Hindu language, which became the official language of the Gupta court. Kalidasa's most important work was a long poetic play called *Sakuntala*. He and other poets read their works at court.

In science, too, the Gupta period was a golden age. Indian scientists learned from the Greeks and the Arabs and added their own ideas and theories. An astronomer named Aryabhata believed that the earth was a sphere—at a time when Europeans were sure it was flat and sailors were terrified of long voyages in case they fell off its edge. Aryabhata and others even suggested that the earth moved round the sun—an idea that was not accepted in Europe for hundreds of years.

Indian mathematicians devised the decimal system of numbers, which spread to Egypt in the 500s. A thousand years later it was adopted in parts of Europe. They also worked out a system of algebra many years before this was developed in Europe.

The richest collection of Gupta art was discovered in the Ajanta caves of western India. These thirty caves had been carefully excavated to create Buddhist temples as places of worship and retreat for holy men. They were intricately decorated with beautiful wall paintings. First, the rough cave surface was covered with a layer of clay or cow dung. When this was smoothed down, it was coated with fine white clay or gypsum, and it was on this surface that the paintings were done. The paintings themselves tell us a lot about the life of the wealthy people in Gupta times. One of the paintings from the Ajanta caves is shown in Fig. 1.17 on the next page.

Fig. 1.16 The exterior of the Ajanta caves.

Fig. 1.17 Part of the wall paintings inside the Ajanta caves.

The fall of the Guptas

The Gupta empire was at its height during the reign of Chandragupta II. His successor, Kumara-gupta, who ruled from 415 to about 455, was not as strong a leader. During his reign tribes of Huns raided the northern borders of the empire. At first the Gupta soldiers were able to resist these attacks, but in the reign of Skandagupta, the next Gupta emperor, the Hun raids became fiercer and more frequent. Later emperors could no longer repel the attacks and the Huns poured over the border into India just as they did in Europe.

The Gupta empire was shattered. Although the Gupta dynasty continued ruling for many more years, it controlled only small areas of India. The Guptas were no more important than other princes and rulers. India remained a disunited country and in about 700 was invaded once again, this time by Moslems.

Time to understand

An important source of information about Gupta India was the journal of Fa Hsien, a Buddhist monk from China who travelled to India to study the scriptures and literature of his religion. Fa Hsien was in India from 401 until 410 and as he travelled from place to place he recorded his impressions of Indian life.

The passage below was written by Fa Hsien. Read it carefully and answer the questions that follow it.

> To the south of this, the country is called Madya Dêsa (i.e. the middle country). The climate of this region is exceedingly equable, there is neither frost nor snow. The inhabitants are prosperous and happy. There are no Boards of Population and Revenue. Those only who farm the Royal demesnes, pay a portion of the produce as rent. Nor are they bound to remain in possession longer than they like. The King in the administration of justice, inflicts no corporal punishment, but each culprit is fined in money according to the gravity of his offence; and even in cases where the culprit has been guilty of repeated attempts to excite rebellion, they restrict themselves to cutting off his right hand. The chief officers of the king have all alloted revenues. The people of this country kill no living creature nor do they drink intoxicating liquors . . .. In this country they do not keep swine or fowls, they do not deal in living animals, nor are there shambles or wine shops round their markets. They use shells for money in their traffic.

1 Who was the ruler of Gupta India when this passage was written?
2 Can you explain the meaning of these words and phrases?
   a equable
   b Royal demesnes
   c corporal punishment
   d gravity of an offence
   e to excite rebellion
   f alloted revenues
   g intoxicating liquors
   h shambles
3 Make a list of the things Fa Hsien liked about Gupta India.

4 Did Fa Hsien approve of eating meat? How can you tell?

5 What do you think would have been the job of Boards of Population and Revenue?

6 Imagine that a stranger from another country came to your town. What do you think would be his or her main impressions? Write a paragraph or two describing what you think would most strike a stranger about the appearance and customs of your town.

How do we know?

Our information about the fall of Rome, the barbarian kingdoms and the Byzantine empire comes from many sources. Throughout this chapter you have already seen and studied several *pictures* and *paintings* from the period. You have also examined some *written records*. These tell us a great deal about how people lived, what they wore, how they looked, what their towns and cities were like, and how they understood the world. Another important source of information about this period in history are *archaeological discoveries*.

The map in Fig. 1.18 plots the discoveries of two archaeological relics—the cauldrons or metal

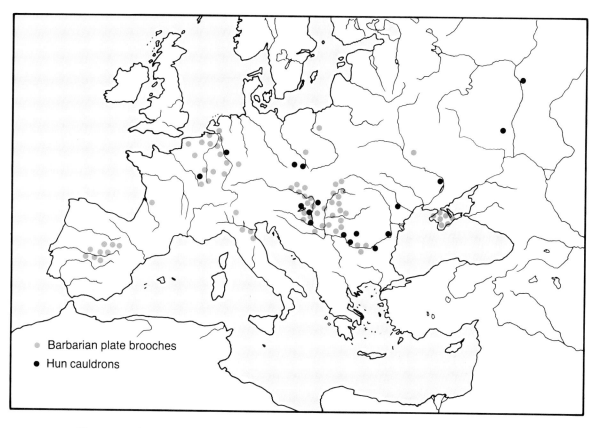

- Barbarian plate brooches
- Hun cauldrons

Fig. 1.18 The distribution of barbarian brooches and Hun cauldrons in Europe.

stewing pots carried by Huns on their raids across Europe, and the decorated metal brooches with which barbarians pinned their cloaks together. Use the map, the pictures and what you have read in this chapter to answer the questions below.

1 In which direction were the Huns moving? In which direction were the barbarians moving? Were these two movements linked? How?

2 Compare this map with a map of modern Europe. In which of today's countries have the greatest numbers of cauldrons and brooches been found?

3 Why do you think the Huns left some of their cauldrons behind? Do you think they might have been too heavy to carry?

4 Why do you think so many barbarian brooches were left behind? Would they have been easy to lose?

5 Why have the barbarian brooches been discovered much further west than the Hun cauldrons? Which German tribe would have left the brooches found in the most western part of the map? (*clue*: look back to the maps in Figs 1.7–1.10)

6 Look carefully at the places where the cauldrons and brooches have been found. Then write three or four sentences about what these discoveries tell you about the movements of the barbarians and the Huns. Pay particular attention to what happened around the rivers shown on the map.

7 Does this map prove that cauldrons and brooches were left *only* at the places marked? Why?

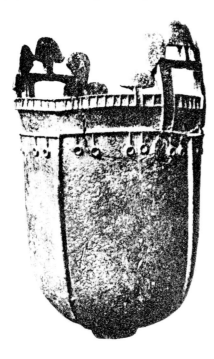

Fig. 1.19 A Hun cauldron or stewing pot.

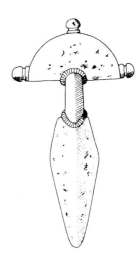

Fig. 1.20 A barbarian's plate brooch.

18

2

Anglo-Saxon England

IN CHAPTER ONE you learned how barbarian tribes invaded the western Roman empire, pushing against the frontiers until they collapsed and destroying what had been the world's most powerful empire. This chapter examines how this happened in England. It looks at the way barbarian tribes—the Angles, Saxons and Jutes—invaded England, the battles they won and lost, the kind of society they established and how they adapted to life in their new home.

Throughout Europe other barbarian tribes were also adjusting to more settled lives, and what happened in Anglo-Saxon England is just one example of this general change. For Australians it is an important example because the Anglo-Saxon period laid the foundations of many of the traditions and customs of Britain. Hundreds of years later, when a British colony was set up in New South Wales, it was natural that these customs and traditions were brought by the first settlers to their new homeland.

The coming of the Anglo-Saxons

The Anglo-Saxons were the third main group of people to invade England. More than a thousand years earlier the first wave of invaders, the Celts, began settling in Britain from their homelands in Europe. Then, in 55 BC, Julius Caesar led the first Roman attack on the island. Although the Celts, now called 'Britons', fought bravely against the Roman invasion, they proved no match for the strong and well-armed Roman armies.

The map in Fig. 2.1 shows the areas of Europe from which the Anglo-Saxons, the third wave of invaders, came. Although the tribes have different names—Angles, Saxons and Jutes—they were, in fact, closely related people from the marshy plains of Germany and southern Denmark. Some were farmers, others were warriors and pirates whose fierce sea raids struck terror into those they attacked.

From the year 200 onwards, these people made crossings to Britain in their narrow longboats. The voyage was hard and dangerous and often the thirty or forty warriors on board were swamped as the seas broke over their low rowboat. They made these perilous journeys for several reasons. Sometimes bands of warriors were called in by Roman generals in Britain to help defend the country from the attacks of the Picts and Scots in the north. Sometimes they were looking for new and better land in which their growing numbers could settle. Sometimes they were simply in search of plunder.

While the Roman empire was strong and its soldiers in Britain were loyal and obedient, these Anglo-Saxon raids could be beaten back. By 400, however, the empire was fighting for its life, soldiers were being called back to help defend it

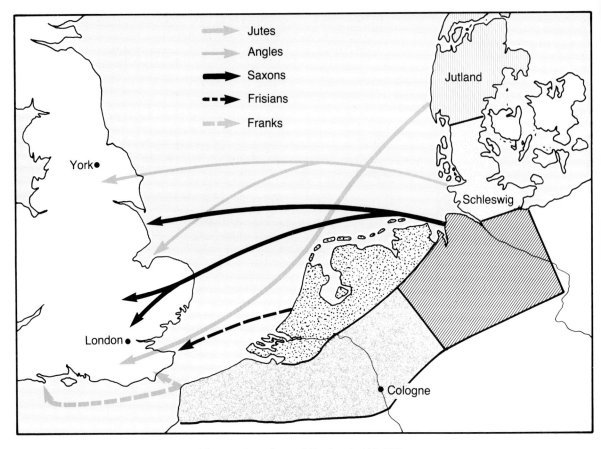

Fig. 2.1 Invaders of England, 400–500.

and the forts and signal stations that had been built to keep the barbarians out of Britain were falling into ruin. In 410 the emperor Honorius wrote to the rulers of Britain's main cities, telling them that in future they would have to fend for themselves; no longer could they rely on the Roman empire to protect them.

Without a central government, power fell into the hands of a number of local or regional leaders, or warlords. They were more concerned with fighting each other than with uniting to defend Britain against enemies from across the Channel. Indeed, one warlord, Vortigern, who controlled much of southern England, promised part of his land to Saxon fighters in return for their help in defeating his enemies in England. Under their leaders, the brothers Hengest and Horsa, the Saxons fought for a time for Vortigern. Then, when their numbers were strong enough, they turned against him, overran

his armies and took much of his land for themselves. From this base they were able to move further into England, sometimes conquering British leaders, sometimes simply setting up their villages and farms where they found unused land.

Other Anglo-Saxon groups landed along the English coast, sailed up the rivers or marched along the roads the Romans had built. Sometimes they arrived peacefully; sometimes they settled only after bitter conflict. The Britons did not give in without a fight, although their towns and villages were often burnt to the ground and many were captured as slaves. Some fled west into Wales and Cornwall and in about 500 a leader called Aurelianus organised troops to fight the invaders.

This resistance was carried on by Artorius, who is believed to be the legendary King Arthur of folk tales. Huge earthen mounds or dykes were built to try and repel the invaders, but by this time they were too strong to be pushed back. By the year 600 the Anglo-Saxons had conquered about half of England, including all the southern part.

In the early 600s there were seven Anglo-Saxon kingdoms, each ruled by a king and ready to fight its neighbours if attacked. By 800 these seven kingdoms had merged into three—Northumbria, Mercia and Wessex. By the year 900 much of England was controlled by King Alfred, the king of Wessex. You can read more about this man and his battles against the Danes, the next group of invaders, later in this chapter.

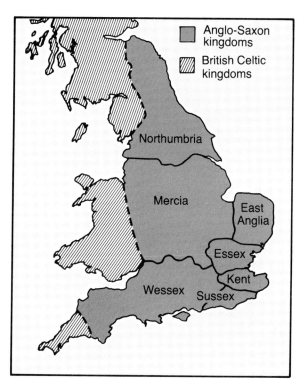

Fig. 2.2 The divison of England, early 600s.

Time to understand

1 Fig. 2.3 shows the kind of longboat in which the Anglo-Saxons crossed to England. Imagine you were one of the crew of an Anglo-Saxon raiding party. Explain what risks and dangers you faced on your voyage to England and why you were prepared to make such a perilous journey.

2 King Arthur has become one of England's best known folk heroes. What does the term 'folk hero' mean? What kind of people become folk heroes? Find some books about King Arthur in your library and read a few of the legends about him and his knights of the round table.

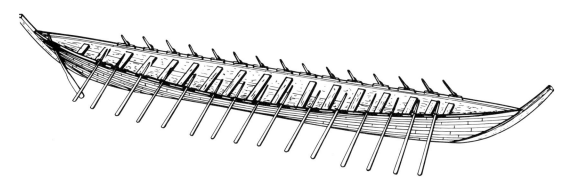

Fig. 2.3 A Saxon boat. It was 26 metres long and less than 4 metres wide, with neither sail nor mast.

Kings and their subjects

Anglo-Saxon fighting men who led successful raiding parties often set themselves up as local kings when they settled down in Britain. Some even forged family trees to prove that they were descended from the Anglo-Saxons' king of the gods, Woden.

The diagram in Fig. 2.4 shows how Anglo-Saxon society was organised. You can see that it was arranged like a pyramid, with the king at the top, his powerful nobles and advisers just underneath, then the wealthy freemen and the craftsmen. Near the bottom of the pyramid were the serfs or peasants who were poor and powerless. Below them were slaves who could be sold

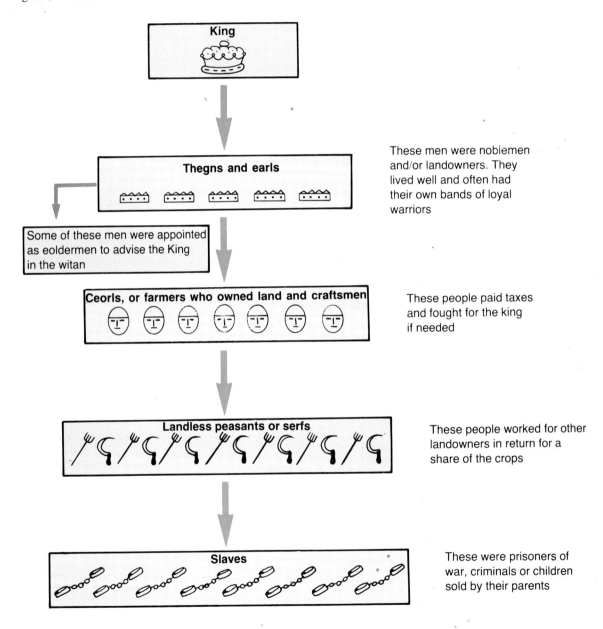

King

Thegns and earls

These men were noblemen and/or landowners. They lived well and often had their own bands of loyal warriors

Some of these men were appointed as eoldermen to advise the King in the witan

Ceorls, or farmers who owned land and craftsmen

These people paid taxes and fought for the king if needed

Landless peasants or serfs

These people worked for other landowners in return for a share of the crops

Slaves

These were prisoners of war, criminals or children sold by their parents

Fig. 2.4 The Anglo-Saxon social hierarchy.

or traded by their masters and who had no rights at all. This system of social organisation is called a *hierarchy*.

The king's most powerful thegns and eorls were appointed to his council, or *witan*. They were called eoldermen. This group of men advised the king and decided who his successor would be.

Village life

The illustration in Fig. 2.6 on the next page shows what an Anglo-Saxon village may have looked like. Most Anglo-Saxons lived their lives in villages that were probably similar to this. How they lived depended very much on whether they were rich or poor.

Each village was a complete community and most of the things the villagers needed could be produced within the village. Each household had a strip of land that was used to grow crops— barley, perhaps, or oats, wheat or rye—and the rest of the land was shared by all for timber-cutting or raising sheep, cattle or pigs. Village craftsmen tanned hides to make leather for clothes or made tools and ornaments from iron bought from travelling pedlars.

Men and women were both expected to work very hard. Men cut timber, built houses or pushed the heavy ploughs that turned woodland into farmland. Women's tasks included milking and caring for the animals, spinning, weaving, brewing, cooking and preserving meat with salt. The day began at dawn and the main meal was eaten at about three in the afternoon. At dusk

Fig. 2.5 A Saxon house. This hut measures 6.5 metres by 4 metres. The frame is made of saplings and thatched with reeds or turf. Inside is a loom for weaving cloth, broken cooking pots and animal bones. There are no windows.

Fig. 2.6 An Anglo-Saxon village.

the villagers returned to their tiny huts, miserable rectangular wooden buildings huddled together for safety. Often a pit was dug in the middle of the hut to make the interior of the hut larger and more comfortable.

You can see from Fig. 2.7 that the homes of the thegns and eorls were much grander than those of the other villagers. Made of logs, they were larger and more sturdy. Inside were benches and long trestle tables with a roaring fire in the centre and walls hung with shields and weapons. At the end of the day, the thegns would sometimes hold feasts, at which plenty of food was eaten and large amounts of mead were drunk while the men and women listened to story-tellers or told stories themselves.

Time to understand

Using the diagram in Fig. 2.8 and the picture of a villager's hut in Fig. 2.5 as guides, make a model

Fig. 2.7 Inside a thegn's home.

of a Saxon house. Make the framework of twigs and sticks. The frame can be covered with a mixture of twigs and clay and the roof thatched with straw. The door was kept open during the day to let in light and covered with an animal skin at night. You can use a piece of leather, vinyl or material for the door of your model.

Town life

Although Anglo-Saxon towns were small and primitive by our standards, they were very important because they were market centres. Many kinds of goods were traded in these market towns. Farmers brought sheep and wool, leather and cloth, eggs, corn, cattle and vegetables. Fishermen brought their catch; craftsmen brought jewellery, iron and pottery; and pedlars brought goods from all over the country. At the larger towns like London and Southampton, there was even a flourishing import and export trade as English wool, tin, lead and silver were exchanged for gold, wine, glass, fur, timber and weapons.

Fig. 2.8 Building a Saxon hut.

A change in religion

Like other barbarian invaders, the Anglo-Saxons were pagans. They believed in a whole range of gods and goddesses, chief of which were the ancient gods of the sky and of fertility, Tiw, Woden, Thor, Frey and Freya.

As the Anglo-Saxons settled in various districts, they often built sanctuaries on hilltops as places of worship of their gods. When a rich and powerful man or woman died, he or she was given an elaborate burial or cremation. Women were buried with household goods and possessions; men were buried with weapons which would protect them in the next life. If the dead person were wealthy enough, his wife or servant was often killed too.

The wealthy dead were sometimes put into a special 'mortuary house' piled with wood and gifts. Then a great fire was lit and the body burned to ashes. Later the bones were collected and put into an urn, then buried in a pit or mound. These urns were often elaborately decorated and from them we have learned a great deal about Anglo-Saxon art. Another form of burial for the rich and powerful was the 'ship burial', in which the dead man (usually a king) was buried along with his ship and a whole array of treasure.

All this was to change after the year 597. It was then that St Augustine was sent to England by Pope Gregory I to convert the pagan Anglo-Saxons to Christianity. Augustine held his first church service in the ruins of a church in Canterbury that had been built in Roman times.

Probably the most difficult task for Augustine and his followers was to persuade the Anglo-Saxons that they should give up all their gods and worship instead one single god. They had to try and convince the Anglo-Saxons to use their temples as Christian churches and to remove all the statues of pagan gods such as Woden and Thor. It took more than two centuries before it could be said that England was a Christian country. Gradually the Christian message was accepted, first by one king, then by another. Sometimes there were bitter battles, as a newly converted Christian tried to convince his pagan neighbours to accept the faith.

Missionaries from Ireland

At about the same time as Augustine and others were arriving in southern England from Europe, another group of missionaries was arriving in northern England and Scotland. Their leader was St Patrick, who had been a child during the last years of Roman Britain and who spent most of his adult life in Ireland, converting the Celts to Christianity. Ireland became a land of devout Christians who supported a number of monasteries and monks.

Monks were people who decided to give their lives to the service of God. For many of them, this meant living a life of simple poverty, owning nothing and spending their days in prayer and meditation. Although monks often lived as a group in a monastery, they sometimes took vows of silence and spoke to each other only occasionally.

Other monks took on the task of spreading the Christian faith, and monks like these crossed the sea to England and Scotland to preach the Christian gospel. First came St Colomba who, in 563, founded a monastery on the island of Iona off the coast of Scotland. Others followed, including St Aidan, who set up a monastery on the island of Lindisfarne off the east coast. Their kind of Christianity, known as the Celtic Church, was different from the kind of Christianity being preached by St Augustine and his followers in the south of the country. The two groups of Christians disagreed about all kinds of matters, including the form of the church service, the shape of a monk's haircut and the date of Easter.

After years of dispute and bitterness, a meeting or *synod* was arranged at Whitby in northern England in 663 to decide once and for all which form of Christianity should be accepted in England. Bishops from both the Celtic and the Roman church argued their views. After many hours of talking and arguing, the Roman church proved stronger and was officially accepted as the correct form of Christianity for England.

Time to understand

1 The Anglo-Saxons made and decorated their burial urns without any idea that hundreds of years later they would be dug up, studied by archaeologists and historians, and used as sources of information about the way the Anglo-Saxons lived. Think about the things you use every day. Pick two or three different objects and imagine that they have been discovered a thousand years from now.

   Write an archaeologist's report on the objects that have been discovered. In it, describe the objects, explain what the archaeologist thinks they were used for (he or she may be wrong!) and make notes about what each object tells the archaeologist about Australian society in the 1980s.

2 Why do you think the Anglo-Saxons built their sanctuaries on the tops of hills? Are churches built on hilltops too?

3 According to legend, there are no snakes in Ireland because St Patrick banished them from the land. Use an encyclopaedia to find out more about this man who has become the patron saint of Ireland.

Education and learning

Before the coming of Christianity, the Anglo-Saxons had little need for education. Farming methods were passed on from father to son, while mothers taught their daughters all the skills they needed to know. Folk legends and stories were handed down orally—they were not written down but passed from one generation to the next by repeated tellings.

St Augustine believed that the only way he could be sure that Christianity would survive in England was to teach the religion to the children. Whenever he established a church, he also set up a schoolroom, where boys from the age of seven were taught Latin and philosophy, church history and sometimes a little science and mathematics as well.

But the really strong centres of learning in Anglo-Saxon England were in the north, in the monasteries that had been founded by Celtic missionaries. Since the end of the Roman empire, the traditions of learning had been kept alive by Celtic Christians in Ireland, and it was this knowledge that was spread into England. Theodore of Tarsus was appointed by Pope Gregory I to organise the church in England and in the late 600s he founded two monasteries in Northumbria in northern England: one was at Monkwearmouth (674) and one at Jarrow (685). Monasteries like these became so famous that pupils travelled to them from all over Europe.

The most famous student of the monasteries was Bede. His parents took him to the monastery at Monkwearmouth in about 678 when he was seven years old. He spent the rest of his life there and at nearby Jarrow, reading, studying and writing. Although he never travelled out of Northumbria, Bede became the greatest scholar of his time. He learnt by studying the books that were collected in the monastery library and by writing to other learned men throughout Europe. Bede wrote books on astronomy and grammar, the Bible and science, but is best known for his *Ecclesiastical History of England*. Written in Latin, this was the first important history of the English people.

Another outstanding English scholar was Alcuin, who lived between about 735 and 804. Alcuin was educated at the cathedral in York and later became master of the school there. His fame as a teacher and scholar spread and he attracted students from many parts of Europe. Alcuin later went to Europe and served Charlemagne as a teacher. You can read more about him in Chapter Three.

One of the greatest poems from Anglo-Saxon times is *Beowulf*, a story which was once told in the halls of thegns and kings by travelling minstrels. Unlike many of these early tales which were never recorded, *Beowulf* was written down by a Christian monk. It tells the story of how Beowulf, the hero, killed a monster that had been terrifying a neighbouring king. Later Beowulf and his men killed the monster's mother who had come to take revenge upon them. Because of his strength and courage, Beowulf

Fig. 2.9 The ruins of a Celtic Christian monastery at Cashel in Ireland. The round tower was used as a lookout and a place of refuge when the monastery was attacked. Why did it have so few openings?

Fig. 2.10 A statue of St Aidan on Holy Island, Lindisfarne. St Aidan founded a monastery there in 635. It was destroyed by the Danes in the ninth century and rebuilt in the eleventh century. Now only ruins remain.

became king of his own land, and died bravely trying to defend it from the attacks of a mighty dragon. At the end of the poem, Beowulf's body is burnt on a funeral pyre with his warriors chanting around it.

Time to understand

1 Bede is usually known as 'the Venerable Bede'. What does the word 'venerable' mean? What does this title tell us about Bede's reputation as a scholar?

2 The legends of the Anglo-Saxons have been written down in modern English. Find a book of Anglo-Saxon legends in your library and read some of these ancient stories. You may also be able to find a modern version of the story of Beowulf or the poems of Caedmon, an Anglo-Saxon poet.

3 Below is an extract from a modern translation of *Beowulf*. Explain what you think the lines are describing. Do you think they describe the scene well? Why?

> Away she went over a wavy ocean,
> boat like a bird, breaking seas,
> wind-whetted, white-throated,
> till curved prow had ploughed so far—

Fig. 2.11 The Alfred jewel. Its inscription reads, 'Alfred ordered me to be made'.

Fig. 2.12 The Celtic monks erected crosses like this in Ireland and England to explain Bible stories. This one still stands in Castedermot, Ireland. Notice the circular pattern on the base which was common in Celtic and Anglo-Saxon art.

Fig. 2.13 An elaborately decorated gold buckle.

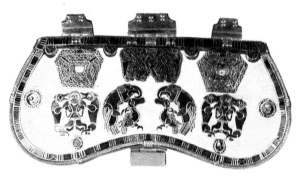

Fig. 2.14 A gold purse lid, decorated with garnets and glass.

Fig. 2.15 The first page of the Lindisfarne Gospel. Works like this took many hours of painstaking labour.

the sun standing right on the second day—
that they might see land loom on the sky line
then the shimmer of cliffs,
sheer moors behind,
reaching capes. The crossing
was at an end.

Art and craft

The illustrations on page 29 (Figs. 2.11–2.15) show just a few of the Anglo-Saxon works of art that have survived. As you can see, their art took many forms. Jewellery was very popular and men and women who could afford them wore beautifully crafted brooches and necklaces. Other practical things such as urns, jars, beakers, cups and drinking horns were also elaborately carved and decorated, often with complex geometric patterns.

The coming of Christianity brought new artforms to Anglo-Saxon England. Missionaries had to try to teach Christianity to people who could neither read nor write and who spoke a different language. They could not understand Latin, the language of the church, either. The missionaries often drew pictures to tell the stories of the Bible and to teach about God. Sometimes these pictures were carved into stone crosses.

Fig. 2.15 shows an illuminated manuscript from the Anglo-Saxon period. These beautiful books were made by monks who set themselves the task of copying out important religious writings by hand. Sitting alone in his *scriptorium*, or writing cubicle, each monk would spend week after week carefully copying a whole book. Because these works were so highly regarded, they were copied with loving care. Gold was used to highlight the first letters of some words and illustrations were coloured very carefully. Among the greatest of these illuminated manuscripts was the Lindisfarne Gospel, a translation of parts of the Bible, that once lay on the altar of the monastery on Holy Island, Lindisfarne.

Time to understand

1 The art of the Celts and Anglo-Saxons was very intricate, detailed and carefully patterned. The pictures in this part of the chapter will give you some idea of the kinds of patterns that were used by these people.

Intricately woven knots were a feature of art at this time. The buckle in Fig. 2.13 is one example of this style of decoration.

Try your hand at creating designs based on Celtic knots. The diagrams in Fig. 2.16 and Fig. 2.17 will give you some ideas about how to create them. They are not easy! If you remember that in objects like the buckle in Fig. 2.13 the knots had to be sculpted in gold, you will begin to realise what a great achievement these objects were.

2 Another common feature of art at this time was the series of circles, sometimes joined together, sometimes broken to form spirals and other patterns. You can see an example of this on the base of the cross in Fig. 2.12.

The diagrams in Fig. 2.18 show how these skills were combined to make beautiful decorated initial letters (A, R and C) in an illuminated manuscript. Design your own manuscript in the same style.

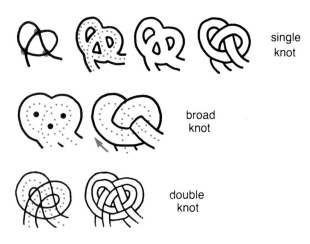

single knot

broad knot

double knot

Fig. 2.16 Celtic knots.

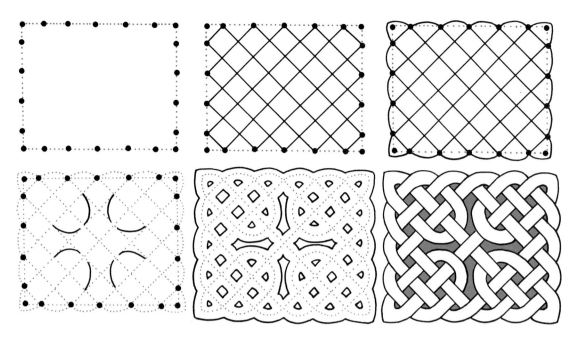

Fig. 2.17 Celtic knot patterns.

Fig. 2.18 Illuminated capital letters from the Book of Kells.

The Vikings

You have probably heard of the Vikings, the fierce and courageous warriors from Scandinavia (Norway, Sweden and Denmark) who sailed on voyages of exploration and plunder in their fast, high-prowed boats. At first, like many of the Anglo-Saxons hundreds of years earlier, the

Vikings came to Britain only to plunder. Their earliest known raid was in 793 when they attacked and partly destroyed the monastery at Lindisfarne.

For year after year these raids continued. At first only two or three boats would come; gradually the fleets grew in number until about 300 men arrived at once. Churches and monasteries along the northern coast and on rivers were attacked, their people were killed and their priceless objects stolen.

In 855 the Vikings, or Danes as they were also known, spent the winter in England. By 866 they had captured all the Anglo-Saxon kingdoms except Wessex. Just as the Anglo-Saxons had settled in England in the 500s, now the Danes settled down to become farmers in a new homeland. Some of their words became part of the English language—words such as 'sky', 'fellow', 'anger' and 'husband'.

Time to understand

A great deal has been written about the Vikings. Use some of this information to make a project about these warlike invaders. First, look through the books your library holds about the Vikings and check articles in encyclopaedias and other reference books. Then decide whether you will work alone or as part of a group. If you are working in a group, divide up the topic so that each person has a particular subject to find out and write about.

Some of the subjects you could explore are:
— the homelands of the Vikings
— how they lived: their homes, clothes, customs and laws
— why the Vikings sailed to other countries
— Viking ships
— Viking battles
— what happened when the Vikings successfully raided an area
— the areas the Vikings explored
— Viking heroes
— Viking myths and legends

You could present your project either in a book or as a series of posters that could be displayed in your classroom. Perhaps you could make it more interesting by making models of Viking clothes, homes and ships.

Alfred the Great

The only English king to be given the title of 'Great' was King Alfred, who was truly a remarkable man.

As the son of King Ethelwulf, Alfred had plenty of experience in fighting Danes as a youth. In 871, the year he became king, he fought them in nine battles but was eventually forced to ask for a five-year truce to allow him to rebuild his kingdom. In 876, when the truce ended, the Danes were stronger than ever. A Danish army led by Guthrum came to meet Alfred's men by land, while a mighty fleet was raiding along the south coast.

Caught off guard by a surprise Danish attack in January 878, Alfred was forced to flee. From his hiding place he organised guerilla raids on the Danes and rebuilt his army until it was strong enough to win decisively at the battle of Ethandune. Alfred had the enemy in the palm of his hand and Guthrum, the Danish leader, offered to leave hostages if he and his men were allowed to leave England forever. Instead, Alfred offered Guthrum a bargain: if the Danes became Christians and stopped their attacks, he would divide his lands and allow them to remain.

Immediately, Guthrum agreed to this bargain, which was much more generous than he could possibly have expected. He and his leading warriors were baptised (with Alfred acting as godfather), there were days of feasting, and Guthrum was presented with gifts. The kingdom was divided and the Danes agreed to live in the area given to them. This area became known as the Danelaw. The map in Fig. 2.19 shows what part of England it was.

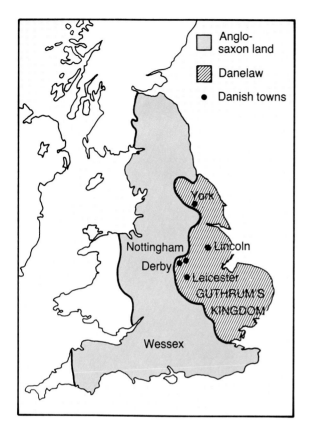

Fig. 2.19 The Danelaw, 886.

The end of Anglo-Saxon England

Alfred the Great died in 900 but the problem of uniting the Danes with the Anglo-Saxons did not die with him. His successors were not strong rulers and the Danes continued to attack the north of England. After many more years of raids and battles, England was once again united, this time under a Danish king, Knut or Canute. In 1016, when Canute came to the English throne, England became part of the great Danish empire which the Vikings had established.

However, when Canute's son and heir died in 1042, his empire collapsed. Ethelred's son Edward was appointed as king. Edward had been brought up in the courts of Normandy in France during the reign of Canute and was a devout Christian. During his reign the power of the church was increased and Westminster Abbey was commenced. Although he was a strong Christian, Edward (known as 'the Confessor' because of his faith) was not a strong ruler.

During the reign of Edward the Confessor (1042–1066), England was really ruled by the king's most powerful noble, Earl Godwin of

Fig. 2.20 Normans (on horseback) attack Anglo-Saxon foot soldiers at Hastings—a scene from the Bayeux Tapestry, which you can read about on page 35.

Fig. 2.21 King Harold is killed; the Normans are victorious.

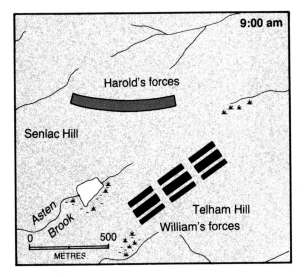
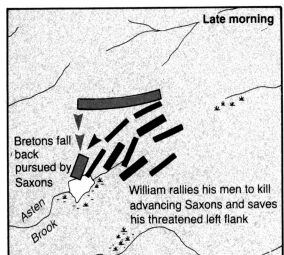
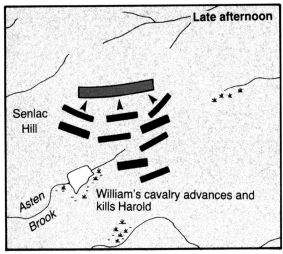

Fig. 2.22 The Battle of Hastings, 14 October 1066.

Wessex. During this time, Earl Godwin's son, Harold, was shipwrecked off the coast of France. When he was rescued, Harold was taken to the court of William, Duke of Normandy. According to William, Harold promised to help him become the king of England when Edward died.

Edward died in January 1066 and the English council, or *witan*, chose Harold as the next king because Edward had no son of his own. Although he was not of royal blood, Harold was a strong leader and immediately raised an army to fight a Viking invasion led by his own brother, Tostig, and the king of Norway.

Determined to win the English crown for himself, and believing that he had a right to it, William planned an invasion. In October 1066, a few days after Harold's army had won a victory over Tostig in the north of England, William's army landed at Pevensey in Sussex. Harold and his men marched south. They were tired and had lost many men in the battle they had just fought. Meanwhile, William's army prepared for battle.

On 14 October 1066 a great battle was fought near Hastings in southern England. The diagrams in Fig. 2.22 show how the armies were arranged and how the battle was lost and won.

In just one day England ceased to be simply an Anglo-Saxon society. Now the Anglo-Saxons, themselves once conquerors, were conquered again from Europe.

How do we know?

An interesting source of information about Anglo-Saxon England is the Bayeux Tapestry. The story of the Battle of Hastings and the Norman conquest of the Anglo-Saxons is recorded in this tapestry, which is now displayed at Bayeux in France. In its 70 metres of embroidered linen, the tapestry records the events of this exciting and important battle. The tapestry is like a comic strip, with a series of pictures embroidered on to strips about 50 centimetres wide and sewn together to make a single story. Above and below each scene are a series of small pictures which themselves provide a good deal of information about birds and animals, farming and hunting.

Who made the tapestry? We do not know, but three facts might help us make a guess:
— Bishop Odo of Bayeux (William's brother) plays a more important part in the tapestry than he probably did in real life.

— Some of the embroidered letters are made in the English rather than the French way.
— English women were well known at the time for their fine embroidery.

Do you think this is enough evidence for us to be able to say: *Bishop Odo wanted the tapestry to be made. He arranged for English women to go to Bayeux to do the embroidery and made it clear that he should have an important part in the finished product*?

Imagine that all these guesses are wrong. Using the three facts listed above, make up another explanation for the making of the Bayeux Tapestry.

Figs 2.20 and 2.21 on page 33 show two scenes from the Bayeux Tapestry. Explain what is happening in each one and what you can learn from it about the Anglo-Saxons and Normans.

3

The Middle Ages

THE PERIOD of about a thousand years between the fall of the Roman empire (in the 400s) and the Renaissance (in the 1400s) is known as the Middle Ages. This time is also often called the medieval period, a name which comes from the Latin word for 'middle'. You can see from the time-line in Fig. 3.1 that this long period can be divided into two parts: the Early Middle Ages, until about the year 1000, and the Later Middle Ages, from about 1000 to about 1450.

The Early Middle Ages have also been called the Dark Ages because it was in these years that Europe lost much of the culture, law, government and learning that had flourished during the years when the Roman empire controlled Europe. As we shall see in this chapter, Europe was not entirely 'dark' at this time. The Christian Church kept the flame of learning alive and preserved many books that would later be read and studied by scholars.

The empire of Charlemagne

If you look back to the map in Fig. 1.9 on page 10 you will see that the Franks were one of the barbarian tribes which attacked the western Roman empire in the fourth century. Although the other barbarian tribes gradually fell apart and disappeared, the kingdom of the Franks thrived and grew. Under a series of warrior kings in the 500s and 600s, the Franks attacked and conquered their neighbours, whose lands were added to the Frankish kingdom.

During the reign of Clovis (481–511), the Franks had become Christians. They had a great sense of loyalty to their king. When a king died, his lands were divided up between his sons so that each got a share of the kingdom. When Clovis died in 511, the kingdom was divided into four, as you can see from the map in Fig. 3.2. Later, it was divided again in several different ways.

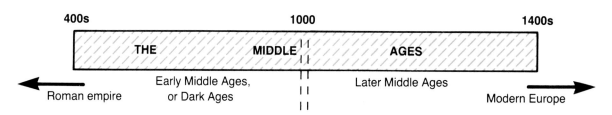

Fig. 3.1 The Middle Ages, or medieval period.

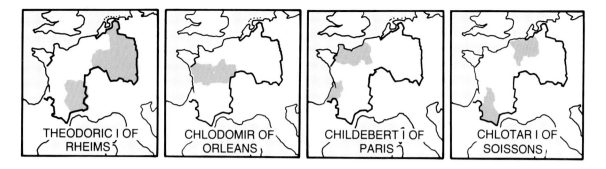

Fig. 3.2 How the lands of Clovis were divided upon his death in 511.

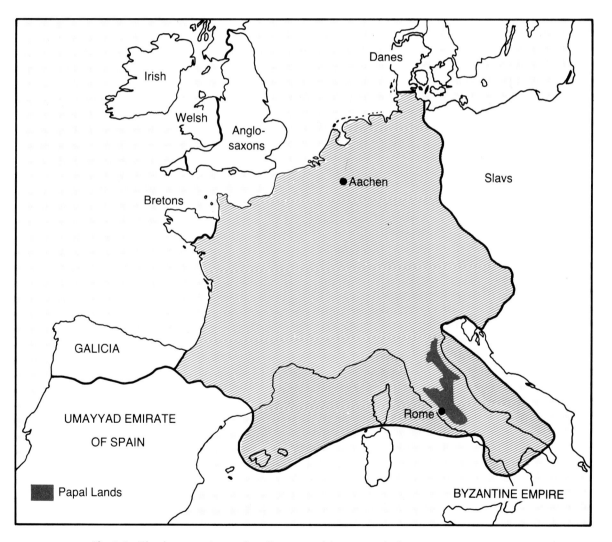

Fig. 3.3 Charlemagne's empire. Compare this map with the maps in Fig. 3.2. Which land had Charlemagne added?

Although Clovis had been a strong ruler, his sons and descendants became gradually weaker. Perhaps there was a hereditary sickness in the family, for many of them died when they were teenagers. As the king's family weakened, real control of the Franks fell into the hands of the 'mayors of the palace', particularly Pepin, who reunited the kingdom in 687. Pepin's son, Charles Martel (Charles the Hammer), ruled the Franks in this fashion from 719 until 741, but he was not prepared to call himself king of the Franks, because the descendants of Clovis were still supposed to have this title.

The Franks were both Christians and warriors. It was natural, then, that when another barbarian tribe, the Lombards, threatened to attack Rome in 750, the Pope called upon the Franks for help. Charles Martel's son, Pepin the Short, came to the assistance of the Pope and in return for his promise to help the Pope fight the Lombards, the Pope allowed him to become king of the Franks in 751.

Charlemagne (whose name means 'Charles the Great') was the son of Pepin the Short. Born in 768, he soon became renowned as a strong and successful military leader. In battle after battle, he fought and defeated neighbouring tribes as well as other peoples who were threatening the Frankish kingdom. The map in Fig. 3.3 shows how Charlemagne increased the size of his kingdom by these conquests. At its greatest his empire consisted of the whole of present-day France, most of Germany, parts of Spain and much of Italy.

On Christmas Day in the year 800, when Charlemagne was attending a church service in Rome, Pope Leo III crowned him as the new Roman emperor. Here is how one witness described the occasion:

> On the most holy day of the birth of our Lord the king came to mass in the basilica of the blessed apostle Peter. Pope Leo placed a crown on his head and joined by all the Romans proclaimed, 'Long life and victory to Charles Augustus crowned by God, the great and pacific Emperor of the Romans.'

It seemed that the great days when the Roman empire controlled the whole of Europe had been restored. In fact, this was not to be.

The real problem was the Franks' system of dividing up the kingdom between the king's sons. When Charlemagne died in 814, the whole kingdom went to his surviving son, Louis the Pious. It remained united until Louis died in 840 but then the old battles began again and the empire was divided between Louis' three sons. The map in Fig. 3.4 shows what had happened by 870. The three new kingdoms were roughly equal to today's countries of France, Germany and Italy. Although the empire was briefly united again in 884, it was split forever in 888.

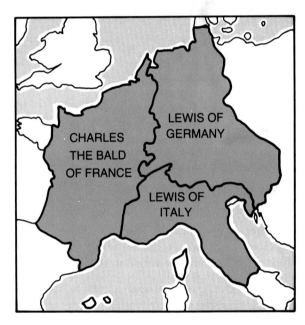

Fig. 3.4 How Charlemagne's empire had been divided by 870. The three divisions are roughly equal to today's France, Germany and Italy. Which other countries are also in this area today?

Charlemagne's empire was no more, and Europe was being threatened on all sides by invaders: Vikings, Muslims and Magyars. People could no longer look to their king for protection; instead, they came to rely on local military chiefs to defend them. Although the kings continued to rule, they had very little real power. Western Europe broke up into a number of small units, each of which tried to defend itself. Germany, for example, was divided into five small kingdoms each ruled by a duke. In Italy the units were much smaller and sometimes consisted of just one city and the country around it.

Time to understand

1 Why do you think many kings in the Middle Ages were given names like 'Pepin the *Short*' and 'Louis the *Pious*'? Draw cartoon figures of Charles Martel, Pepin the Short, Charles the Great (Charlemagne), Louis the Pious, Charles the Bald.

2 Look again at the map of Charlemagne's empire in Fig. 3.3. Do you think the Bretons would have had a peaceful life? Why? The land of the Bretons is now part of France. Use an atlas to find out its modern name.

3 Read again the account of the crowning of Charlemagne on page 38.

a Why do you think Pope Leo chose Christmas Day for Charlemagne's coronation?

b What does the word 'basilica' mean?

c Why did the people call Charlemagne 'Charles Augustus'?

d The writer describes Charlemagne as a 'pacific' emperor. What does 'pacific' mean?

e Was Charlemagne a 'pacific' king? Can you suggest why he was called 'pacific emperor'? (The following section, Charlemagne's society, will help you answer this question.)

Charlemagne's society

One winter day in 780, Alcuin, the head of the school and library at the cathedral in York (whom you read about in Chapter Two) crossed the English Channel to Europe. Now nearly fifty years old, Alcuin was travelling to Rome to present the good wishes of the new Archbishop of York to the Pope and to be honoured himself by the Pope for his work at York. The journey was long and tiring as Alcuin and his small group of companions rode on horseback through the cold lands of Europe.

After several weeks of church services, ceremonies and debates in Rome, Alcuin set out for home. In March 781 in the Italian town of Parma, he met the most powerful man in Europe—Charlemagne, king of the Franks, who was on his way to Rome to celebrate Easter. Charlemagne, who could not write himself, was impressed by Alcuin, the greatest teacher of his time. He invited Alcuin to return to Europe to study at his court and help teach his people. The invitation was accepted and thus, as a result of an accidental meeting, Europe's most powerful king and its greatest scholar were brought together.

What sort of man was Charlemagne, this king whose power had caused the Pope to crown him

Fig. 3.5 Charlemagne, king of the Franks and the most powerful ruler in Europe. What are the two things he is holding? Do you know what they represent?

as a new Roman emperor? He was tall and athletic, and according to his friend and secretary, 'well-built with large piercing eyes . . . His manner was impressive and held both authority and dignity'. Charlemagne was a warrior-king and each spring he and his followers prepared for war. For more than forty years he led his followers into battle, attacking the pagan tribes on the edges of his kingdom and converting them, by force if necessary, to Christianity. He was as cruel and ruthless as other warriors and once executed 4500 pagan tribespeople in one ceremony because they refused to become Christians.

Yet during the winter months, Charlemagne cast aside his tasks as a fighter and set his mind to ruling his vast kingdom efficiently. At his court in Aachen, he gathered officials upon whom he could rely. There was a chamberlain to take care of the royal treasury, a count of the palace to help administer justice, a quartermaster to arrange lodgings, others to look after food, horses and all the other things that were necessary to keep government running smoothly.

Charlemagne was a great talker and, again according to his secretary, 'was able to express whatever he wanted to say with great clarity'. He learnt Latin so well that 'it was all one if he expressed himself in that or in his mother tongue'. Yet, although 'he was accustomed to place tablets and sheets of parchment beneath the pillows of his bed in order to profit from his moments of leisure to practise tracing the letters', he took up writing too late in life and never learnt to do it.

A newcomer to learning himself, Charlemagne gathered some of Europe's finest scholars to his palace school at Aachen. There, during the winter, he and his sons, his courtiers and their children listened, studied and discussed. From 782 until 796 Alcuin was the school's master.

Inspired by their king's enthusiasm for learning, many bishops set up their own schools to educate not only the sons of the wealthy, but also village children. In the larger monasteries, groups of scribes were employed in copying and decorating manuscripts, which were then supplied to other churches. Just as Charlemagne wanted to bring order and unity into his kingdom, so he wanted to bring order into the copying of manuscripts to ensure that mistakes were not made which might remain in the manuscripts forever. A uniform script was developed to try to overcome this problem.

After Charlemagne

After Charlemagne's death, when his empire was torn apart by battle and jealousy, most of the schools disappeared. Only a few remained to keep the light of learning glowing through the Dark Ages. Even during his reign, most of Charlemagne's subjects had nothing to do with education. Their lives were concerned with the much more basic question of how to grow enough food from the land they farmed. Harvests were often very poor and much of the land of Europe was simply wasteland, useful only for hunting, gathering berries and fruit, grazing animals and collecting timber. Many people spent their whole lives on the verge of starvation. For them, learning even the simplest skills of reading and writing was out of the question.

Time to understand

1 Charlemagne used his mark (shown below) to sign orders and decrees. Do you think a head of government today could get by without being able to write? Why? Design your own mark which you would use if you were unable to sign your name.

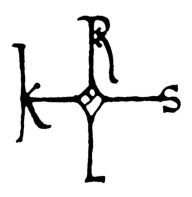

Fig. 3.6 Charlemagne's mark.

2 The picture in Fig. 3.7 shows part of a page from Alcuin's Bible. It is written in the new, uniform writing that Alcuin developed to try to prevent mistakes when monks were copying manuscripts. The name of this new writing was *miniscule writing*. Use a dictionary to find out the meaning of the word 'miniscule'. Why do you think Alcuin's style of writing was given this name?

Fig. 3.7 Part of Alcuin's Bible.

3 Copy out a paragraph of this book (or make up a paragraph of your own) in tiny writing like miniscule writing. Decorate the first letter as the scribes of Charlemagne did. You can also add other decorations to make your paragraph resemble part of an illuminated manuscript.

The feudal system

During the Middle Ages, land and government were very closely linked. Kings, dukes and other noblemen owned most of the land of Europe. They were also the rulers of the lands they owned. The system that linked land and government together is called the *feudal system*. The diagrams in Figs. 3.8 and 3.9 show how the feudal system worked. Charlemagne and other strong kings were able to keep their power because of their position as feudal lords. When their empires broke up, as the empire of Charlemagne did after about 900, dukes and other nobles became feudal lords and expected that all those people who depended upon them would give them the same loyalty as they had given their earlier kings.

Kings and dukes relied upon the support of counts and other wealthy noble families. Unable to pay them with money, they provided them with parts of their royal estates. In return, the nobles were expected to provide knights and other soldiers for the king or duke, to advise him if asked, and to help with money and gifts if necessary. These nobles were called *vassals* and the land they were granted was known as a *fief*. The fief included not only the land but also the people who worked on it. Perhaps 90 per cent of the people in Europe were farm workers. A few owned their own land but most worked on land owned by nobles or other people. These farmers were called *serfs*. They were not allowed to leave their land and had to spend their entire lives working on it.

The serfs spent a fixed amount of time each year working for the noblemen. In return, the noblemen protected them in time of war—which was frequent in medieval times. Not all the serfs and peasants worked on the land: some served the noblemen as blacksmiths, millers, shoemakers, thatchers or other tradesmen.

The feudal system, then, was a system of *responsibilities* and *obligations*. The vassals were supposed to assist their king when called upon, although in the later Middle Ages few kings were powerful enough to insist on this and the vassals themselves became the most powerful people in the kingdom. In turn, these most powerful

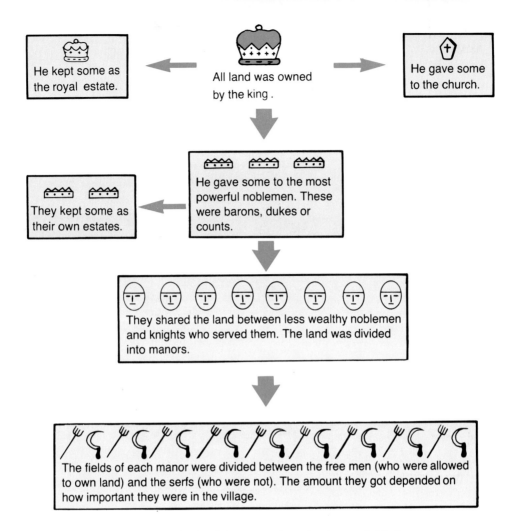

Fig. 3.8 The feudal system: how land was divided.

vassals created their own vassals who served them, just as they were supposed to serve the king. And so on down the line, until at the very bottom of the pyramid were the landless serfs, forced to work not only to feed themselves but also to serve their masters in return for protection from attack.

Life in a village

Most of the people of medieval times lived in self-contained villages on the estates of noblemen. These estates were called *manors* and each was governed by the nobleman who owned the land. He was the lord of the manor and often lived in a castle to protect himself from enemy raids. The lord's castle was, in fact, the last place of defence and it was there that the whole village congregated in time of battle.

The diagram in Fig. 3.10 on page 44 shows a plan of a medieval village. Although villages varied in size, they usually contained the same kinds of buildings. Why do you think many villages were built near rivers? Why was the manor house or castle in the middle of the village? Why was the farmland divided into strips?

King

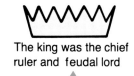

The king was the chief
ruler and feudal lord

Barons and noblemen

Provide knights for
king's army

Pay taxes and dues to
king to pay for armies
and court

**Poorer noblemen and
knights
(Lords of the Manor)**

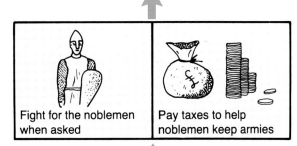

Fight for the noblemen
when asked

Pay taxes to help
noblemen keep armies

Serfs

Unable to own land or
leave the manor without
permission

Able to use
storehouses, ovens,
mills and other facilities
provided by lord of the
manor

Pay dues at certain
times and fines if found
guilty of offences by
lord of the manor

Work for lord of the
manor a set number of
days each year. Had to
fight for him when
required

Fig. 3.9 The feudal system: responsibilities in exchange for land.

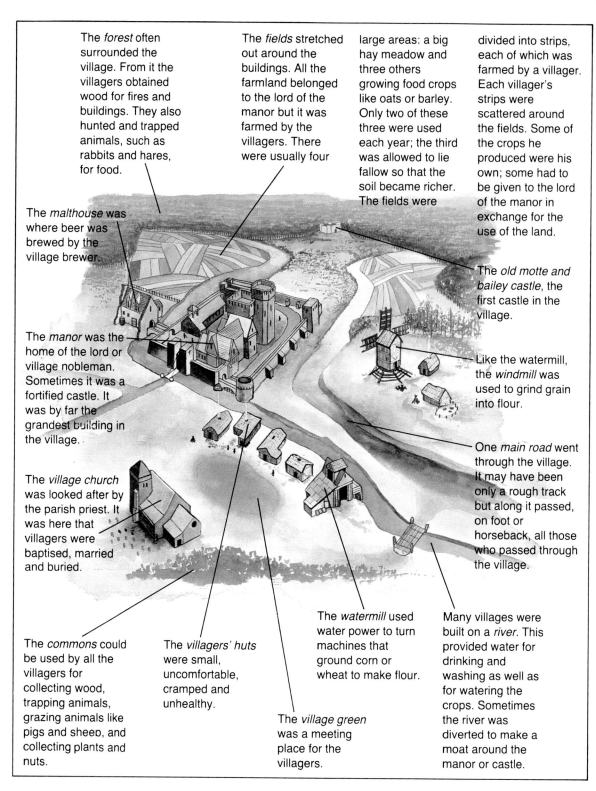

The *forest* often surrounded the village. From it the villagers obtained wood for fires and buildings. They also hunted and trapped animals, such as rabbits and hares, for food.

The *fields* stretched out around the buildings. All the farmland belonged to the lord of the manor but it was farmed by the villagers. There were usually four large areas: a big hay meadow and three others growing food crops like oats or barley. Only two of these three were used each year; the third was allowed to lie fallow so that the soil became richer. The fields were divided into strips, each of which was farmed by a villager. Each villager's strips were scattered around the fields. Some of the crops he produced were his own; some had to be given to the lord of the manor in exchange for the use of the land.

The *malthouse* was where beer was brewed by the village brewer.

The *old motte and bailey castle*, the first castle in the village.

The *manor* was the home of the lord or village nobleman. Sometimes it was a fortified castle. It was by far the grandest building in the village.

Like the watermill, the *windmill* was used to grind grain into flour.

The *village church* was looked after by the parish priest. It was here that villagers were baptised, married and buried.

One *main road* went through the village. It may have been only a rough track but along it passed, on foot or horseback, all those who passed through the village.

The *commons* could be used by all the villagers for collecting wood, trapping animals, grazing animals like pigs and sheep, and collecting plants and nuts.

The *villagers' huts* were small, uncomfortable, cramped and unhealthy.

The *watermill* used water power to turn machines that ground corn or wheat to make flour.

Many villages were built on a *river*. This provided water for drinking and washing as well as for watering the crops. Sometimes the river was diverted to make a moat around the manor or castle.

The *village green* was a meeting place for the villagers.

Fig. 3.10 A medieval village.

Fig. 3.11 A motte and bailey castle. A wooden keep stands on top of the motte, or mound. The lower area was called the bailey. In it were huts, workrooms and stores. The whole castle was surrounded by a ditch or moat.

Fig. 3.12 Caerphilly Castle in Wales was begun in 1271. Notice how wide the moat is. How important would a wide moat like this be when a castle was attacked?

Fig. 3.13 Blacksmiths at work.

Time to understand

The picture in Fig. 3.13 shows blacksmiths at work in a village forge. Many of the surnames that are still used in Australia have come from the work done by people of the Middle Ages. 'Smith', for example, which is the most common surname in Australia, comes from the medieval word for tradesman. As well as blacksmiths, there were goldsmiths, arrowsmiths, and whitesmiths (who made things out of tin).

These surnames have come down to us from the Middle Ages. Try to find out what work each of these people did:

Thatcher	Wright	Weaver
Webster	Packer	Carpenter
Butler	Franklin	Marshall
Cooper	Miller	Taylor
Turner	Chapman	Tanner
Chamberlain	Clark	Carter
Mason	Kitchener	Page

(A book about English surnames will help you in this search.)

Medieval castles

The Middle Ages was a violent and dangerous time and death was no stranger to most families. It was to protect themselves, their families and their supporters that noblemen built castles on their land.

The first castles were not homes but were used only when an enemy attacked. Later castles were grander, stronger and larger. They were not only places of safety from attack but were also the homes of many people. Some of these castles still stand in Europe and England, although many are in ruins.

Fig. 3.11 on page 45 shows an early kind of European castle—a *motte and bailey* castle. The *keep* was the most important part of this kind of castle and it was not until an enemy actually took the keep that he could claim victory.

As weapons became more powerful, the design of castles had to change to keep them safe. Stone was used instead of wood because it was stronger as well as being fireproof. The keep became larger and more elaborate. A gatehouse and drawbridge were added to castles to make them safer. Sometimes secret passageways and underground tunnels were built to enable the lord of the castle to escape if his enemy proved too strong for him. Sometimes, too, an old castle would be completely rebuilt according to new ideas about the best methods of defence. For example, after the Crusades (which you will read about in Chapter Seven), some European noblemen changed their castles to make them more like those they had seen in their travels. A number of thick round towers replaced a single keep because round towers were not as easily battered with a battering ram. The inside wall of the castle was built higher than the outside walls so that archers could fire right over the castle walls at the enemy. Moats became wider and sometimes rivers were diverted so that the castle was virtually on an island in the middle of the river.

These later castles were quite luxurious inside, for they were the main way a nobleman could show how rich and powerful he was. Their important rooms, such as the great hall, were large and impressive, with elaborate furnishings and decorations. Flags and banners hung around the hall, which was used for feasting and entertainment as well as meetings. But for those whose job it was to cook food, keep the castle clean and do all the work that was needed to make these grand occasions possible, the castle was not as comfortable. The rooms were dark and cold, sleeping accommodation was just a bundle of rags on the floor or a mattress of straw, and life was very hard indeed.

The medieval church

As we have already seen in this chapter, the church was one of the most powerful organisations in medieval times.

Just as everyday life was organised in a pyramid system, with the king at the top and the serfs at the bottom, so the church was arranged in a pyramid, with the Pope at the top and the parish priests at the bottom. You can see from the diagram in Fig. 3.14 how this worked. In fact, the feudal organisation of society was closely linked with the organisation of the church because wealthy bishops were also feudal lords who had their own lands and peasants to work for them. Their influence was much wider than that of church leaders today and many of them were more concerned with gaining even more wealth and power than with their duties as churchmen.

The illustrations in Figs 3.17–3.20 show some of the most important activities of the medieval church.

After the collapse of Charlemagne's empire, the church became even more powerful than it had been earlier. It was now the only bond that linked Europeans, the only organisation that was spread throughout the continent. Instead of being loyal to a country or state, people were

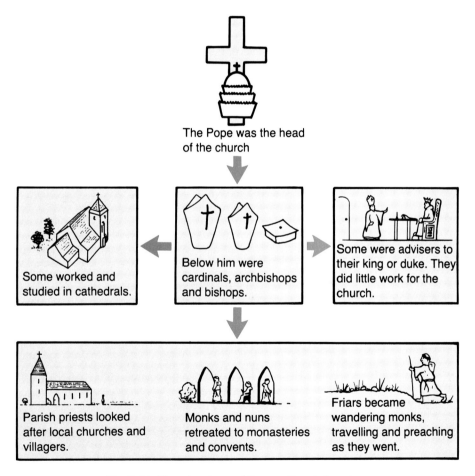

Fig. 3.14 The structure of the medieval church.

Time to understand

Work in groups to make a model of a motte and bailey castle. You will need cardboard, newspaper, strong glue, matchboxes and matches.

First find a strong piece of cardboard about 30 centimetres wide and 50 centimetres long. On it, draw two circles, one slightly larger than the other.

Crumple pieces of newspaper and stick them on each circle to make two mounds. The higher mound, which should be on the smaller circle, is the motte. It can be up to eight centimetres high. The other mound is the bailey. It can be two or three centimetres high. When you have made the motte and bailey high enough, cover them with strips of paper and paint them green.

You can then build up the outside of the cardboard, leaving a space around the motte and bailey to form the ditch. Cover the outside with paper and paint it green. Paint the ditch blue.

Matchboxes glued together and covered with thin cardboard can be used for the keep (which should be on top of the motte) and for two or three barns or stables in the bailey. Rows of matches glued around the motte and bailey will make a very good *palisade*, or fence, or you could use long pieces of cardboard painted to resemble palings. Use cardboard too for the bridges and arches.

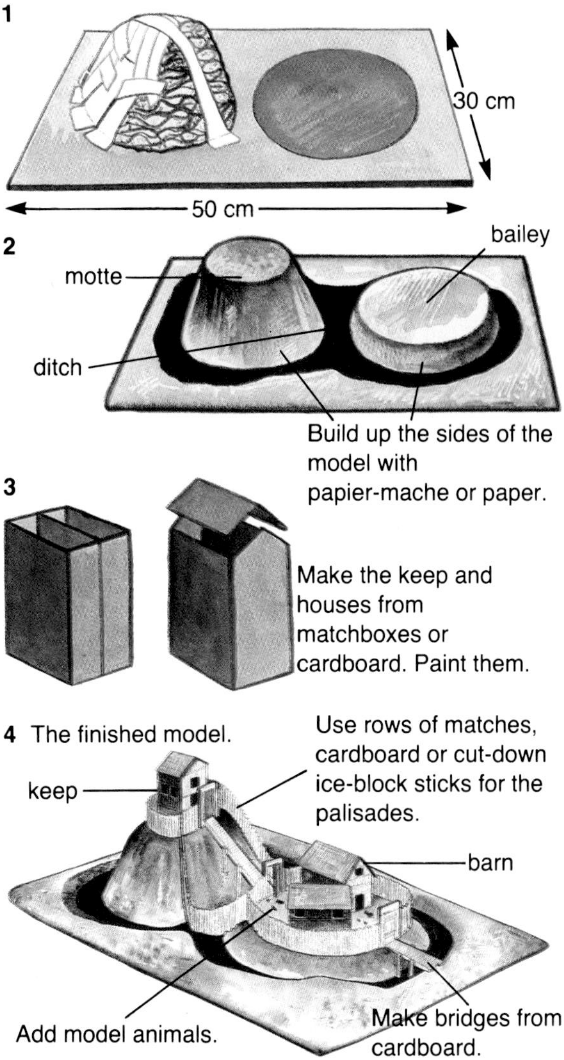

Fig. 3.15 Making a motte and bailey castle.

1

30 cm

50 cm

2

motte

bailey

ditch

Build up the sides of the model with papier-mache or paper.

3

Make the keep and houses from matchboxes or cardboard. Paint them.

4 The finished model.

keep

Use rows of matches, cardboard or cut-down ice-block sticks for the palisades.

barn

Add model animals.

Make bridges from cardboard.

loyal to their church. People saw the Popes as representatives of God, more important than kings, who came and went. The church was wealthy and many fine cathedrals were built, some of which still stand. In these churches, people could find release from the boredom of their everyday lives.

Often understanding very little of the church services themselves, people came to rely on the power of holy relics—'bits and pieces' which were said to have belonged once to saints or even to Jesus himself and which were supposed to

Fig. 3.16 The cathedral at Bourges in France. It was planned in 1172, started in 1192 and first used in 1224. It is built in the Gothic style.

48

Fig. 3.17 The church kept learning alive. Monks copied manuscripts like this one by hand. The church also ran schools where boys were taught to become priests and monks.

Fig. 3.18 Friars were wandering monks who travelled from place to place preaching to the villagers and townsfolk. Unlike other monks, they were poor. The two main groups of friars were the Franciscans (founded by St Francis) and the Dominicans (founded by St Dominic). Why were these churchmen called 'Europe's own missionaries'?

Fig. 3.19 The church provided sanctuary in a time of uncertainty and upheaval. This door-knocker is part of the main door to Durham Cathedral in England. To gain sanctuary, a person had to knock at the cathedral door.

Fig. 3.20 The church was important in everyday life. Baptism, for example, washed away sin. If a baby died without being baptised, he or she could not go to heaven.

49

have magical healing qualities. These relics were often kept in beautifully made caskets and people would travel long distances to see shreds of clothing, locks of hair, fingers, hands or even feet which they believed would bring them good fortune throughout their lives. These journeys were called *pilgrimages* and those who went on them were called *pilgrims*.

Time to understand

1 The diagram in Fig. 3.21 shows the main parts of a medieval monastery. The list below gives some of the activities of the monks. Try to work out in which part of the monastery each of the following activities would have been carried out.

a corridors where monks walked and meditated
b caring for the sick
c worshipping God
d keeping food and equipment
e providing accommodation for travellers
f preparing meals
g dining room
h monks' sleeping quarters
i holding meetings

2 Orderic Vitalis was a monk who wrote down his story of how he was taken from his home at the age of ten to train in a monastery. His story is on the next page.

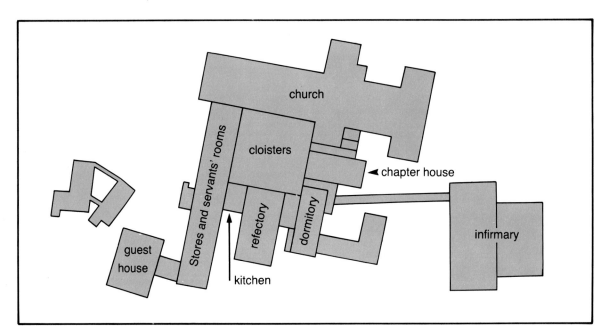

Fig. 3.21 Fountains Abbey, an English monastery.

There was once a little boy named Orderic. He lived by the river Severn at Shrewsbury, and his father, Ordelerius, was a Norman who had come over the sea from Normandy with Earl Roger Montgomery, one of William the Conqueror's barons. Perhaps Ordelerius married an English girl, for the little Orderic felt he belonged to England and lived happily with his father and mother until he was ten. But one day a strange monk named Rainald arrived from France and talked to his father in a language he could not understand. Then Ordelerius told his son that he was going to send him far away across the sea to be a monk. Orderic wept to leave his father and mother and the river Severn and the land of England. His father wept, too, as he tied up Orderic's little bundle of clothes and gave him into the care of Rainald.

So Orderic travelled across the sea to Normandy—like Joseph being taken into Egypt, he said. There, at the monastery of S. Evroul, he was given a new name, Vitalis, and began to learn how to be a monk. All round him strange monks spoke a strange language he could not understand, and at first he was very frightened and lonely for he was only ten years old. But soon he learnt the language [Latin] and began to enjoy the new life. He grew up happily and lived sixty years in his monastery, doing a lot of writing in the cloister, except when, in winter-time, his fingers were so numb that he could not write. He wrote history books and loved talking to old knights who visited the monastery, about the exciting fights they had. He never saw his father and mother again, but he never forgot England and the happy life he had lived by the river Severn.

a Why do you think Orderic's parents decided to send him to France to become a monk?

b Do you know the story of Joseph being taken into Egypt? If you do not, try to find out from a book of Bible stories. How was the experience of Orderic similar to that of Joseph?

c Why did the monks speak Latin and not French?

d From his story, what sort of person do you think Orderic would have been?

e Can you find out how old people are when they decide to become monks today? What sort of training do they do?

3 Monks, like many other people in the Middle Ages, believed that evil thoughts and bad behaviour were the work of devils. Read how one monk explained it and draw a picture to illustrate the passage.

All our little daily slips and mistakes are their doing. Sometimes they make my hands so heavy that I can hardly raise them. When we snore or cough or sneeze in church, it is their work. One troop of devils will spend all their efforts weighting my eyes and closing my eyelids, and another will come and snore in front of my nose, so that the brother next to me thinks I am doing it. The other day I saw a devil carefully plastering up a brother's ears so that he should not listen to the Rule being read in chapter.

Learning for life

Although students grumble sometimes about having to go to school, Australians accept that children need to be educated so that they can take their place in adult life. Because we need skills like reading, writing and mathematics in order to live comfortably in Australia, these subjects are taught at school.

Children in the Middle Ages were also taught the skills they would need as adults. Only occasionally did these skills include reading and writing, and mathematics was taught even less often.

The few boys (and even fewer girls) who were taught to read and write were educated in one of three ways. Some were instructed by their parish priest so that they could help in church services and perhaps take a minor position in the church. Others went to monastery schools where they learnt about the church, its history and teaching, and were taught Latin, the language of the church.

A few boys were sent to cathedral or grammar schools. These were run by churchmen and, like the monastery schools, spent a lot of time teaching about the church. Their pupils spent many hours a day learning Latin grammar. Lessons began at six in the morning and continued until eleven, with a fifteen minute break at about nine for prayers and breakfast. Dinner was at eleven, with a typical menu being 'peasouppe, bredde and ale'. Then the boys had two hours off before beginning lessons again at one and continuing until five o'clock. The only holidays from this routine were on Sunday afternoons and on festival and saints' days.

Classrooms were often uncomfortable and lessons were very dull. Here is a poem one boy wrote about his teacher:

The birchen twiggis be so sharpe
It maketh me have a faint heart
I would my master were an hare
And all his bookes hounds were
And I myself a jolly hunter
To blow my horn I would not spare
For if he were dead I would not care.

However, not all schoolmasters depended only on the cane to punish their pupils. One wrote: 'Knowledge is not imparted by blows . . . You may break an entire forest on the backs of your wretched pupils but you will achieve nothing without the co-operation of their minds.'

The children of freemen and serfs rarely went to school. Instead, they learnt from an early age country skills such as scaring birds off the crops, picking up sticks and stones, helping with the harvest and haymaking. As they grew older they were given more responsibility and were expected to work harder. Children whose fathers were expert thatchers, hedgers or carpenters were taught these crafts. Girls really had a double education, for they were expected to be skilled at farming and also to be experts at cooking, spinning, weaving, making clothes, salting meat and curing illnesses with herbs.

The sons and daughters of the manor house had a quite different education. It was expected that boys would become knights and girls would become ladies. From the age of seven, boys were often sent to another household to train as pages. If his family was rich enough, a boy might be sent to the king's court.

A page had many things to learn. Of special importance were good manners, fighting, hunting and riding. An old book called *The Babees Book* describes just how a page should behave. He must get up early, wash (and keep his nails clean), and say his prayers or, better still, go to church. He must be polite to everyone and not look 'lumpish'. He must serve at table and look after all the diners, especially his master. He must never fill his mouth 'full as a pigge'. Nor must he scratch himself or sniff in public.

At fourteen the page became a squire. This was like an apprenticeship to a knight, for the squire was given more responsibility than the page. He was expected to do more, too. A squire had to be brave and courteous, to sing and play at least one musical instrument, to recite poetry and be skilled at carving meat and serving wine. In addition, he was supposed to know the rules of hunting and jousting, how to hunt with falcons and be an expert horseman.

While the boys of the manor were struggling with this strict education, their sisters were being taught at home by their mothers. They learnt

Fig. 3.22 A squire holds a horse for his master. How would you describe the clothes the knight is wearing?

how to organise servants, how to sew and do fine embroidery, to sing and play music and to ride. They learnt to be ladies. It was expected that if they did not marry they would enter a convent and become a nun.

In the towns, other children were apprenticed to a master craftsman to learn a trade. When they were about seven years old their parents signed an agreement by which their education was placed in the hands of a master. It was his responsibility to teach the children a trade—carpentry, perhaps, or stonemasonry, or shoemaking. He also agreed to give his apprentices food and lodgings and to discipline them if they got into trouble. In return, the apprentice was expected to do whatever work the master demanded and to obey him in all ways.

After seven years as apprentices, the boys became journeymen. Now they were free to earn money by charging by the day for their work. They could change masters if they wanted to, or even move to another town to find work. But the journeymen were not fully qualified. Only when they produced a piece of work of very high standard—called a 'masterpiece'—and paid quite a high subscription to join their trade association or guild, could the journeymen call themselves 'master craftsmen'.

Time to understand

1 Why do you think the church played such an important part in education during the Middle Ages? What part does the church play in education in Australia today?
2 Read again the words of the schoolmaster quoted on page 52. Do you think he was right?
3 Why were the children of freemen and serfs rarely sent to school?
4 Why do you think it was specially important for a page to learn good manners, fighting, hunting and riding? What do you think are the four most important things for children in modern Australia to learn before they are fourteen years old? Why?
5 An apprenticeship system is still used to teach some trades. Can you name some modern

trades that are learned through apprenticeship? Do you think this a good way to learn a trade? Why? How are the training and conditions of today's apprentices different from those of apprentices in the Middle Ages? Are there any similarities between apprenticeship today and in the Middle Ages?
6 The French word for 'day' is *journée*. Can you work out how journeymen got their name?
7 What was the original meaning of the word 'masterpiece'? Does it have the same meaning today?

The Black Death

In many ways, western Europe seemed to be doing very well in the late 1200s. The population of most countries had grown quite quickly and the area that Europeans controlled and farmed was expanding too. Towns were getting bigger and trade was flourishing. The two main trading districts, Flanders and Lombardy, were exporting goods far beyond Europe and, in return, Europe was buying goods from China, India and beyond. The church was more united than it had been for several hundred years. Laws were being written down, universities were growing and books were being written, not only in Latin but also in French, Italian and English—languages that more people could understand.

All this was to change after 1348, the year that brought the Black Death to Europe. Here is how Boccaccio, an Italian writer of the time, described the sickness:

In men and women alike there appeared at the beginning of the sickness, certain swellings, either on the groin or under the armpits. Some grew to the size of an apple, others grew like an egg. These were named plague-boils. These death-bearing plague-boils continued to appear on every part of the body. Then they began to change into black blotches, and these were a certain sign of coming death.

The illness usually lasted for only two or three days. As the plague-boils spread, the victim started vomiting blood. Then he or she became delirious. Death soon followed.

Europeans in the Middle Ages had no idea what caused this terrible disease, nor did they know how to cure it. Today we know that what they called the Black Death was, in fact, bubonic plague. It appeared in China in about 1334 and spread to the seaports of Italy by 1347. In the following year it was killing people throughout France and Italy. It then moved north to Scandinavia and east to Russia. The disease was spread by parasites living on the common black rat.

The doctors of the Middle Ages were powerless when the Black Death struck Europe. A few worked out that the only chance of surviving was to keep well away from other people, but they had no idea why this worked. Others invented all

Fig. 3.23 A plague doctor. His strange costume was supposed to keep the disease away.

kinds of strange mixtures and remedies, such as drinking large amounts of vinegar or avoiding moist foods. Of course none of these 'cures' was successful.

We do not know exactly how many people died in the Black Death but it seems that about one-third of the total population of Europe was killed by the disease. This caused enormous problems, as those who survived tried desperately to bury the victims. One doctor wrote:

> Many died without anyone to serve them, and they were buried without priests to pray over their graves. A father did not visit his son, nor a son his father. Charity was dead . . . even the doctors did not dare visit the sick from fear of infection.

After the first great attack of bubonic plague in 1348, the disease continued to be a problem throughout the rest of the Middle Ages. Although none of the later plagues was as destructive as this first one, the possibility of sudden death through disease was another hazard that people learned to cope with.

The Black Death changed Europe in many ways. With perhaps a third of the population dead, there were not enough workers to produce food from Europe's farms. Food was short and prices were high. Poor land was abandoned and villages were allowed to fall into ruin as their remaining people left and went to a town or city, or perhaps to a bigger village. Landowners whose land had once been farmed by serfs now found that there were not enough workers to keep their farms going. Serfs discovered that they had new bargaining power. Sometimes the landowners had to rent out their land to their serfs; sometimes they sold it. No longer were serfs prepared to spend many days a month working for a landowner: if they thought their work was too hard, they simply moved somewhere else. Many went to the towns to fill the gaps left by town workers who had been killed by the Black Death.

Traders and town workers found that there was no longer a big market for their goods. There were perhaps one-third fewer people to buy things and this made it much more difficult to sell or trade. Some crafts declined because the old people who understood how to do them had been killed by the plague.

Europeans in the Middle Ages were, as we have seen, very religious people. Many believed that the Black Death was a punishment from God for their evil ways. They reacted to this belief in several ways. Some, because of the horrors they had seen, became obsessed by death. They felt that they could do nothing but wait for death to catch up with them. Some even started worshipping the Devil instead of God. Some believed that the best thing they could do was to live their lives to the full. They gave up religious worship and took on the idea of 'Eat, drink and be merry' because they felt they could do nothing to stop the death that would eventually come to them.

For other people though, the Black Death was something that strengthened their religious belief. They became fanatical, believing that if they could get rid of all their evil doings and thoughts, they would be more likely to go to heaven when they died. Some of these fanatics joined the Order of Flagellants, who marched through towns beating each other with chains and whips. By doing this they believed they could get rid of the evil inside them.

Just as it takes people many years to recover from a major war, so it took the people of medieval Europe many years to recover from the sorrow, distress and problems caused by the Black Death. In fact, the Middle Ages were never really the same again. Feudalism was no longer accepted as the only way to organise the use of land and many of the old ways were never really re-established.

Fig. 3.24 Flagellants in England. They often paraded in front of churches and cathedrals.

How do we know?

Historians, as we have seen, can use many different ways of learning about the past: reading words that were written by people who lived many years ago, studying objects that have been discovered from earlier times and looking carefully at pictures that were drawn by artists long ago. Even if we have all these kinds of evidence, we still have to *imagine* what it was like living in a different country in a different time.

In this chapter we have learnt quite a lot about castles in the Middle Ages. What would it have been like trying to attack a strong castle like the one in Fig. 3.12? How would you have felt if you were inside the castle trying to stop your enemies from capturing and perhaps destroying it? Would it have been easy to take control of the castle of an enemy? Or would it have been a hard, long drawn-out and dangerous job?

To answer these questions, we have to combine what we know about medieval castles with our own imagination. The activities below will help you to do this.

Attacking and defending a castle

Imagine you are an enemy of the nobleman who lives in the castle in Fig. 3.25. You are organising

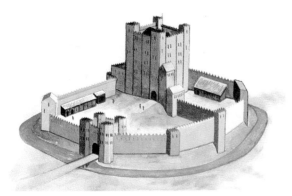

Fig. 3.25 The castle.

Fig. 3.26 Filling in part of the moat.

Fig. 3.27 A belfry.

an attack on the castle. Below are the moves you make and some of the responses made by your enemy. Look carefully at the pictures and answer the questions about each stage of the attack.

1 Filling in part of the moat (Fig. 3.26).
   a Why would you do this?
   b How would you do it?
   c What problems might you face?

2 Pushing a belfry into place (Fig. 3.27).
   A belfry was a huge tower on wheels. When the moat was filled in, it was pushed as close as possible to the castle walls.
   a How do you think a belfry was made?
   b What would it help you to achieve?
   c Why were there several levels inside the belfry?

3 Defending the castle from the walls (Fig. 3.28).
   a Why was the castle built with spaces between the walls?
   b How effective do you think arrows would be against the enemy in the belfry?
   c Sometimes the defenders threw rocks over the battlements or poured boiling oil over their enemies. How effective do you think these tactics would have been?

4 Tunnelling under the castle walls (Fig. 3.29).
   a When do you think this would have been started?
   b What would the attackers hope to achieve?

5 Bringing in a battering ram (Fig. 3.30).
   a What did the attackers have to do before they could use a battering ram?
   b Explain how a battering ram was used.
   c What did the attackers hope to achieve by using a battering ram?

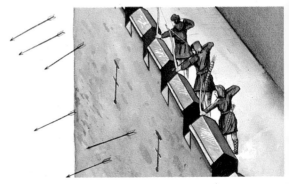

Fig. 3.28 Defending the castle from the walls.

6 Using a balista (Fig. 3.31).

A balista was a giant cross-bow which fired a heavy bolt, often tipped with an inflammable material.

a Why would the bolt be tipped with an inflammable material?

b Where would be the best place for it to land?

c Was there any way the defenders could destroy the power of the balista?

7 Bringing in a trebuchet (Fig. 3.32).

A trebuchet was like a huge catapult. The long arm was winched down and, when released, hurled a missile into the castle, over the walls. Sometimes the missile was a cannonball; sometimes it was a dead and rotting animal like a horse.

a Why were dead animals hurled over the castle walls?

b Why was the trebuchet weighted at the opposite end from the missile?

c Would there have been any disadvantages in using this weapon?

Look again at the castle in Fig. 3.25. Using what you have learned about attacking and defending a castle, write an account of how you would attack this castle. Your army is camped outside the castle and you have stopped anyone getting in or out of the castle so that when you start your attack the people inside the castle know that they cannot call on outsiders for help. They may also be getting hungry because your soldiers are not allowing any food to be taken into the castle.

Some of the methods you choose to attack the castle may be successful; others may not be successful. Will you win?

Fig. 3.30 Bringing in a battering ram.

Fig. 3.31 Using a balista.

Fig. 3.29 Tunnelling under the castle walls.

Fig. 3.32 A trebuchet.

4

China: a world apart

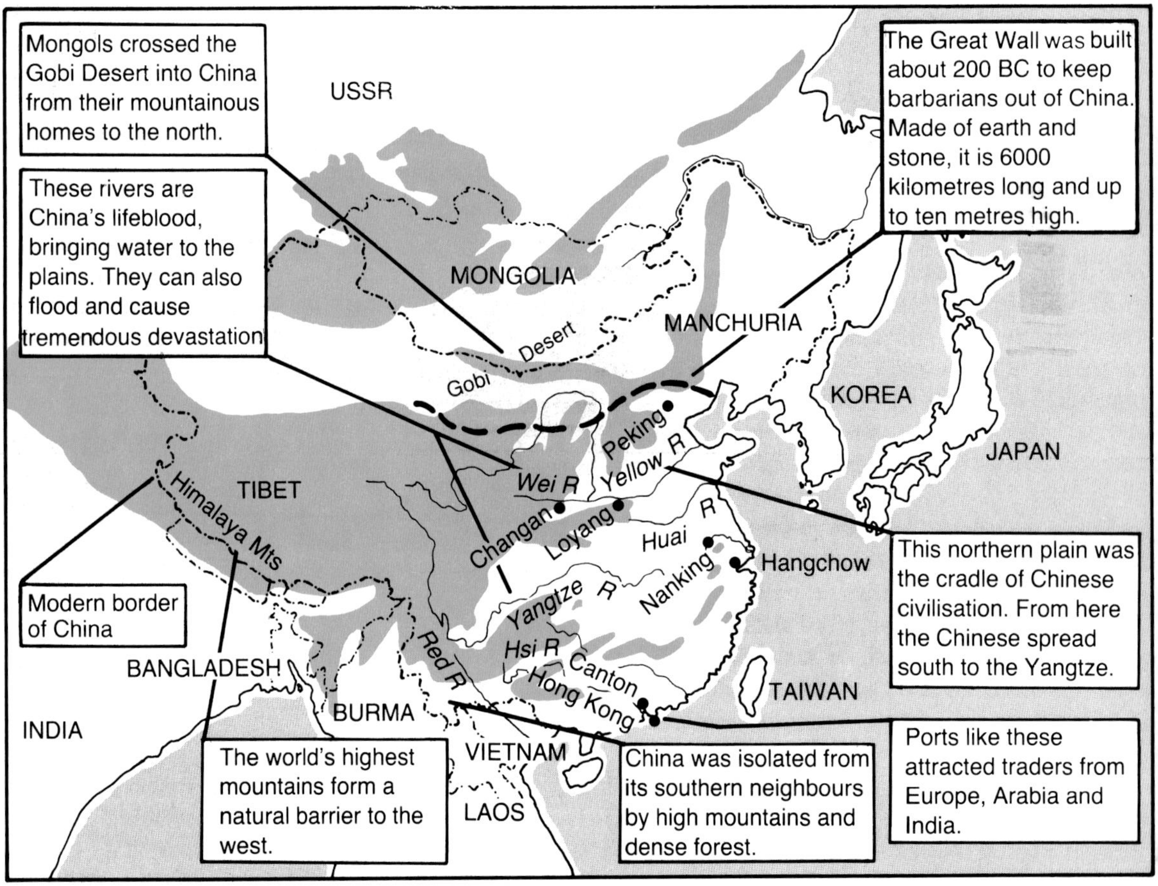
Mongols crossed the Gobi Desert into China from their mountainous homes to the north.
These rivers are China's lifeblood, bringing water to the plains. They can also flood and cause tremendous devastation
Modern border of China
The world's highest mountains form a natural barrier to the west.
China was isolated from its southern neighbours by high mountains and dense forest.
Ports like these attracted traders from Europe, Arabia and India.
This northern plain was the cradle of Chinese civilisation. From here the Chinese spread south to the Yangtze.
The Great Wall was built about 200 BC to keep barbarians out of China. Made of earth and stone, it is 6000 kilometres long and up to ten metres high.
USSR
MONGOLIA
MANCHURIA
Gobi Desert
KOREA
JAPAN
Peking
Yellow R
Wei R
TIBET
Himalaya Mts
Changan
Loyang
Huai R
Hangchow
Nanking
Yangtze R
Hsi R
Canton
Hong Kong
Red R
TAIWAN
BANGLADESH
BURMA
INDIA
VIETNAM
LAOS

Fig. 4.1 China, a world apart.

LOOK CAREFULLY at the map of China in Fig. 4.1. From it you can see that China is a large land, a land that today is the home of a quarter of the world's people. The map also shows the most important features of China's geography. As you read this chapter, it is important to keep these geographic facts in mind, because much of what happened in China in the period we shall be studying—the long period between 200 and 1644—was influenced by China's geography.

Most of China's land is either too mountainous or too poor for farming and only about one-tenth is fertile enough to support crops. For thousands of years the people of China have tried to survive on this fertile area, the land watered by the Yellow and Yangtze Rivers and their tributaries.

During the period we are studying, the Chinese farmers, or peasants, worked seven days a week just to grow enough food to feed their families. Yet they were expected to provide some grain to pay their landlords and even more to pay the taxes the rulers demanded of them.

This struggle to survive became very much worse in times of drought and flood, or when the crops failed. It was worse, too, when rulers or local officials demanded higher taxes or levies to pay for wars, luxurious palaces or expensive building projects. When this happened, many peasants were forced to hand over their land to

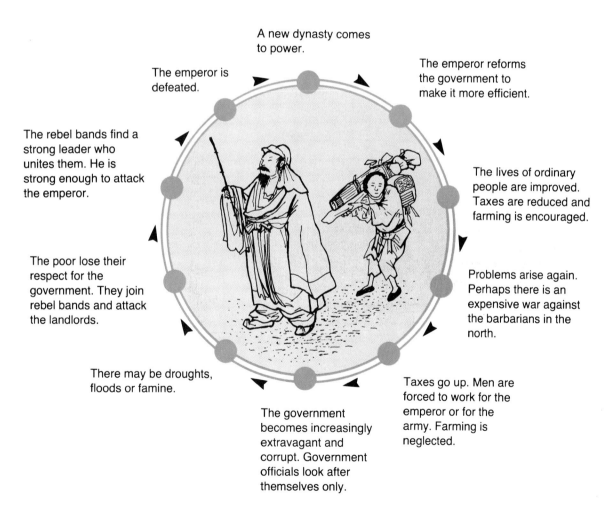

A new dynasty comes to power.

The emperor is defeated.

The emperor reforms the government to make it more efficient.

The rebel bands find a strong leader who unites them. He is strong enough to attack the emperor.

The lives of ordinary people are improved. Taxes are reduced and farming is encouraged.

The poor lose their respect for the government. They join rebel bands and attack the landlords.

Problems arise again. Perhaps there is an expensive war against the barbarians in the north.

There may be droughts, floods or famine.

Taxes go up. Men are forced to work for the emperor or for the army. Farming is neglected.

The government becomes increasingly extravagant and corrupt. Government officials look after themselves only.

Fig. 4.2 The cyclic pattern of Chinese history.

the landlords. Some joined roaming bands of outlaws, wandering the countryside attacking officials and landlords and surviving on what they could steal.

If these bands became strong and powerful, if they had strong leaders and determined followers, they were sometimes able to attack and defeat the rulers of China. The outlaw leader then became a ruler himself and formed a new ruling family, or *dynasty*.

This pattern of the rise and fall of dynasties was repeated many times in China's long history. In this chapter we shall see how a few of these dynasties came to power, how the people of China lived during their periods of rule, and how they eventually collapsed when new groups rose up and threatened them.

A time of disunity, 220–581

Our study of China begins in the year 220, the year in which the Han empire, which had been established long ago in 206 BC, collapsed. Although the Han emperors had controlled only part of what is now China, they had brought unity and stable government to the area they ruled.

This unity was destroyed when the empire broke up. Instead of one emperor, China was ruled by a number of military leaders, or warlords. For more than 350 years the people of China suffered as these rulers struggled to keep and strengthen their power. Hundreds of thousands of peasants died in these battles and old stories tell of rivers being blocked by their bodies.

Because no single warlord was strong enough to keep them out, nomadic or barbarian tribes from the north attacked parts of China, sometimes defeating the local rulers and setting up short-lived governments of their own. Among these invaders were tribes from Mongolia, Manchuria and Tibet.

During these years, the extravagance and wealth of the rich contrasted very strongly with the suffering and poverty of the poor. While most Chinese struggled to stay alive and cope with the ever-increasing demands for taxes and military service, the wealthy landowners built strongly fortified homes to protect themselves

and their families from attack. Government officials, called *mandarins*, who were supposed to administer law and order, collect taxes and look after local affairs, worked only to help the landlords. They lived in luxury and grew their fingernails enormously long to show that they had nothing to do with hard work.

Chinese achievements

Despite the troubled times, Chinese culture survived the long period of disunity. In Europe, the barbarians destroyed what remained of the Roman empire, but in China the barbarian invaders (such as the Mongols and Turks)

Fig. 4.3 This water-lift was invented in China in the third century. The men worked the pedals to move the pieces of wood which brought water up from rivers to the fields. Why do you think this invention was also called 'the dragon's backbone'?

adapted to Chinese ways and became part of Chinese society without destroying it.

During this period, Chinese inventions included a weaving loom that wove silk six times faster than the old-style loom, a water-lift to raise water from rivers for irrigation, and water mills. Chinese mathematicians worked out the exact value of pi (π), which helped them to do complex calculations. A farming encyclopaedia and geography of China were also written. Another invention of the period was the wheelbarrow—an implement that was not used in Europe until the time of the Renaissance, ten centuries later!

Time to understand

1 The diagram in Fig. 4.4 shows a Chinese wheelbarrow.
   a Write two or three sentences describing a wheelbarrow.
   b What sort of things are wheelbarrows used for today? Do you think they were used for the same purposes in early China? Why?
   c What would have been used to do this work before the invention of wheelbarrows? Would these implements have been as efficient as wheelbarrows?
   d How do you think the wheelbarrow was invented? What sort of person might have invented it? Why?
   e Can you suggest why wheelbarrows were not used in Europe for many hundreds of years after they were invented and used in China?

Fig. 4.4 A Chinese wheelbarrow.

The Sui reunite China, 581–618

The long period of war and confusion ended when Yang Chien, a warlord from the north, managed to bring much of China under one ruler again. After a series of victories, he was able, in 581, to proclaim himself as the first emperor of a new dynasty, the Sui. Twenty years later he was murdered by his son, Yang Ti, who became the second Sui emperor.

Yang Ti was a cruel and vicious man who was determined to strengthen his power and prestige at all costs. He had grand plans for buildings and battles, plans that would be successful only if millions of people were forced to work for him. Human life meant nothing to Yang Ti and his supporters.

The most ambitious, and certainly the most useful, of Yang Ti's building projects was the Grand Canal, which was needed to move the grain grown in the fertile plains to the poorer areas. The food that passed along the canal fed Yang Ti's armies which were stationed on the borders to stop barbarian tribes from seizing land.

The canal was more than twelve metres wide with tree-lined avenues along its banks. More than two million people, both men and women, from the ages of fifteen to fifty, were called up to build it. When it was finally opened, the emperor and his courtiers made a journey along its length, forming a line of boats a hundred kilometres long that were towed by 80 000 peasants.

Yang Ti was assassinated in 618 by a group of rebellious army officers. One of them, Li Shih Min, was powerful enough to put his own father on the throne of China and start a new dynasty which he called the Tang. Nine years later, in 627, he became emperor himself, taking the name of Tai Tsung. A new dynasty had begun.

Time to understand

1 Although Yang Ti was a cruel and unpopular emperor, he was very fond of books. He issued a decree offering a length of silk to anyone who could lend a book to the imperial palace. The book was then copied out by the palace

Fig. 4.5 A boat on the Grand Canal. The map in Fig. 4.6 shows where the Grand Canal was built. It was later extended and deepened.

scribes and returned to its owner. In this way, over 400 000 books were copied, many of which would otherwise have been lost forever. The palace of Yang Ti had the greatest collection of books anywhere in the world: in fact, there were more books in China than in the rest of the world put together.

Imagine that Yang Ti had the resources of modern newspapers in which to advertise his offer. Design an advertisement explaining the offer, what would happen to the books and why the offer was being made. Make your advertisement as convincing as possible: remember that you are trying to persuade people to part with a precious item, even if only for a short time.

How do you think Yang Ti *really* made his offer known?

2 The Grand Canal in China is nearly ten times as long as the combined length of the Suez and Panama Canals. Find out more about each of these canals. Where are they? Why was each one built? How long is each one? When was each built? You may be able to find illustrations of each canal showing the kind of country it passes through.

The Tang dynasty, 618–907

The period of Tang rule—from 618 until 907—was a time of relative peace for war-torn China. The Tang empire was much larger than the lands controlled by either Charlemagne or Alfred the Great—both of whom were ruling at about the same time as the early Tang emperors. With peace came prosperity for more people; and with prosperity came a golden age of culture rather like the Gupta period in India which you read about in Chapter One.

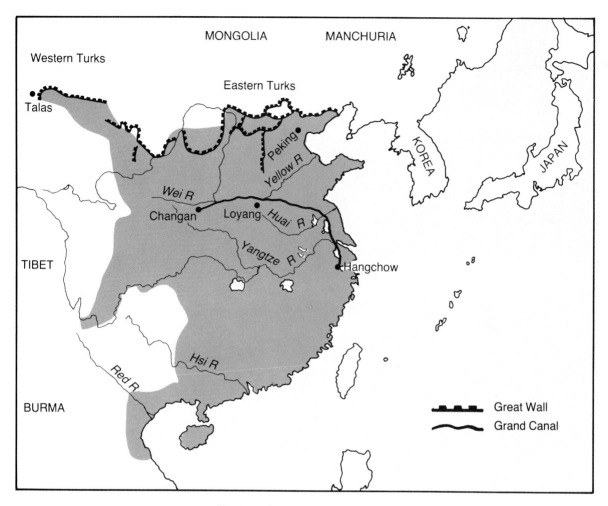

Fig. 4.6 The Tang empire, 700.

The Tang emperors encouraged agriculture. Taxes were reduced, irrigation canals were dug and campaigns were waged against insect pests like locusts, which could devastate a crop in a few hours. In addition, the emperors encouraged farmers to open up new land. This policy helped not only the farmers but the emperors as well. New land meant more farms, and more farms meant more taxes; all of which helped to pay for Tang government.

Education and exams

In order to govern efficiently, the Tang emperors realised that they needed an efficient and competent public service. For several hundred years, local officials had not organised government affairs properly because most of them were concerned only with looking after their own interests and keeping on the right side of the local warlord or military leader. The Tang emperors changed this by bringing back and improving a system of selecting government officials that had first been developed during the Han empire many years earlier. This was a complicated system of examinations, in which students were tested on ancient Chinese tradition, law and the Confucian religion. The Confucian religion had been established in China around 500 BC and was supported and encouraged by the emperors so that it had become the 'official' religion of China.

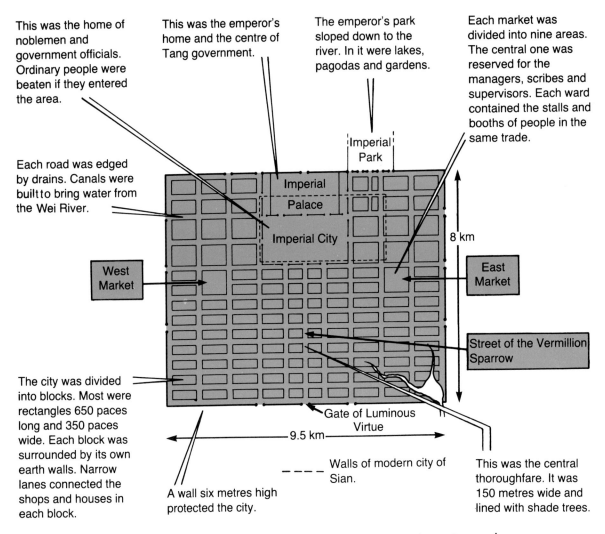

This was the home of noblemen and government officials. Ordinary people were beaten if they entered the area.

This was the emperor's home and the centre of Tang government.

The emperor's park sloped down to the river. In it were lakes, pagodas and gardens.

Each market was divided into nine areas. The central one was reserved for the managers, scribes and supervisors. Each ward contained the stalls and booths of people in the same trade.

Each road was edged by drains. Canals were built to bring water from the Wei River.

Imperial Park

Imperial Palace

Imperial City

8 km

West Market

East Market

Street of the Vermillion Sparrow

The city was divided into blocks. Most were rectangles 650 paces long and 350 paces wide. Each block was surrounded by its own earth walls. Narrow lanes connected the shops and houses in each block.

Gate of Luminous Virtue

9.5 km

A wall six metres high protected the city.

---- Walls of modern city of Sian.

This was the central thoroughfare. It was 150 metres wide and lined with shade trees.

Fig. 4.7 Changan, 'the city of lasting peace'. This city was at the eastern end of the trading route from Europe.

Only the most hard-working and able students gained success in these examinations. They were appointed at first to minor government positions but if they were capable or lucky, they could be promoted to become regional governors or given other posts of power, wealth and influence. Thus, while in Europe men gained power by success in battle, in China they were able to gain power by success in study and examination.

While the examination system encouraged the study of the ancient Chinese classics, it had the disadvantage of being very formal and inflexible. Students were expected to learn large slabs of Confucius' writings, and to understand the meaning of every word. There was no interest in encouraging students to think for themselves, to be creative or to question the world they lived in. Because of this, the examination system discouraged change. In fact, it continued until 1905.

The 'city of lasting peace'

The long period of peace that the Tang brought to China made possible the growth of Changan, the capital city, and other cities.

Fig. 4.8 Emperor Tai Tsung, founder of the Tang dynasty.

The diagram in Fig. 4.7 shows the layout of the city of Changan, 'the city of lasting peace' and the most magnificent city in Asia during Tang times. More than a million people lived inside the city walls and almost as many made their homes in the suburbs that stretched outside the city. Today the city of Sian is on the site of Changan, but it is much smaller than the old city.

Changan was a great trading centre, with people from many parts of the world selling goods of all kinds in the markets and bazaars. While the marketplaces were bustling with life, the imperial city was out-of-bounds to ordinary people. It was a place of great beauty and luxury, the centre of Tang government and the home of the emperor and his courtiers.

A golden age of culture

In Chapter One you read about the Gupta period in India, a time when stable government and a long period of peace gave rise to a golden age of culture. The same thing happened in China during the Tang period. The eighth century was a high point of Chinese painting, sculpture, decorative writing and poetry.

The illustrations in Figs 4.9–4.11 on page 66

show a few of the works of art that were produced during the Tang period (you can read more about each one in the captions for each picture). On these pages you can also read some of the poetry of Li Po and Tu Fu, two famous poets of Tang times.

> When I wake and look out on the lawn
> I hear midst the flowers a bird sing;
> I ask, 'Is it evening or dawn?'
> The mango-bird whistles, 'Tis spring'.
>
> Over powered by the beautiful sight
> Another full goblet I pour
> And would sing till the moon rises bright—
> But soon I'm as drunk as before.
>
> *Li Po*

> The silk shared out in the Vermilion Hall
> Was woven by the hands of poor women
> Women whose men were whipped in their own homes
> By tax collectors who took the silk to court.
>
> So many courtiers now throng around the court
> That honest men must tremble;
> And it's said that the gold plate from the treasury
> Has gone to the kinsmen of the Lady Yang.
>
> *Tu Fu*

People of the Tang

Wu Chao was the only woman ever to rule China as empress. She began her political career in the court of Li Shih Min when she joined the emperor's harem at the age of thirteen. By a combination of shrewdness, political skill and intrigue, she gradually gained more power, until in 690 she was appointed as the empress. Wu Chao ruled China from then until she was forced to give up the throne in 705. She was a strong and able ruler but, partly because she was a woman and partly because of her ruthless punishment of enemies, she was feared and disliked at court. Wu was a supporter of the Buddhist faith and encouraged many of the artists who created sculptures and paintings of the Buddha.

Li Po was one of the best-known poets of the Tang period. He and other poets were supported and encouraged by empress Wu's grandson,

Fig. 4.9 A model horse.

Fig. 4.10 A Tang painting showing warriors in action.

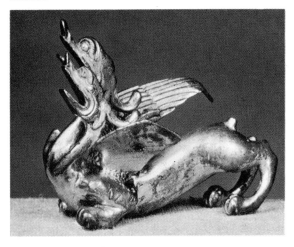

Fig. 4.11 A three-headed monster of the Tang dynasty, beautifully sculpted in gold.

Hsuan Tsung, who was emperor from 712 to 756. Li Po spent part of his life at court, entertaining and being entertained, drinking and writing poetry. He belonged to a group called the 'Eight Immortals of the Wine Cup' and spent much of his time drunk. According to legend, he died by drowning as he was hanging over the side of a boat trying to catch the reflection of the moon in the water. Li Po's poetry was cheerful, carefree and romantic. He wrote about nature, friendship and the pleasures of good company.

Tu Fu, another poet, was a friend of Li Po, but he was a more serious and thoughtful man. Unlike Li Po, he did not live at court and was often short of money to feed his children. Tu Fu hated the suffering and cruelty of war and the corruption of life at court. He felt strongly about the poverty and suffering of ordinary people and wrote about their experiences in his poems.

An Lu Shan was a Turk who had been captured in battle and sold as a slave to a Chinese officer. He gained influence in the Tang court and was appointed as a provincial governor, and even given the title of prince. Thousands of men joined his army and, when he was strong enough, An Lu Shan marched to Changan and attacked the imperial palace. The emperor was powerless against him; there were murders and massacres, mutinies and rebellions. The peasants no longer supported the Tang because taxes were once again high to pay for the extravagant court life. The peasants also resented being called up for military service to protect China from the barbarians. The rebellion which An Lu Shan began was to bring about the end of the Tang dynasty.

Time to understand

What does the expression 'public servant' mean in Australia? What sort of work do public servants do? How are Australian public servants chosen today? Does the way today's public servants are selected resemble the way government officials were selected in Tang China?

Although the Chinese examination system seemed to be a fair way of selecting government officials, it is worth considering these facts:

- Women were not allowed to sit for the exams.
- Merchants, boatmen, beggars and actors were not allowed to sit for the exams.
- Many years of study were needed before a student was able to take the exams. Poor people could not afford to do without their sons' work for the long years of study.
- High officials could recommend their sons for government jobs even if they had not passed the exams.

Was the examination system *really* fair? Consider each of the above points and make your own conclusions. Do Australians who want to become public servants have the same restrictions as the Chinese of the Tang period?

The Sung dynasty, 960–1279

Another period of war and turmoil followed the collapse of the Tang dynasty. This was the period of the 'five dynasties and ten kingdoms' as generals, warlords and governors tried to seize power for themselves. None of them was strong enough however, until 960, when Chao Kuang established the Sung as China's rulers.

The new emperor and his successors faced many problems, particularly the constant threat of attack from the nomadic tribes on China's borders. In fact, the Sung never controlled as much of China as earlier emperors. Despite the efforts of reformers in the government, the emperor was not strong enough to keep control

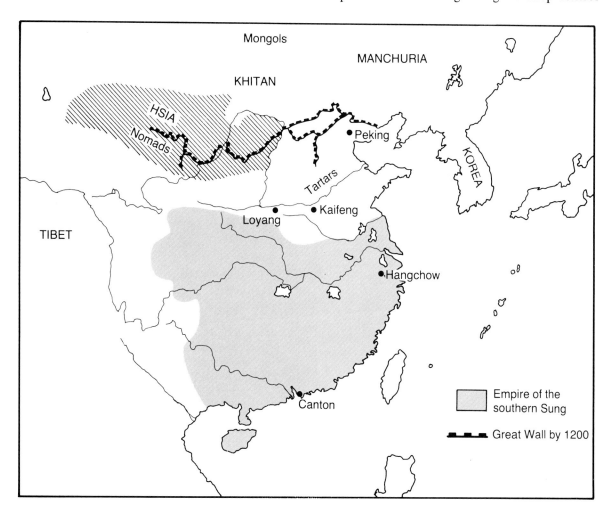

Fig. 4.12 The land controlled by the southern Sung, 1126–1279.

of northern China, and in 1126 the Sung capital, Kaifeng, was raided by nomadic tribes known as Kin Tartars. The emperor was forced to flee to the south, where a southern Sung empire was set up at the city of Hangchow.

With all the problems the Sung emperors faced, it is suprising that the period was one of great achievements. In some ways, the Sung period was like the Renaissance in Europe about 400 years later. It was a time when great and beautiful works of art were created, some of which have survived until today. It was a time, too, when people were interested in science and the world around them. Chinese scientists developed a vaccine against smallpox. The abacus, or counting frame, was invented, as well as an accurate clock and paper money.

Printing

Printing was developed in China hundreds of years before it was known in Europe. The invention of printing depended on two things: paper and ink. Both had been invented in China by the sixth century and by about 650 the art of block printing was underway. The diagrams in Fig. 4.13 show how this early kind of printing was done.

The earliest known printed book is the *Diamond Sutra*, which dates from 868—almost six hundred years before a book was printed in Europe.

The examination system stimulated the growth of printing because students needed to study the works of Confucius in order to sit for the exams. Between 932 and 953, 130 volumes of the Confucian classics were printed from woodblocks. The invention of printing also made possible the printing of paper money and playing cards—both of which existed during the Sung period.

The examination system

The examination system for selecting public servants and government officials was strengthened in Sung times. Strict rules were made about when and where the exams were to be held and what was to be tested. Students were locked into tiny cubicles for several days to do their exam papers; some died of exhaustion or went mad with the strain.

Commerce and city life

During the years when the Sung emperors controlled southern China, there was a great increase in trade and commerce. Land trade was mainly of horses from the north, which the Sung wanted for their cavalry. In exchange, the Sung rulers supplied the northern nomads with tea, silk and other goods. Sea trade was increasing, too, with huge junks (Chinese ships), each crewed by several hundred men, sailing to India, Africa and South-east Asia. They carried Chinese pottery, artworks, silk and paintings to other countries and brought back spices, ivory, cotton and timber.

With the growth of trade and commerce cities also grew. The growing population increasingly settled in cities like Hangchow, Canton and Chuanchou. These were among the world's largest cities at the time and, like Changan, had long, wide streets. Street-cleaners were employed to keep the cities clean. There were fire brigades, restaurants, amusement places, fairs and markets, schools and orphanages. Rice and pork were sold around the city, with street merchants carrying small amounts of each for sale to householders. Craftsmen worked at their trades, organised into guilds or associations for each craft.

Yet not all Chinese people shared in this wealth. Poverty was an ever-present problem, both in the country and in the cities. One poet wrote of the beggars who thronged cities like Hangchow:

In filthy knotted rags and broken hats,
They carry threadbare rugs and tattered mats;
    With batons of bamboo,
    And battered rice bowls too,
They swarm the rich man's gate and raise
    A frightful how-d'ye-do.

The end of the Sung

Like the other dynasties you have read about in this chapter, the Sung dynasty collapsed as a result of two important things: a foreign threat which was becoming increasingly powerful, and

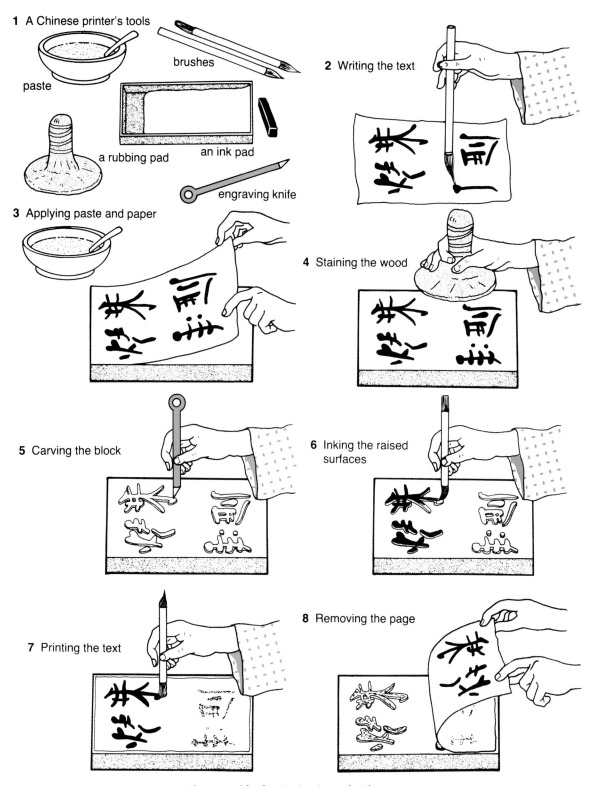

1 A Chinese printer's tools

paste

brushes

a rubbing pad

an ink pad

engraving knife

2 Writing the text

3 Applying paste and paper

4 Staining the wood

5 Carving the block

6 Inking the raised surfaces

7 Printing the text

8 Removing the page

Fig. 4.13 Block printing in early China.

69

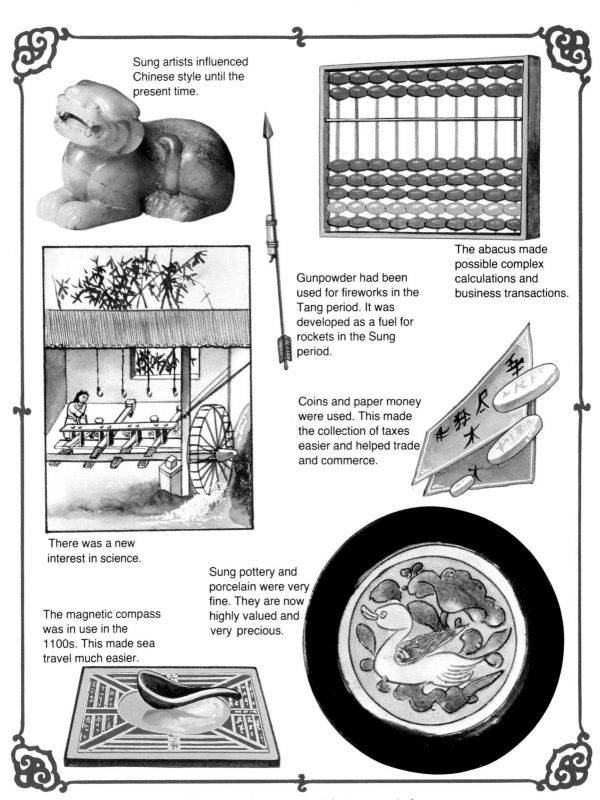

Sung artists influenced Chinese style until the present time.

The abacus made possible complex calculations and business transactions.

Gunpowder had been used for fireworks in the Tang period. It was developed as a fuel for rockets in the Sung period.

Coins and paper money were used. This made the collection of taxes easier and helped trade and commerce.

There was a new interest in science.

Sung pottery and porcelain were very fine. They are now highly valued and very precious.

The magnetic compass was in use in the 1100s. This made sea travel much easier.

Fig. 4.14 Achievements of the Sung period.

The border tribes made frequent raids into Sung territory. The emperor had to bribe them to stop them from attacking his kingdom.

A large amount of Sung government funds was spent defending the empire against barbarian invasion.

As taxes rose, farmers had to sell their land or borrow from moneylenders at high rates of interest.

The government became corrupt. Officials were more interested in increasing their own power than in doing any work.

An official named Wang An Shih tried to introduce reforms. The opposition was so strong that he was forced to resign.

Fig. 4.15 Some reasons why the Sung empire collapsed.

growing discontent among the people governed by the Sung. The diagram in Fig. 4.15 explains these problems in more detail.

cards the Chinese used? Where did the pictures on modern cards come from? When were they first used?

Time to understand

1 Using the diagrams in Fig. 4.13 on page 69, try to print a design or piece of writing using the block printing method. Do you think it is an efficient way of printing?
2 The abacus is one of the oldest calculating machines. Do you know how it works? If not, try to find out by looking up 'abacus' in an encyclopaedia.
3 You might be able to find out more about the history of playing cards in an encyclopaedia. Can you find any pictures showing the kind of

The Mongols

As we have seen throughout this chapter, the nomadic tribes on China's border were always a threat to the peace of China and no emperor could really be sure that his rule would be strong enough to resist attack. These border people were tough and hardy: they had to be because of the harsh land they lived in. The plains and grasslands of the north were not very fertile and it was almost impossible to survive by growing crops. Instead, the nomads moved around, grazing their horses and cattle, plundering and steal-

Fig. 4.16 A Mongol horseman. Under Genghis Khan the Mongol cavalry was the strongest in the world.

Genghis Khan wanted to conquer the world. A ruthless and skilled leader himself, he developed a mighty cavalry of magnificent horsemen and set out to achieve his dream. Town after town, city after city fell to his men. They moved south into China, conquering the city of Peking in 1215, and west into southern Russia and Persia.

In 1227 Genghis Khan died on a campaign in China. His empire was divided between the four sons of his chief wife, creating four Mongol kingdoms, or *Khanates*: in China, Persia, southern Russia and central Asia. The conquests continued and the Mongol empire grew.

It was Genghis Khan's grandson, Kublai Khan, who finally conquered southern China. The Mongols developed the art of siege warfare and forced the walled Chinese cities to surrender when huge catapults hurled rocks or simple gunpowder bombs over the walls. In 1276 Hangchow surrendered to the Mongols and three years later the last Sung emperor, a young boy, died when the government minister who was carrying him jumped with the boy into the ocean at Canton rather than allow the young emperor to be captured by his enemies.

Kublai Khan moved his capital to the city of Peking. From there he controlled an empire that was even larger than that of his grandfather, Genghis Khan.

In the Chinese way, Kublai Khan declared himself to be the emperor of a new dynasty, the Yuan, or Beginning. He and his courtiers lived in the Chinese style, but his rule was not trusted by the Chinese themselves, who could not forget that the Mongols were enemy barbarians.

The Polos

The huge empire of Kublai Khan made travel between Europe and Asia easier than it had ever been in the past. Two men who took advantage of this were the merchants Maffeo and Niccolo Polo from Venice in Italy. On their first journey to China they met Kublai Khan, who took a great interest in the land they had come from and asked them questions about the religion and rulers of Europe.

ing from their enemies and growing food wherever they could.

These people had developed into fine horsemen and fierce warriors. By Sung times they were such a threat that the emperor paid their leaders a *tribute* or bribe in the hope that they would be satisfied and keep away. As we have seen, however, the nomads broke into northern China and took control of part of the Sung empire in 1126.

The Mongols were a tribe of nomads from Manchuria and Mongolia, north of China. At the end of the 1100s their leader, Temuchin, was able to unite the Turks, Tartars and other nomads of the region with the Mongols, and in 1206, at a gathering of tribes, he was accepted as ruler of all the chiefs. Temuchin took the name of Genghis Khan, meaning 'universal ruler'.

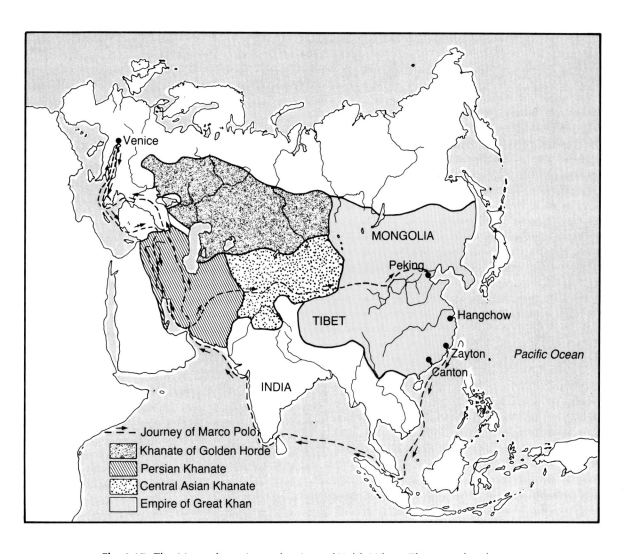

Fig. 4.17 The Mongol empire at the time of Kublai Khan. The map also shows the route taken by Marco Polo.

In 1271 the brothers set out once again for China, this time accompanied by Niccolo's seventeen-year-old son, Marco. The journey to Peking took them over three years. Young Marco Polo learned the language of the Mongols and was employed by Kublai Khan as a government official, being sent on missions around his kingdom. After seventeen years in China, the Polos left again for Europe, escorting in a fleet of junks a seventeen-year-old princess who was being sent as a new wife for the ruler of Persia.

In 1295 the travellers reached their home city of Venice. Few people believed the strange stories they had to tell about the mighty empire in the east. When Marco Polo was taken as a prisoner in a war between Venice and another Italian city, he told his story to another prisoner who wrote it down in French. It was later published as a book called *The Travels of Marco Polo*. Once again, few people believed what Marco Polo had written in his book; they thought he was making it all up. When he was dying, the traveller said that he had not told even half of what he had seen.

Fig. 4.18 A porcelain dish of the Ming period. Chinese porcelain was of such high quality that we still use the word 'china' to refer to fine pottery today.

Fig. 4.19 A Ming tapestry.

Fig. 4.20 A basket of flowers, painted during the Ming period.

After the Mongols

Kublai Khan died in 1294. As had happened so often in the past, the death of a powerful leader was followed by a period of struggle and war as various groups tried to gain power. At this time, the situation was worsened by famine and flooding of the Yellow River.

Chu Yuan Chang, a peasant who had spent several years begging for his living as a Buddhist monk, became the leader of a secret society called the Red Turbans. In 1356 the society was strong enough to capture the city of Nanking. From there he was able to push the Mongols further and further north. In 1368 Chu Yuan Chang was powerful enough to declare himself to be the emperor of China. He took the name of Hung Wu, meaning 'great military power'. The dynasty he started was called the Ming and its capital was the city of Nanking. The Ming dynasty lasted until 1644.

As had happened so often in the past, the early years of the Ming dynasty were a time of reform, a time when the new emperor tried to improve the lives of his people. Taxes were reduced and peasants were encouraged to farm new land or land that had been idle during the time of war. The government began projects to conserve water. Craftsmen were encouraged. The illustrations in Figs 4.18–4.20 show some of the works of art that were produced during the Ming period.

The Ming emperors ruled wisely for about a hundred years. By then, however, the weaknesses in the government were becoming more evident. The emperor's advisers were concerned not with the welfare of the people, but with their own power and influence. The emperors themselves were becoming less powerful as their advisers gained more influence in government policy. While greed and selfishness ruled at the royal court, the people were becoming poorer. Tax collectors travelled the country trying to force just a little more from people who were almost at starvation point. Female babies were drowned when their parents could not support them; other children were sold as slaves.

In 1644 the Ming dynasty was destroyed, once again by enemies from the north. Tribespeople from Manchuria united, just as the Mongols had done in 1206 under Genghis Khan. They fought their way southwards and captured Peking, the Ming capital. The emperor committed suicide by hanging himself from a tree behind the imperial palace. The tree is still there, bowed and bent. According to Chinese legend, it dare not raise its head because it was the means by which the emperor, the 'Son of Heaven', died.

The Ming dynasty collapsed. Once again barbarian conquerors controlled China.

How do we know?

We have already seen how important documents written at one time can be for those who, perhaps hundreds or thousands of years later, want to find out about the time when the documents were written. The two documents below were written many hundreds of years apart—the first is part of a long poem written by a Chinese woman between 200 and 300; the second is an extract from *The Travels of Marco Polo*. Yet these two documents have one thing in common, for each tells us something about Chinese women in the period we have studied in this chapter.

An unhappy life

At thirteen I knew how to weave silk.
At fourteen I learned to sew.
At fifteen I could play the small lute
And at sixteen I knew how to sing well.
At seventeen I was made your wife and moved into your parents' house.
From care and sorrow my heart was never free thereafter,
For you cared for nothing but your work.
I was left alone.

It was not often that we two were together.
From dawn till night I toiled and got no rest.
And yet the Great One, my mother-in-law,
scolded me for being lazy.
Husband, I find it hard to be your wife in your
parents' house.
For it is not in my power to do all the tasks I am
given!
Go then, quickly, speak to your mother
Or let me go back to my home!'
Her husband listened to her words,
Then went to his mother's room. 'Mother,' he
said,
'Luck was with me when I took this girl for my
wife.
We have lived here and served you two years or
three.
In nothing has the girl offended or done you
wrong.
What has happened to bring trouble between
you?'
Then spoke his mother:
'Come, my son, such love is foolish.
Your wife neglects all rules of behavior
And in all her ways follows only her own whim.
I have long been displeased with her.
Send her away quickly. Do not let her stay.'

1 From the evidence of this part of the poem, what skills and qualities were Chinese girls and women expected to have?
2 What do you think the writer meant by saying that she was 'made your wife'? Do you think she had any say in the choice of a husband?
3 Why did she call her mother-in-law the 'Great One'?
4 Why did the woman find it hard to live in her husband's parents' house?
5 Why did the Great One make life hard for the young wife? Can you suggest some of the 'rules of behaviour' that she may have neglected?

6 Can you think of a way this story may have ended:
a happily?
b unhappily?

The young women of China

They do not keep watch at the windows gazing at passers-by or exposing themselves to their gaze. They do not listen to improper stories. They do not gad about to parties and entertainments. If it happens that they go out to some respectable place, as for instance to the temples of their idols or to visit the houses of relatives, they walk in the company of their mothers, not glancing brazenly about them, but some of them wear pretty hoods over their heads . . . On their way they always walk with their eyes cast down in front of their feet. In the presence of their elders they are respectful and never utter a needless word—indeed they do not speak at all in their presence unless addressed.

a What qualities did Marco Polo admire in China's young women?
b Do you think that Marco Polo would have approved of the behaviour and attitudes of the young wife in the previous poem? Why?
c From the evidence of the poem and this extract, had the position of women in China changed very much between about 200 and the time of Marco Polo's visit? About how many years apart were these two documents written? Can you suggest why women's lives had not changed very much?

5

Japan: the 'walled garden'

IN THE LAST CHAPTER we began our study of China by looking at the geography of the country. In the same way, we shall start our exploration of Japanese history by learning about the main features of the landscape of Japan.

The map in Fig. 5.1 shows the four main islands that make up the country of Japan. As well as these four big islands there are about 300 smaller islands in Japan. According to an old legend they were formed when an ancient god plunged his spear into the sea and dragged it out again. The drops of water became the islands of Japan. Altogether the Japanese islands form an archipelago that stretches for more than 2400 kilometres.

About 80 per cent of Japan consists of steep hills and mountains, some of which are volcanoes. Because of this, most Japanese people live either on the narrow coastal strip or along the valleys that rivers have cut out between the mountains. Only about 15 per cent of Japan's land can be used for farming. Japanese farms, therefore, are very small but are intensively and carefully farmed. Hills and mountains are terraced so that crops like rice, wheat, barley and vegetables can be grown on them.

You can see from the small map in Fig. 5.1 that Japan is close to, but separate from, the rest of east Asia. Across the Sea of Japan, 160 kilometres to the west, lies the country of Korea, while China is about 800 kilometres away.

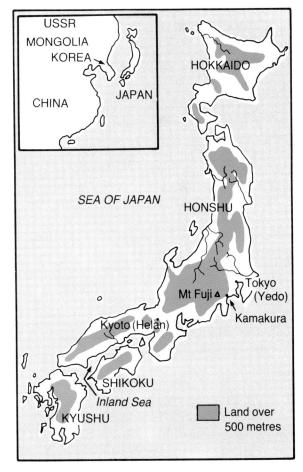

Fig. 5.1 The land of Japan.

Fig. 5.2 Terraced ricefields make the most of Japan's mountainous land.

The fact that Japan is surrounded by water has been very important in the country's history. The ocean has been like a barrier, keeping foreigners out of Japan. Although, as we shall see in this chapter, Japan has been strongly influenced by Chinese culture, it has been invaded by foreigners only three times: once by the Mongols in the thirteenth century, once by the Americans and Europeans in the nineteenth century, and again by the countries that defeated Japan in the Second World War.

Time to understand

1 What are the names of Japan's four main islands?
2 What is an archipelago? Find out the names of three other archipelagos. Where are they?
3 Use an encyclopaedia or other reference book to find out about the 'Pacific ring of fire'. Try to find a picture showing the countries affected by the 'ring of fire'. Can you find out what scientists believe to be the cause of the 'ring of fire'?

4 Find out the name of Japan's highest mountain. How high is it? What is Australia's highest mountain? How high is it? Draw a diagram of the two mountains on the same scale to show the relative height of each one.

Ancient Japan

People have lived in Japan since the Stone Age. By about 250 AD they had developed a culture known as 'mound building'. Like the ancient Egyptians who buried their dead leaders in pyramids, the mound builders of Japan buried their chieftains in huge mounds. Archaeologists have dug into these mounds to find evidence about the life of the mound builders. In the mounds they have discovered pieces of pottery, mirrors and bronze objects from China. This evidence indicates that Japan had contact with the culture of China at the time. The link was probably through Korea, which at that time was a colony of China.

The mound builders were a tough, warlike people, quite at home on horseback and accustomed to brawling and fighting to solve their problems and disagreements. The ruling family probably changed often as local leaders fought to become chief.

The *uji* system

The most powerful rulers of the mound building period were the Yamato family. Gradually they took control of neighbouring groups until they held a loose control over most of Japan. But they never had complete control of the country. Instead, Japan was broken up into a number of clans called *uji*, each of which controlled part of the land. The members of each *uji* believed that they had the same ancestor; they also worshipped the same god. Sometimes, the god they worshipped was in fact the ancestor of their clan.

The Yamato became powerful by taking control over other *uji*. Later, however, some *uji* became so strong that they really ruled the country. Although the Yamato were still supposed to be the rulers of Japan, it was the *uji* who held real power.

Shinto, the Japanese religion

The religion of the early Japanese has been called *Shinto*, a name which means 'way of the gods'. The basis of Shinto was the worship of nature. By praising and worshipping natural things such as waterfalls, trees and rocks, the believer could worship the god who had created them.

We have seen that in the *uji* system, the founder of the clan was often worshipped as a god. This helped to strengthen the power of the *uji* chieftains. Obviously, it was harder to disobey

Fig. 5.4 A Shinto shrine.

a ruler if his ancestors were the gods you worshipped.

Because the Yamato clan was the most powerful, the founder of that clan held a particularly strong place in the Shinto religion. The founder of the Yamato was said to have descended from the Sun goddess, the most powerful of all the Shinto gods. And because the rulers of the Yamato were descended from the Sun goddess, they too had to be worshipped and obeyed.

Fig. 5.3 This clay figure of a man in armour was dug up by archaeologists studying burial mounds. It dates from the period of the mound builders. What can we learn about these people from this discovery?

Time to understand

The ancient Egyptians and the Japanese mound builders knew nothing of each other: in fact they were separated not only by distance but also by thousands of years. Can you suggest why each of these people built large burial tombs for their leaders?

Japan and China

Relics discovered by archaeologists show that there were links between Japan and China as early as the first century AD. Sometime during the 400s the Japanese learned of Chinese writing and began adopting and adapting it for themselves. During the sixth century—in the 500s—Japan's links with China grew. This was the time of the Sui empire in China and the beginning of strong rule by the Chinese emperors. Perhaps the Yamato rulers in Japan admired the strength and power of the Chinese emperors and wanted to make their own rule as efficient. Perhaps they were aware of the problems that other ambitious *uji* would bring them.

Among the ideas that spread from China to Japan was the Buddhist religion. Many of the *uji* opposed Buddhism because they felt that it threatened their power. But one clan, the Soga, accepted the new religion.

Buddhism became increasingly popular and in 587 the emperor himself was converted. By this time the Soga clan had become very influential at court. In 593 a Soga leader, Prince Shotoku, became the real ruler of Japan, although he never became emperor.

Prince Shotoku, 593–622

Prince Shotoku admired the culture, government and art of China and tried to copy it in Japan. Shotoku adopted the Chinese calendar and re-organised the court to make it more like the Tang court of China. He set up grades of officials, each rank distinguished by the colour of the caps worn by its members. All government officials had a rank, from the 'Senior First Rank' at the top down to the 'Junior Eighth Rank Lower Grade' at the bottom.

Because of his interest in and admiration for China, Prince Shotoku organised embassies to

Fig. 5.5 This huge statue of Buddha was built by Emperor Shomu at Kamakura in 743. It is 26 metres high and made of 500 000 kilograms of tin, lead and copper and another 250 kilograms of gold.

Fig. 5.6 Prince Shotoku and his sons. How would you describe their clothes? Do you think that all Japanese people dressed like this?

travel from Japan to China. The first was sent in 607. Many more followed.

The embassies to China were large and expensive and those who went on them had to brave great danger. By the 700s each embassy consisted of four new ships and up to 600 men. The ships sailed through rough and dangerous waters and shipwrecks were common. Despite this, the embassies were important to Japan because they made possible the introduction of new ideas about art, music, government, writing and religion from the Chinese empire. As well, the embassies brought back examples of Chinese inventions that were copied in Japan.

Time to understand

Prince Shotoku has been called the 'prince charming' of Japanese history. His abilities and achievements were exaggerated as the years passed until people believed that he could do almost anything. According to tradition, he could speak as soon as he was born, and could listen to ten people at once and make the right decision about each one. Some believed that he knew what was going to happen before it actually happened.

1 Can you suggest why legends like this grow up around some leaders? Why do they not grow up around all leaders?
2 Do you know of any other leaders who were supposed to have magical qualities? Who were they? What qualities were they supposed to have?

Japanese feudalism

In Chapter Three you read about the feudal system in medieval Europe. You will remember that it was a way of organising society in several layers or groups of people, each linked to the group above or below by duties and responsibilities.

A similar kind of feudalism developed in Japan in the Middle Ages. We have seen that the emperors were not strong enough to control all the local noblemen. Although these noblemen officially accepted the emperor as the supreme ruler of Japan, in fact they went their own ways, giving little thought to obeying the emperor's laws and edicts. They paid no taxes on their large areas of land and as a result became very rich. With this wealth came great power. It was the local nobleman rather than the emperor who offered protection to the people. As a result, the people supported various noblemen rather than the emperor, in the many wars of the period.

The nobles set up bands of warriors to protect them and to keep order in their district. These warriors were given land and peasants to work on it. In return, they pledged to support the particular nobleman completely, both in peace and in war. The warriors became known as *samurai*; the noblemen they served were called *daimyo*.

Many samurai divided up the land they had been given by the daimyo and gave some to less important warriors. These men promised to support the richer samurai in the same way as the richer samurai had promised to support the daimyo. If this happened several times, some samurai ended up as the leaders of large bands of less powerful warriors.

Time to understand

Look again at the diagram of the feudal system in Europe in Fig. 3.9 on page 43. Using this as a model, draw another diagram showing how the feudal system in Japan worked.

The samurai

The samurai were a privileged class in Japan. They were not as powerful as the daimyo they served but were higher on the social ladder than the other groups of people—the artisans, craftsmen, peasants and merchants.

As warriors, the samurai had to have great fighting skills. Their symbol was the sword, and they were expected to wield it perfectly. The

Emperor

The emperor's palace was at Kyoto. Although he was officially the ruler of Japan, he had very little real power. He played a ceremonial role in religious rituals.

Shogun

The shogun's palace was at Edo (now Tokyo). He was the most powerful man in Japan and the country's real ruler. The position was passed from father to son.

Daimyo

The daimyo were feudal lords. They held most of Japan's land and were powerful local rulers.

Samurai

The samurai were a class of warriors who served the local daimyo. Some were very wealthy and were served themselves by poorer samurai. They were respected by the peasant farmers.

Farmers

Most farmers were peasants whose lives were hard. They worked just to keep themselves alive and to pay their taxes to those above them.

Craftsmen

Craftsmen in the towns were not regarded very highly because they were outside the traditional village system.

Merchants

Merchants were thought to be of little value because they did not produce anything. Although they were not highly regarded, some merchants were very rich.

Fig. 5.7 The social ladder of feudal Japan.

samurai tried to live their lives according to a code of conduct called *Bushido*, 'the way of the warrior'. According to this code, the samurai had to be courageous in battle but kindly in peace. He should be able to stand pain without flinching and should lead a simple, honourable life without indulging in excesses.

The most basic principle of Bushido was that of loyalty. A samurai had to be completely loyal to his master, even if death was the result. He had to defend the honour of his family name, again even if it meant death. If necessary he had to be prepared to commit *seppuku* or *hara-kiri* rather than accept disgrace or betray his master. This was a ritual way of committing suicide. The disgraced samurai knelt down and slit his stomach with a dagger. Another samurai then cut off his head with his sword. This, according to Bushido, proved that the samurai was completely devoted to his master and wiped away the disgrace that had befallen him.

Time to understand

The advice below was given by a Japanese samurai in 1348. Read it carefully and answer the questions that follow.

> There must be no negligence in the samurai's service. He must get up at four in the morning and practise martial exercises. Then he may have a meal and afterwards shoot with bow and matchlock and ride horseback. And those who

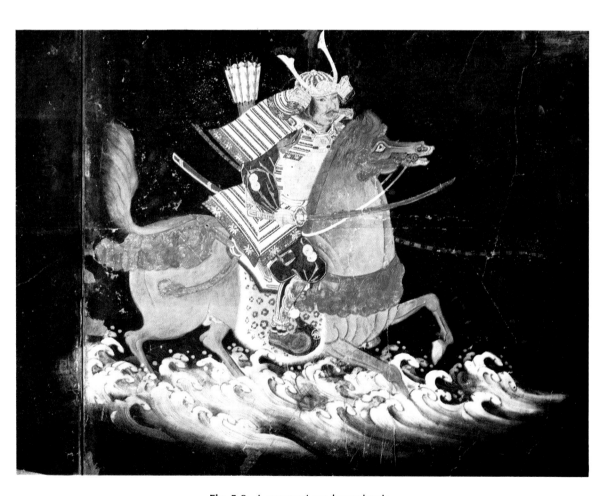

Fig. 5.8 A samurai on horseback.

are proficient in these exercises will be promoted accordingly.

If he wishes for diversion he may find it in hawking, stag-hunting and wrestling. With such things he must amuse himself.

His clothes must be of cotton and pongee. It is an offence to spend money on clothes so that one is embarrassed in other ways. Weapons must be provided in accordance with one's standing, and retainers have to be kept. And in time of war money has to be spent. In ordinary social intercourse there must be only one guest beside the host, and unhulled rice only is to be eaten. However, when military exercises are held there may be a large gathering.

Military rules and etiquette are what a samurai has to know. Those who are given to unnecessary luxury will be held culpable. A stop must be put to all frivolous posturing and sword dancing. When a sword is drawn it is to kill someone. Serious concentration is the secret of everything, so those who go in for these frivolous pastimes will be required to commit *seppuku*.

A samurai must be diligent at his studies. He must read military works and particularly pay attention to matters of loyalty and filial duty.

There must be no making poems and verse-capping. If a man is inclined to luxury and aesthetic pleasures he will become debilitated and no better than a woman.

1 Find a word in the extract that means the same as each of these explanations:
   a hard-working
   b rules of behaviour
   c weakened
   d neglect of duty
   e able to be blamed
   f plain woven silk
2 How should a samurai spend the early hours of the day? Why was he advised to do this?
3 What was hawking? Why would this be a useful skill for the samurai to have?
4 What did the writer mean by saying that 'It is an offence to spend money on clothes so that one is embarrassed in other ways.'? Do you think this advice is true today?
5 What are retainers? Why did the samurai have to keep retainers? What sort of people would have become retainers of the samurai?

6 What advice did this writer give about luxurious living and idling away the time? Why do you think this advice was necessary?
7 What is meant by 'filial duty'? Why was this important to the samurai?
8 Use a dictionary to find the meaning of the word 'aesthetic'. What sort of pleasures might be called 'aesthetic' pleasures? According to the writer, what would happen if the samurai became interested in aesthetic pleasures?
9 What do you think this writer believed to be the place of women in society? Did he have a high opinion of women?
10 In many ways the samurai of Japan were similar to the knights of medieval Europe. How many similarities can you think of? How much of the advice given for the samurai in the extract above would also be useful for European knights? Why do you think the two groups had such similar ideals?
11 Imagine you have to give some advice to young people leaving school today. Write a paragraph or two setting out the things you think they should and should not do in order to make a success of their lives. Do you think any of the advice given to the samurai in the 1300s would still be useful today?

The Fujiwara, 645–1185

After the death of Shotoku, government was in the hands of the emperor Tenchi and a nobleman named Kamatari, who was given the name of Fujiwara. Together they set about making even more changes to Japan. In 646 they issued an edict that set out what have become known as the *Taika* reforms (*taika* means 'great change'). According to this decree, land could no longer be owned by individuals. Instead, it was owned by the emperor and rented out to other people. Governors and other officials were appointed by the emperor and had to obey the emperor's orders.

For the next hundred years or so, Japan was officially ruled by a series of emperors. In fact, these emperors were so strongly influenced by members of the Fujiwara family that it was they who were the real rulers of Japan. We saw how this pattern was established much earlier in Japanese history when leaders of the *uji* had a strong influence over the emperors.

The shoguns

In China, a weak emperor was constantly threatened by other leaders who wanted to become emperor themselves. If a person had enough support, he could attack the emperor, defeat him and set up his own family as the ruling family. He became emperor and his children followed him until they too were threatened by another powerful leader.

In Japan, things were different. There were weak emperors in Japan just as there were in China. But instead of defeating them and taking control for themselves, strong families left the emperors theoretically in control. In practice, however, the emperor was without power and it was the strong families who ruled Japan. The Fujiwara, for example, were never the emperors of Japan, yet they had much more real power than the emperors who were supposed to be ruling at the time. The Fujiwara family ruled but did not reign.

The Fujiwara remained in power from 645 until about 1185. They did this by arranging marriages between Fujiwara girls and the sons of emperors and also by controlling most official positions, both at court and in the regions.

Ruling families like the Fujiwara were given the name of *shogun*, a word which means 'great general'. The shogun was a combination of prime minister and military leader, with more power than either. Later shogun families were the Ashikaga, who held power between 1338 and 1573, and the Tokugawa, who ruled from 1603 until 1867.

Time to understand

Explain the meaning of the statement that 'The Fujiwara family ruled but did not reign'. Do you know of any world leaders today who 'rule but do not reign'? Do you know of any who reign but do not rule'?

The Mongols attack Japan

By about 1260 Kublai Khan had conquered just about all the territory surrounding him and it was then that he turned his attention to Japan.

The attack came in 1274 when Kublai Khan sent from Korea a force of over 25 000 men in more than 400 ships. The governor of the port where they landed fought with his 200 samurai until all had been killed. The battle raged for the rest of the day, with more Japanese samurai and their followers fighting hard and well in defence of their country. The Mongols were skilled with bows and arrows and on horseback, but the Japanese were better with swords and light armour. As a storm blew up that night, the Mongols retreated to their ships. During the night the wild weather destroyed many of their ships and caused the deaths of thousands of men.

Kublai Khan then sent more ambassadors to demand that the Japanese shoguns come to Peking and accept his rule. Twice the ambassadors were beheaded, and the Japanese busied themselves preparing their defences.

The second Mongol invasion came in 1281. This time it consisted of 140 000 men in 3500 ships. But the Japanese were ready for the attack. They had fortified the coast and built walls around their towns. They fought the Mongols on land and at sea. A huge wall around the bay where the Mongols landed made it hard for the cavalry to make a full-scale attack, while the light Japanese boats made constant raids on the larger Mongol junks moored in the harbour.

For almost two months the fighting continued. Then a typhoon struck, destroying what remained of the Mongol fleet. Only a few of the once mighty fleet managed to straggle home, in complete defeat.

Fig. 5.10 over the page shows part of the Mongol Scroll, a pictorial record of Japan's battle against the Mongols. This is a valuable record of the attack. It shows the Japanese samurai in

Fig. 5.9 Yoritomo, who was the first ruler to be given the title of shogun. He was given the title in 1192 when he had set up a capital at Kamakura and divided Japan into districts, each ruled by a lord who owed allegiance to him. The shogun system lasted until 1867.

battle against the Mongol soldiers and the ships of both sides. It even shows some of the explosive missiles, or bombs, that the Mongols flung over the Japanese walls with catapults. The Mongol Scroll is so accurate that it must have been painted either by someone who saw the Mongols or someone who was able to refer to drawings made at the time of the battles.

Time to understand

1 Using the picture in Fig. 5.10 and what you read about the Mongols in Chapter Four, make a comparison of the weapons of the Mongol attackers and Japanese defenders in the thirteenth century. Which side was better prepared for the battles that were fought in this invasion? Were the soldiers on either side at all like the knights of medieval Europe? Why?

2 Imagine it is the year 2001. You are the only witness to a battle between a group of Austra-

Fig. 5.10 Part of the Mongol Scroll showing the battle between the Mongol cavalry and Japanese soldiers. Can you see the Mongol fire-bomb in the centre of the picture?

lians and an alien force trying to invade the country. Sketch what you see. Remember that your drawing may be the only record ever made of this important event, so make it as detailed and exact as you can. What particular things do you think future generations may find particularly interesting? Do you think they would want to know about something that is so obvious and commonplace to you that you did not bother putting it in your drawing?

The Ashikaga shoguns 1338–1573

We have seen how it was traditional in Japan for the emperor to have no real power while the shoguns really ruled the country. This pattern

Fig. 5.11 A daimyo and his escort arriving at the city of Edo. Edo was the second capital of the shogun (the first was Kamakura). In 1869 it was renamed Tokyo and is now the capital of Japan.

continued for many hundreds of years until 1318 when a young man named Go-Daigo became emperor. Go-Daigo was determined to overthrow the power of the shoguns and restore power to the emperor. He fought and was exiled, but escaped from exile and was joined by a strong military leader called Ashikaga Takauji. As the emperor and his new ally advanced to Kamakura, the shogun and 800 followers committed *seppuku* rather than face capture and torture.

As soon as Ashikaga Takauji was sure of his position, he turned against the emperor Go-Daigo. Many years of civil war followed until 1392 when an uneasy peace was reached. By this time Ashikaga was well established as shogun. In fact, his family kept the position of shogun until 1573. Ashikaga's capital was part of the city of Kyoto known as the Muromachi district. For this reason, the period of the Ashikaga shoguns has become known as the Muromachi period.

Bad times

Japan was not a peaceful country during the Muromachi period. The daimyo and their samurai followers fought battle after battle against each other as they tried to increase their own power and influence. Small landowners, hit by high taxes and the effects of all these wars, frequently lost their land by giving it over to the local daimyo in return for protection. Many became vagabonds, called *ronin*, who wandered the highways in gangs attacking and robbing travellers.

Peasants and merchants

The almost constant state of war made life very hard indeed, even for those peasants who were able to stay on their land. Armies trampled over their crops and tax collectors became more and more demanding, until almost all their rice had to be sent to the local daimyo to support his army. Sometimes the peasants banded together to attack those who were making their life difficult. 'Down with the samurai', they cried as they too joined in the warfare. At other times they attacked the pawnbrokers and moneylenders who were growing rich on the troubled times.

Fig. 5.12 Planting rice. The man is carrying seedlings raised in the nursery-bed while the women plant them in the wet fields.

Sometimes a farmer had to pay his debts by selling one of his children as a slave, so it is no wonder that the farmers and peasants hated the moneylenders so much.

The Ashikaga shoguns were always trying to find ways of raising more money to support themselves and make sure they remained powerful. Taxes were as high as they could possibly be, but much of the rice that was collected was kept by the daimyo and not passed on to the shoguns.

The Ashikaga shoguns may have been poor, but the emperors were even poorer. One emperor had to sell his hand-written books in order to make ends meet. When another emperor died, it was two months before his family could raise enough money to give him a proper burial. Despite problems such as these, the emperors kept the position as the head of Japan, even though they were in fact without power.

Time to understand

At this time in Japanese history, the tea ceremony was an important ritual among some classes of society. Try to find out something about this ceremony. What sort of people took part in tea ceremonies? How was the ceremony carried out? How did it start? What was its significance for those who took part? A book about Japanese history or customs will help you to find the answers to these questions.

The Japanese family

Just as there are many differences between the lives of rich and poor Australians and between Australians who live and work on farms and those who live and work in a town or city, so were there many differences in the way Japanese families lived in the period we are studying.

Many families included more than just a married couple and their children. The brothers and sisters of the husband, his parents and other relatives often lived in the same house. This extended family was headed by the husband, although it was often his mother who really dominated the household. Some husbands were very strong-minded and their wives and children obeyed them without question; others discussed family affairs with their wives and children.

Women

We have seen how strong the samurai tradition was in early Japan. Because of this, women were considered to be inferior to men. The values of the samurai stressed military skills and loyalty to a male leader. It is no wonder, then, that women's place was in the background, caring for children and being dutiful wives but having little to do with other matters.

This was particularly so with women of the upper classes. They were expected to be skilful at calligraphy (handwriting), painting and music, but were secluded and often quite isolated from other people, talking only to their servants and immediate family.

Fig. 5.13 Japanese women in their traditional role.

Time to understand

1 *The Greater Learning for Women* was written in 1672 to explain what was required of a samurai's wife. According to this book:

The worst faults of a female are laziness, discontent, a lying tongue, jealousy and silliness. These faults are found in seven or eight of every ten women. These faults make women inferior to men.

What do you think? Do you think more women than men have the faults described in the book? Why did the writer believe they did? What does this extract show about the attitudes to women at the time?

2 Women in traditional Japan wore quite a lot of make-up. It was fashionable to paint the face white, pluck the eyebrows, and put a red spot like lipstick on the lower lip. The teeth were painted black. One woman in the sixteenth century who rebelled against these fashions was criticised by other women who said that her eyebrows looked like caterpillars and her white teeth resembled a skinned animal.

How do these ideas about make-up compare with modern Australian ideas about what makes women look attractive? What do you think would happen if an Australian woman painted her face white, blackened her teeth and plucked her eyebrows out? Would she be criticised by other Australian women? Why?

Children

Many Japanese babies did not survive the first few months of life. Although the Japanese people of the time were very cultured and capable of producing beautiful works of art, they were less aware of and concerned with the basic hygiene and cleanliness that was necessary to ensure the survival of babies. Few Japanese parents could afford to call a doctor to help a woman in childbirth and if there were any problems either the baby or the mother (and often both) died.

Those babies who did survive were considered to be babies until the girls were six years old and the boys were seven. For the first few years of life, Japanese children wore a short *kimono*, or robe tied around the waist and long baggy pants. Boys and girls were treated in a similar way, although the first-born son and heir of the family was given a little more respect and greater privileges than his brothers and sisters.

At the age of six, little girls put on their first long kimono, tied with a sash called an *obi* which was fastened in a large bow at the back. When they were seven, boys too were allowed to wear different clothes. This was the *hakama*, a pair of breeches worn over a kimono. After the ceremony at which these changes were made, the children were taken to a Shinto shrine to pay homage to the god or *kami* who protected them from danger.

Children in Japan had to be educated, just as children do now. The form of their education

Fig. 5.14 A child being fed with chopsticks. Weaning was an important time for Japanese families and friends gathered to watch the baby eat its first grain of rice. They offered prayers for the baby's health.

Fig. 5.15 Japanese boys playing on stilts.

varied according to the family's social standing and whether the child was a boy or a girl. The sons of samurai of low rank were often sent to the household of a richer samurai family. Here they served as pages, learning about the samurai traditions as they helped the master with his tasks. This system of education was similar to that of the noble families of Europe who sent their sons to the castles of richer noblemen to become pages, squires and then knights.

Other boys served as assistants to craftsmen. They learned the skills that they would later use in their adult lives. Among the craftsmen of highest rank were those who created beautiful works of art, either painting, pottery, sculpture, making musical instruments, or working with leather, metal or paper. The skills needed to do this work well took many years to learn.

Farmers' children had very little choice about their education because as soon as they were old enough to work they were expected to help on the land. Of course, the jobs they were given became harder as they grew up until they knew as much as their fathers about farming, caring for animals, feeding and caring for silkworms and all the other jobs that needed to be done. If the shogun or local daimyo demanded it, peasant children were also expected to help with projects like building pathways, roads, bridges, irrigation channels and other works.

Some boys were sent to a monastery to be educated. They were cared for by the Buddhist monks, who sometimes dressed then in beautiful flowing robes and treated them like pets. At the same time, they were expected to work hard, learning by heart the Chinese Buddhist texts and the *sutras*, or Buddhist holy books.

Girls had less chance of an education because they were expected to remain at home, learning the accomplishments that Japanese women were supposed to have. In addition, they helped their mothers in the home and cared for younger brothers and sisters. The daughters of peasant farmers had extra work to do because they helped with the farm work as well.

At the age of twelve or thirteen, boys and girls were considered to have become men and women. Once again, this change was marked by special ceremonies and new clothes. At these ceremonies the young samurai could exchange his wooden sword for a proper steel sword. He could fight in battle at the age of fifteen.

Time to understand

1 Read again the section in Chapter Three that deals with the education of young people in the Middle Ages in Europe (pages 51–53). Make a list of the similarities between the education of Europe and that of Japan.
2 One of the popular children's pastimes of Japan was *origami*, or paper folding. This craft is still popular today. Find a book on origami at your school or public library and try to make some of the models in it. Why do you think this craft has remained popular?

The Tokugawa shoguns 1603–1867

The Ashikaga shoguns were able to maintain power for over 200 years, mainly because no other family was strong enough to challenge their power. But by the mid–1500s the Ashikaga shoguns faced real problems. Three new leaders were threatening their position. These men were Nobunaga, Hideyoshi and Tokugawa Ieyasu. All three were enemies of the Ashikaga; yet all three were enemies of each other as well. Together they brought about the end of the Ashikaga: 'Nobunaga prepared the cake, Hideyoshi baked it and Ieyasu ate it', according to a saying of the time.

After years of warfare and murder, treachery and violence, Tokugawa Ieyasu emerged as the strongest man in Japan. In 1603 he became the new shogun and his family held the office until 1867.

At first Ieyasu was prepared to allow foreigners to come to Japan to trade. He also allowed Christian missionaries to enter Japan to convert the people to the Christian religion. The most famous of these missionaries was Francis Xavier, who arrived in Japan in 1549. For a time Japan had strong links with Europe, particularly with Portugal which at the time was one of Europe's leading trading countries.

Gradually, however, the shogun became annoyed by the quarrelling and greed of the Europeans. He feared that traditional Japanese ways were being destroyed by the new ideas of the Europeans. Ieyasu issued orders that the missionaries were to leave Japan; those who disobeyed were tortured and sometimes murdered. When a group of Japanese Christians stood up to the shogun in 1638, 37 000 people were executed to prove that the shogun was serious in his determination that Christianity would not be tolerated.

Gradually Japan was closed to other countries. It became like a country surrounded by a high wall. Merchants and missionaries gave up their attempts to enter this closed world and after 1636 Japanese people were forbidden to travel to other countries. Those who were overseas were not allowed to return. An edict declared that ships capable of sailing to other countries could no longer be built. Only a very small number of Dutch and Chinese traders were allowed to stay in Japan, trading from a limited number of ports under a system strictly supervised by the Tokugawa shoguns.

The Tokugawa shoguns stayed in power for more than 200 years. They were successful in keeping Japan apart from the rest of the world. One Japanese writer explained it this way.:

[Japan was] a sort of garden, small and dainty, tended by people who knew nothing beyond the pretty little things within the hedges. She knew nothing of the world and the world knew nothing of her . . . She just kept herself alive.

In 1853 four 'black ships' from America appeared at a Japanese port. The Tokugawa rulers were not strong enough to stop them coming

Fig. 5.16 Japanese look at some of the gifts brought to them by the American fleet.

into the harbour. Nor were they able to stand up to the demands of the ships commander, Matthew Perry. Within a few years Japan had been opened up to the west and the Tokugawa government had fallen.

Time to understand

The orders below were issued to villages in part of Japan in 1649. Read them carefully and answer the questions that follow.

> Farm work must be done with the greatest diligence. Planting must be neat, all weeds must be removed, and on the borders of both wet and dry fields beans or similar food-stuffs are to be grown, however small the space.
>
> Peasants must rise early and cut grass before cultivating the fields. In the evening they are to make straw rope and straw bags, all such work to be done with great care.
>
> They must not buy tea or *sake* to drink, nor must their wives.
>
> Men must plant bamboo or trees round the farmhouse and must use the fallen leaves for fuel so as to save expense.
>
> Peasants are people without sense or forethought. Therefore they must not give rice to their wives and children at harvest time, but must save food for the future. They should eat millet, vegetables, and other coarse food instead of rice. Even the fallen leaves of plants should be saved as food against famine. . . . During the season of planting and harvesting, when the labour is arduous, the food taken may be a little better than usual.
>
> The husband must work in the fields, the wife must work at the loom. Both must do night work. However good-looking a wife may be, if she neglects her household duties by drinking tea or sightseeing or rambling on the hill-sides, she must be divorced.
>
> Peasants must wear only cotton or hemp—no silk. They may not smoke tobacco. It is harmful to health, it takes up time, and costs money. It also creates a risk of fire.

1 What were 'wet fields'? Why were they wet?

2 Why were peasants told to plant crops on the edges of fields? What sort of crops were they to plant?

3 What happened to the grass the peasants cut in the mornings? How do you think the grass was cut?

4 What was *sake*? Why were the peasants told not to buy tea or *sake*?

5 Why were trees and bamboo planted around the farmhouse?

6 Why were the peasants encouraged to eat 'coarse foods' instead of rice? What does this tell us about life in early Japan?

7 What sort of 'night work' do you think men and women were expected to do? What would happen if a wife did not do the work expected of her?

8 Why were the peasants told to wear cotton or hemp clothes? What was hemp made from? Who would wear clothes made of silk?

9 Why was tobacco smoking discouraged?

10 What general impressions does this extract give us about the lives of peasants in Tokugawa Japan? Make a list of the main conclusions you can draw from the extract.

How do we know?

An important way of learning about the past is by studying the literature—stories, poems and plays—written long ago. By doing this, we can discover quite a lot about the things that writers felt were worth writing about, as well as learn about the styles of writing that were popular at different times.

When we are studying a country whose people spoke a language other than English, we have to rely on translations of literature (unless we are lucky enough to understand the language ourselves). When people translate a story, poem or play from one language to another, they must understand not only the language in which the work was written but also the way of life of the people when the work was written. The more translators can find out about the writer, the better, because this will help them understand the kind of person he or she was.

It is difficult to translate poetry from one language to another because the rhymes and rhythms of one language may be quite different from those of another language. In this case, a translator tries to express the feeling and mood of the original poem, even if some of the words are left out or changed around to make it sound better.

The extracts below were taken from Japanese writers in the period we have studied in this chapter. They are all from works of literature— imaginative writing, not the kind of writing that gives information or orders, or records events. Read the extracts carefully and answer the questions about each one.

1 The following poems are written in the *haiku* style: in the original Japanese they have only seventeen syllables each. They were written by Basho, who lived from 1644 to 1694. Basho was a Zen Buddhist and in his poems he tried to express the Zen ideas of simplicity and naturalness. Believing that too many words spoil poetry, the writers of haiku tried to express a great deal with as few words as possible. Read Basho's haiku poems. How successful do you think they are? Try to write your own haiku, using the principles of simplicity and naturalness and suggesting a feeling through clever use of words.

Summer grasses,
all that remains
of soldiers' dreams.

Journey's end—
still alive,
this autumn evening.

Smell of autumn—
heart longs
for the four-mat room.

Sick on a journey—
over parched fields
dreams wander on.

2 The lists below were made by Sei Shonagon, a lady-in-waiting to the empress, in a book called *Pillow Sketches*. This book was written in a style that was later known as 'following the pen'. Stories, lists, poems, descriptions and ideas were written down without any order, just as they struck the writer.

Dreary Things

A nursery where the child has died.

The birth of a succession of female children in the house of a learned scholar.

A letter from one's country home with no news in it.

Detestable Things

A visitor who tells a long story when you are in a hurry.

An exorcist who, when sent for in a case of sudden illness, recites his charms as if he were half asleep.

Babies that cry or dogs that bark when you want to listen.

People who ride in a creaking carriage. Such people must be deaf, and are very detestable.

People who interrupt your stories to show off their own cleverness. All interrupters, young or old, are very detestable.

People who, when you are telling a story, break in with, 'Oh, I know,' and give quite a different version from your own.

Either at home or in the palace to be roused up to receive an unwelcome visitor, in order to avoid whom you have been pretending to be asleep.

People who mumble a prayer when they sneeze.

N.B.—Loud sneezing is detestable, except in the case of the gentlemen of the house.

Fleas are very detestable, especially when they get under your clothing and jump about.

Things Which Give One a Thrill

To see sparrows feeding their young.

To pass by where infants are playing.

To be asked the way by a handsome man who stops his carriage for the purpose.

Cheerful Things

Coming home from an excursion with the carriages full to overflowing, to have lots of footmen who make the oxen go and the carriages speed along.

A river boat going downstream.

Teeth nicely blackened.

To hear a well-voiced professor of magic recite his purification service on a river bank.

a What can you learn about Sei Shonagon from these lists?

b What can you learn about Japan around the year 1000 (when she lived) from these lists?

c Make up your own lists of 'dreary things', 'detestable things', 'things which give one a thrill' and 'cheerful things'. What do you think they would tell other people about you and the society in which you live?

6

Islam: religion and empire

FROM THE MAP in Fig. 6.1 over the page you can see that Arabia is a large peninsula between the Red Sea and the Persian Gulf. Today Arabia is part of the region we call the Middle East, a region which links three continents: Africa, Asia and Europe. Although the Arabian peninsula is large—it stretches for more than 2.5 million square kilometres—it is hot, dry and generally infertile. Much of it is desert which can support only a little stubbly grass. In places where the rainfall is higher, a few palm trees may grow together to form an oasis from the dust and heat.

The Bedouins

Even today the Arabian peninsula can support a limited number of people. In the past, those who lived there were nomads, moving from place to place with their flocks of sheep and goats, constantly in search of fresh food and water for them. These people were called Bedouins, and their descendants still wander the peninsula in much the same way as their ancestors did thousands of years ago.

The sheep and goats of the Bedouins provided meat and milk for food, skins and wool for clothes, and hair from which tents could be woven. The Bedouins lived in tribes, each ruled by a leader called a *sheikh*. When the tribe was on the move, its few goods were loaded on camels, the most valued animals in the desert.

The Bedouins were nomads, then, partly because they had little choice: they were forced to move on when food and water became scarce. But there was another reason for their constant travelling. They were trading people, moving along a number of well-established trade routes with their camel caravans buying and selling goods from the three continents which the peninsula linked.

Bedouin religion

In many ways, the Bedouins were a tough, warlike group of people. Tribal battles and feuds were common, and the caravans of one tribe were frequently attacked and robbed by rival tribes. Yet they had a strong sense of tribal loyalty, a loyalty which was needed if people were to survive in the harsh desert.

The Bedouins worshipped many gods, believing that trees, stone, wood and other natural things all had spirits with supernatural powers. In the sixth century, the richest and most holy place in Arabia was the town of Mecca, about 80 kilometres inland from the Red Sea. Mecca was the most prosperous town on the peninsula for two reasons. Firstly, it was at the crossroads of the main trading routes. Through it passed many of the camel trains that travelled through the region. Secondly, Mecca was the home of

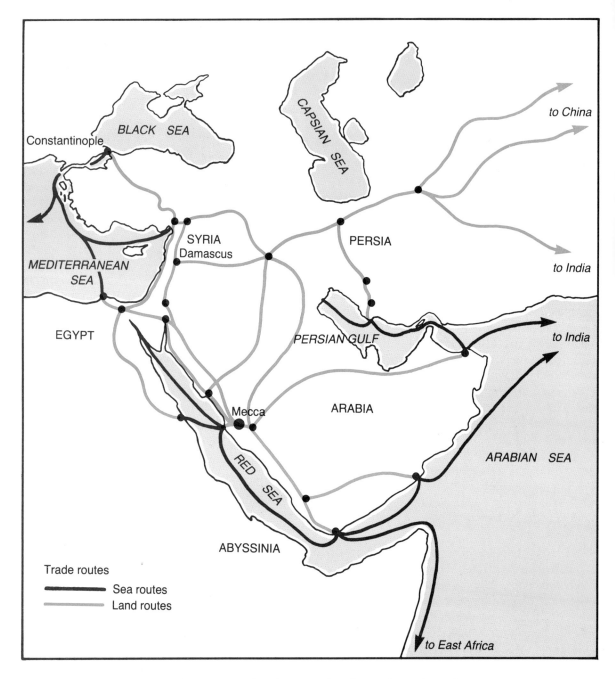

Fig. 6.1 The Arabian peninsula. The map also shows the main trade routes at the time of Mohammed.

Arabia's holiest shrine. In the centre of the town was a small cube-like building called the Kaaba. You can see it in the picture in Fig. 6.2. Inside the Kaaba were more than 300 religious idols and statues, the most precious of which was a meteo-rite known as the Black Stone. People travelled to Mecca from all over Arabia to touch the Black Stone. By doing so, they believed, their sins would be forgiven by Allah, the chief of all their gods.

Time to understand

1 List as many reasons as you can to explain why camels were so highly valued by the Bedouins.
2 Many thousands of pilgrims travelled to Mecca to touch the Black Stone. Can you explain what the word 'pilgrim' means? Do you know of any places today to which pilgrims travel? Why do they go there? How would the large number of Arabian pilgrims have helped the growth of Mecca?
3 Use an atlas to find out how many countries are in the Arabian peninsula· today. In which of these countries is the city of Mecca?
4 What is a meteorite? Why do you think a meteorite might have been thought to have magical powers?

Mohammed: the founder of Islam

Mohammed was born in Mecca in 570. His father, a trader named Abdullah, died before his birth and his mother died when Mohammed was six years old. Mohammed was brought up by his grandfather and later by his uncle, Abul Talib. When he was a young man, Mohammed became a trader, like so many of the people of Mecca. On his journeys to Syria he came into contact with Christians (Syria was part of the Byzantine empire) and became interested in their belief that there was only one god, not the many gods that were worshipped in Mecca.

The pictures on the following pages depict scenes from Mohammed's life. Fig. 6.3 shows angels descending to be present at the birth of Mohammed. They are bringing a mattress and a cover so that his mother can rest comfortably. The Kaaba can be seen in the centre of the picture.

Mohammed was well liked and trusted in Mecca. When he was 25 years old he married a rich widow named Khadija, for whom he had worked as a trader. Although Khadija was much older than Mohammed, their marriage was a happy one. The couple had three sons (all of whom died as children) and four daughters.

Fig. 6.4 shows the wedding ceremony. Khadija is on the right, with her face covered by a veil.

Fig. 6.2 The city of Mecca. The Kaaba is the box-like building on the left. The area is crowded with thousands of pilgrims visiting the shrine.

Fig. 6.3 Mohammed's birth.   **Fig. 6.4** The wedding ceremony.   **Fig. 6.5** Allah's message.

Fig. 6.6 The rich people of Mecca stone Mohammed.

Fig. 6.7 Allah protects Mohammed.

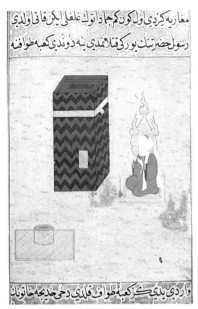

Fig. 6.8 Mohammed praying. **Fig. 6.9** Mohammed's death.

Fig. 6.10 Mohammed preaching in Mecca.

Mohammed is in the centre, dressed in green. His head is surrounded by flames which represent a halo.

Mohammed was now wealthy. He spent much of his time meditating and thinking about religion on a mountain near Mecca. In 610, when he was 40 years old, the angel Gabriel appeared and showed Mohammed a scroll which stated that he was to be the prophet, or messenger, of Allah, as Abraham and Moses had been hundreds of years earlier.

Fig. 6.5 shows Mohammed receiving the news from Allah. He is surrounded by flames and wherever he looks, he cannot escape the face of Gabriel.

For some time Mohammed had no further messages from Allah. He began to doubt his first revelation. Then a second angel came to him and told him to 'rise and warn' the people of Mecca. In 613, therefore, Mohammed started preaching in Mecca. He taught that Allah was the one and only true god and that all who believed in him and obeyed his rules would go to heaven, whether they were rich or poor. The religion that Mohammed preached became known as Islam, 'Obedience to the Will of God', and those who followed it were known as Moslems. Many poor people listened to Mohammed and were converted to Islam. The rulers of Mecca, called the *Quryash*, were angry with this man who called himself the prophet of Allah. They believed that if people became Moslems they would no longer come to Mecca to worship the idols in the Kaaba. Their city would not be as powerful and they would lose all the money they made from the pilgrims.

Fig. 6.6 shows the rich people of Mecca stoning Mohammed. The man trying to stop them is Abu Bakr, a rich merchant who was one of the first people to be converted to Islam.

When Mohammed's wife, Khadija, died, Mohammed felt that it was time to leave Mecca. He was invited to the town of Yathrib, 350 kilometres away. Gradually the Moslems left Mecca. In September 622 Mohammed and Abu Bakr left and journeyed to Yathrib. The year 622 became the first year in the Moslem calendar, marking as it did the *Hegira*, or moving of the Moslems from Mecca to Yathrib.

Fig. 6.7 shows an event which was supposed to have occurred on Mohammed's journey to Yathrib. On the first night, he and Abu Bakr found shelter in a cave. When soldiers from Mecca came by in search of them, they found a spider's web completely covering the entrance to the cave and a dove peacefully settled in its nest just outside. Surely, they thought, Mohammed was not hiding in the cave, because the web would have been broken and the dove taken flight. They did not bother going into the cave. According to the legend, Allah had done this to keep Mohammed safe.

Mohammed became more and more powerful in Yathrib, which became known as Medina, the city of the prophet. The people of Medina—rich and poor alike—were converted to Islam and Mohammed became the city's ruler. He organised raids against the trading caravans of his enemies, the Meccans. In one battle, 300 Moslems from Medina attacked 1000 Meccans. Mohammed prayed as the battle raged and the Moslems were successful. In 627, 10 000 Meccan troops attacked Medina but the people of Medina had dug a deep trench around their city and the attack was a failure.

Fig. 6.10 shows Mohammed preaching in the mosque that was built in Medina.

In 630, 10 000 Islamic troops attacked Mecca and the city fell to Mohammed's forces. Mohammed went into the Kaaba and destroyed all the idols, leaving only the Black Stone as the shrine to Allah. When this had been done, he said, 'Truth has come and falsehood has vanished'. Mecca was now the spiritual home of the Moslems and each Moslem was expected to turn towards Mecca while praying and to make at least one pilgrimage to the city.

Fig. 6.8 shows Mohammed, with his face veiled, praying beside the Kaaba.

With Mecca now conquered, Islamic troops struck further and further into Arabia. By 632 most of the people living in the peninsula had accepted the new faith. For the first time the Arabs had a leader who ruled over more than a single tribe. Mohammed gave the people of Arabia a greater sense of loyalty than they had ever had before: they had a strong leader and a new religion that promised them hope for the future, even if they were poor and suffering in their lives on earth.

In 632, when he was 63 years old, Mohammed fell ill with a fever. He died in the same year. When his followers heard of his death, they were distressed and panic-stricken. Abu Bakr, his closest friend, said to them, 'Whichever of you worships Mohammed, know that Mohammed is dead. But whichever of you worships God, know that God is alive and does not die.'

Fig. 6.9 shows Mohammed on his deathbed. The Angel of Death is on the right.

Time to understand

1 Fig. 6.11 shows Mohammed preparing to enter the city of Mecca in 630.

a Why did Mohammed attack the city of Mecca?

b Was this attack successful?

c Describe the clothes worn by Mohammed and his followers. Why do you think they wore clothes like these?

d The angel Gabriel can be seen above Mohammed's head. Why do you think Gabriel was included in this picture? Does Gabriel look like your idea of an angel? Why?

Fig. 6.11 Mohammed is encouraged by the angel Gabriel as he prepares to attack Mecca.

e Using this picture as evidence, describe the weapons used in the Arabian peninsula in the time of Mohammed.

2 Read again the words spoken by Abu Bakr after the death of Mohammed. Explain in your own words what Abu Bakr meant.

The five pillars of Islam

Mohammed taught that Moslems were expected to obey five main rules, which were called the 'five pillars of Islam'. These were:

1 They must accept the Islamic faith.
2 They must pray regularly.
3 They must give money to the poor.
4 They must fast at certain times.
5 They must make a pilgrimage to Mecca at least once in their life.

The first pillar: faith

To become a Moslem, one simply had to say to another Moslem, 'There is no god but Allah, and Mohammed is his prophet'. Unlike Christians, Moslems did not believe that Jesus was the son of God; instead, they believed that he was a prophet like Abraham, Moses and Mohammed. The teachings of God were recorded in the Koran, the Moslem bible which was compiled soon after Mohammed's death. Both the Christian Bible and the Koran describe what will happen on the Day of Judgment when all people, living and dead, will be judged on the basis of their lives on earth. According to the Koran, the good will have the record of their lives placed in their right hand and go to heaven; the wicked will have it placed in their left hand and be sent to hell.

The second pillar: prayer

Prayer was the way by which Moslems praised Allah, and Moslems were expected to pray five times a day. When it was time for prayer, they were called to the mosque by a prayer caller or *muezzin* who had climbed into the minaret or tower of the mosque. The prayers were in a set order and the worshippers had to do certain acts before praying, such as washing their bodies, taking off their shoes and covering their heads. The prayers had to be made facing Mecca, and mosques were built with a specially decorated niche set in one wall pointing the direction of Mecca.

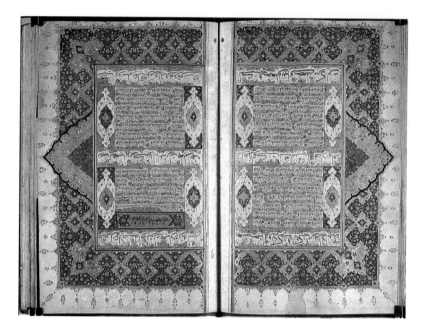

Fig. 6.12 The Koran was written down partly by Mohammed's scribes and partly by those who came after him. It contains the messages given to Mohammed by the angel Gabriel. It is the sacred book of the Moslems and many learn it off by heart. The Koran is about as long as the New Testament of the Christian Bible.

The third pillar: giving alms

Moslems were expected to give some of their wealth to the poor. Part of this offering was rather like a tax. It was collected by government officials who used it to help pay for things like preparing strong armies to defend Islam and spread it to other countries.

The fourth pillar: fasting

For one month each year Moslems had to fast from dawn to sunset. This month was called *Ramadan* and it was supposed to help believers to discipline themselves and to understand the suffering of the poor. Each evening, when the day's fasting was over, people enjoyed a large festive meal and there was often entertainment, story telling and special services in the mosque. This continued through the whole month of Ramadan.

The fifth pillar: pilgrimage

We have seen that people from all over Arabia travelled to Mecca to visit the Kaaba even before the coming of Islam. Mohammed kept up this tradition and made a rule that all Moslems should visit Mecca at least once in their lives. The best time to make this pilgrimage, known as the *Hidja*, was two months after Ramadan. In villages all over Arabia, there was great excitement as the pilgrims left and returned. People from many lands met on these journeys, which helped to strengthen the sense of unity that Moslems felt. The pilgrimage was very strictly organised and pilgrims knew exactly what was expected of them. Outside Mecca they washed and changed into special robes. At the Kaaba the pilgrims kissed the Black Stone, then walked around it seven times reciting prayers. Then

Fig. 6.13 Mosques were generally rectangular in shape with a large courtyard in the centre surrounded by arcades. The sanctuary faced Mecca. The hours of prayer were called by the muezzin from the minaret or tower. Moslems gathered in the arched sides of the mosque to read, talk or even sleep. Mosques were cool retreats from the hot sun. This picture shows the Qum mosque in Iran.

they had to run seven times between two small hills in Mecca. On the ninth day of the pilgrimage the pilgrims gathered outside Mecca to pray together and on the tenth day each pilgrim sacrificed an animal—a goat, sheep or camel—to Allah.

Today there are more than 600 million Moslems throughout the world. They still accept as the basis of their religion these 'five pillars of Islam' set down by Mohammed.

Time to understand

Moslem scholars study the Koran carefully to find guidance about Islamic beliefs. Islam is based on what can be learned from this book which, according to Moslems, records the word of God. The extracts below are taken from the Koran. Read them carefully and answer the questions about each one.

Praise be to God, the Lord of the Universe,
the Merciful, the Compassionate,
the Authority on Judgment Day.

It is You whom we worship
and You whom we ask for help.

Show us the upright way:
the way of those whom You have favoured,
not of those with whom You have been angry
and those who have gone astray.

a In what way is this prayer like a Christian
prayer?
b Would this prayer have suited the Bedouins
in Arabia before the founding of Islam?
Why?

Those that make war against Allah and His
apostle and spread disorders in the land shall be
put to death or crucified or have their hands and
feet cut off on alternate sides, or be banished
from the country. They shall be held to shame in
this world and sternly punished in the next:
except those that repent before you reduce them.
For you must know that Allah is forgiving and
merciful.
 Believers, have fear of Allah and seek the right
path to Him. Fight valiantly for His cause, so that
you may triumph.

a Who was Allah's 'apostle'?
b How were enemies of Allah to be punished?
c Why does the Koran say that Allah is
'forgiving and merciful' despite these harsh
punishments?
d How could a passage like this encourage
Moslems to fight and perhaps die for their
faith?

The spread of Islam

When Mohammed died in 632, his followers were
confused about the future of their religion.
Mohammed had not named the next leader of
Islam, nor had he set down any rules about how
his successor was to be chosen. A group of influential Moslems met and decided that the best
leader would be Abu Bakr, Mohammed's closest
friend and one of the first people to have been

converted to Islam. In which illustration in this
chapter is Abu Bakr shown? What is he doing?
 Abu Bakr took on the name of *caliph*, a title
which comes from an Arabian word meaning
'successor' or 'follower'. Other Moslem leaders
who followed him used this title as well. In the
twenty years after Mohammed's death there were
four caliphs, all of whom had known Mohammed
and were related to him by marriage.
Three of these caliphs were murdered by their
enemies, for this was a time of change and in-
security, of violence and warfare. Nevertheless,
it was a time of great expansion for Islam. You
can see this from the map in Fig. 6.14 opposite.
 The dotted area on the map shows the land
that had been converted to Islam by 632, the year
of Mohammed's death. The striped part shows
the area conquered by the first four caliphs. The
speckled area indicates the area conquered by the
forces of Islam by the middle of the 700s.

The Umayyad caliphs

Muawiya was the first of a long line of caliphs
from the same family, or clan, called the
Umayyads. The Umayyads were the leaders of
Islam from 661 until 750. No longer were the
caliphs chosen one by one according to their
ability; now they were selected only from one
family according to their position in the family.
 Muawiya set up a new Moslem capital in
Damascus, the main city in his home country of
Syria. In time Damascus became one of the
world's greatest cities. Fig. 6.15 opposite
shows the Great Mosque of Damascus which was
built during the Umayyad period. Although the
Umayyad caliphs built elaborate religious
buildings such as this, they also became
increasingly concerned with their own comfort
and built lavish palaces that were havens of
beauty and pleasure in the harsh lands
surrounding them.
 During the time of the Umayyad caliphs, Islam
spread to India in the east and Spain in the west.
Moslem forces came close to capturing Constantinople, the centre of the Byzantine empire.
Cordoba in Spain beame the capital of the
Moslem rulers of Spain and it too had a great
mosque, the Alcazar.

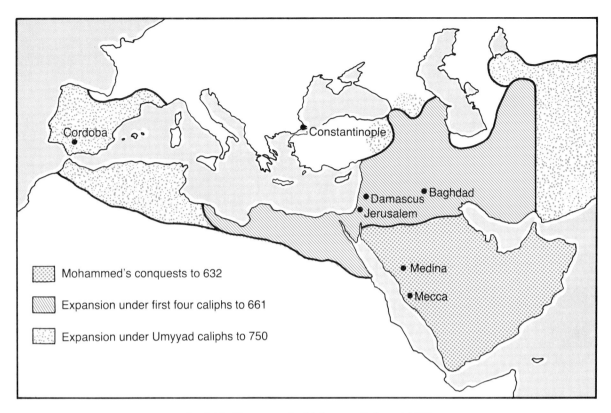

Fig. 6.14 The spread of Islam until the mid-700s.

Mohammed's conquests to 632

Expansion under first four caliphs to 661

Expansion under Umyyad caliphs to 750

Fig. 6.15 The courtyard of the mosque in Damascus. All mosques had a fountain in the courtyard to allow worshippers to clean their bodies before praying.

Spain was invaded and conquered by the Moslems in 711. They pushed further into Europe and it was not until 732 that Moslem soldiers were defeated at Tours by Charles Martel, the grandfather of Charlemagne whom you read about in Chapter Three. This was one of the most important battles in history because from that time onwards the Moslems were fighting to keep their position in Europe. But although they lost many battles, they were not forced out of Spain until 1492, more than 700 years after their defeat at Tours.

Despite the conquests of the Umayyad caliphs, their rule was not peaceful. Many of the people they had fought and defeated were unhappy about being conquered by the Moslems. They resented the fact that they did not have the same privileges as Arabian Moslems, even if they were converted and became Moslems themselves.

The greatest danger to the Umayyads came from the Abbasid group, led by Abbas, a descendant of an uncle of Mohammed. The Abbasids were based in Persia. In 747 they raised their black flag and defeated the Umayyad governor

The Bedouins were good fighters. They knew the desert, moved quickly and made sudden, surprise attacks on their enemies.

Mohammed's followers were fanatics. They were determined to spread their faith. If they won battles, they shared in the looting that followed. They believed that if they were killed in battle they would automatically go to heaven.

The Arabs had no strong enemies. The Byzantine and Persian empires were weakened by fighting with each other. There was no united opposition.

Many people supported Islam because it was an easy faith to accept and understand. They had nothing to lose by becoming Moslems but their lives could be difficult if they resisted the conquerors.

Fig. 6.16 Why Islam spread so quickly.

in Persia. Two years later Abbas was declared to be caliph and in 750 the Abbasid army defeated the Umayyads. The last Umayyad caliph fled to Egypt but was caught and murdered. His head was taken to the new Abbasid caliph to prove that the enemy had been defeated and that he, Abbas, was the new ruler of Islam.

Time to understand

The extract from the Koran below explains the idea of Holy War. In the next chapter of this book you can read about the crusades, the Holy War between Moslems and Christians.

> Warfare is ordained for you, though it is hateful unto you; but it may happen that you hate a thing which is good for you, and it may happen that you love a thing which is bad for you. Allah knoweth, ye know not . . . Persecution is worse than killing. And they will not cease from fighting against you till they have made you renegades from your religion, if they can . . .
>
> Fight in the way of Allah, against those who fight against you, but do not begin hostilities.

Allah loveth not aggressors. And slay them wherever ye find them, and drive them out of the places whence they drove you out . . . If they attack you, then slay them. Such is the reward of disbelievers.

1 What does the statement, 'Warfare is ordained for you' mean?
2 Explain the meaning of 'Persecution is worse than killing'. Do you agree?
3 Who are the 'they' referred to in the section that begins, 'And they will not cease from fighting against you . . .'?
4 From what you have read in this section, do you think Moslems always obeyed the command, 'do not begin hostilities'? How can you tell?
5 How would advice like this help to spread the Islamic empire?

The Abbasid caliphs

The Abbasids were determined to get rid of their enemies, so as to ensure that there would be no challenges to their power. The capital was moved to Baghdad on the Tigris River, which became a bustling and important trading centre where goods from India, Africa, China, Europe and the Middle East were bought and sold at bazaars and markets.

Harun Al Rashid, 786–809

Harun Al Rashid was the greatest of the Abbasid caliphs. From his capital at Baghdad he ruled over the huge Islamic empire and it was during his reign that Islam was at its height. This was the time that has become known as 'the golden age of Islam'. You can read more about its achievements later in this chapter.

Harun Al Rashid knew of Charlemagne, the king of the Franks. The two leaders even exchanged gifts, although the Moslems and the Christians were sworn enemies. One gift from Harun Al Rashid to Charlemagne was an ele-

phant: another was an elaborate clock. Harun Al Rashid's palace stretched over one-third of the area of Baghdad. In its centre was the Hall of the Tree, and in the centre of the hall was a tree made of gold and silver decorated with golden birds that actually sang.

Time to understand

1 The poem below was written by Abu Nuwas, an Abbasid poet. What comment does it make on the kind of life led by Harun Al Rashid?

Vanity: To Harun Al Rashid

Live securely, as you wish;
    the palace heights are safe enough,
With pleasures flooding day and night,
    the smooth proves sweeter than the rough.

But when your breath begins to clog
    in sharp contractions of your lungs
then know for certain, my dear sire,
    your life was vain as idle tongues.

2 Can you suggest why Charlemagne and Harun Al Rashid exchanged gifts even though they were enemies?

3 In splendour, the palace of Harun Al Rashid compared with the imperial palace of the Chinese emperors in Changan, which you read about in Chapter Four. Why did rulers build such extravagant palaces? Who paid for them? Do modern rulers live in the same style as these earlier leaders? Why?

4 In which modern country is the city of Baghdad? Try to find a picture of modern Baghdad. Can you find any evidence in the picture to indicate that it is an important centre of Islam?

Fig. 6.17 Harun Al Rashid, caliph from 786 until 809.

After the Abbasids

In the 900s a rival group of Moslem leaders grew powerful in Egypt and challenged the Abbasids in Baghdad. From this time on, the power of the Abbasids began to weaken. In fact, they had to hire soldiers from the nomadic tribes of Asia to fight their battles and keep their power.

One of these nomadic tribes was the Seljuk Turks, who moved into the Middle East in the 1000s. By 1100 they had defeated the Abbasids to become the rulers of the Middle East. But their power was short-lived. At the beginning of the 1300s, the Seljuk Turks were defeated by another group of Turks—the Ottomans.

The Ottoman leaders, the sultans, fought desperately against the Byzantine empire until 1453 when the last Byzantine emperor was killed and the Byzantine empire fell to the Turks. The sultan moved his capital to Constantinople, from where he ruled over his empire.

The golden age of Islam

As you have already read, Islamic culture and learning were at their height during the Abbasid period, particularly in the time of Harun Al Rashid. In this section we shall explore some of the areas in which Islamic peoples excelled and look at some of their achievements.

An international empire

The Abbasids, as we have read. were from Persia. During their rule the Persians became much more influential than the Arabian Moslems. Persian art, writing and culture became incorporated with the culture of other Moslem countries.

Because the Islamic empire was so large and covered so many different countries, Baghdad and other large cities became 'melting pots' of culture in which the skills, traditions and inventions of many different people were brought together. Persian games like chess and polo were

Fig. 6.18 The Taj Mahal in India is Asia's most famous Islamic building. It was built by Shah Jahan, the grandson of Akbar the Great, as a memorial to his wife. Its designer was blinded when the building was complete so that he could never design a more beautiful building.

spread to other countries. The Arabs tasted new food and learned to eat from tables instead of from cloths on the floor. Persian trousers replaced Arab robes, while ships came to Baghdad carrying silk and jewels, chinaware and spices from Asia, gold and slaves from Africa and goods from as far away as Russia and Spain.

Fig. 6.19 The Alhambra in Granada, Spain, was begun in 1230 as a palace for the Moslem conquerors. It took two centuries to build. This picture shows the Court of the Lions.

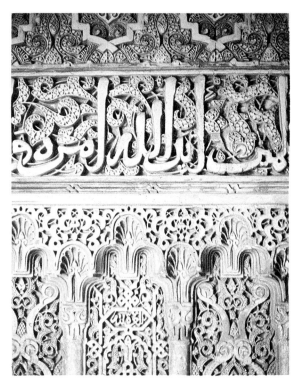

Fig. 6.20 This detail from the Alhambra shows how delicately and intricately its walls were made.

Fig. 6.21 A detail from an Islamic tile, again showing the intricate patterning of Islamic art.

To organise this complex trade, a new system of banking was developed in the Islamic empire. For the first time, a cheque could be written in one part of the empire and cashed at a bank in a city many hundreds of kilometres away in another part of the empire.

Architecture

The early mosques were quite small and simple because they were modelled on the house of Mohammed. As the empire grew and the caliphs became richer, the mosques they built were more and more elaborate. The original mud buildings were replaced with large mosques built of wood and stone, bricks and marble, glass and mosaic. Minarets and domes were beautifully crafted and decorated by craftsmen from many parts of the empire.

We have seen that the early Arabs lived hard and simple lives, often living in only a tent while on the move. As the Islamic empire grew and the Persian influence became stronger, this pattern was changed. Caliphs and other rich Moslems built large and impressive houses and palaces. Like the mosque, they were decorated almost all over with tiles and glass, mosaics and paintings, carvings and glazing.

Art

Mohammed had told his followers that they were not to make idols of their god. Because of this, Moslems rarely painted or sculpted images of people. Instead, they decorated their buildings with beautiful patterns. Many of their other works of art—carpets, plates, materials and vases—were also decorated with carefully designed patterns. You can see an example of this in Fig. 6.21 on page 109.

Just as monks carefully copied out and decorated parts of the Bible and other religious works in medieval Europe, so the followers of Islam copied and decorated the Koran and other religious writings. They believed that beautiful works of art would make the reader think about Allah.

Literature

The literature of Islam began with Arabian poets who wrote about their experiences in a simple and clear way. An example of this early style of poetry are the following lines, written by Maysun, the wife of the first Umayyad caliph.

> Breeze-flowing tents I prefer to ponderous halls
> And desert dress to diaphanous veils.
> A crust I'd eat in the awning's shade, not rolls,
> And watched by a dog that barks not a cat that smiles,
> I'd sleep to the wind's tune, not to the tambourine.

Among the most famous works of Islamic literature was *A Thousand and One Nights*, or *The Arabian Nights*. According to legend, this book was written when Harun Al Rashid condemned a slave girl to death. She made a bargain with the caliph that she could stay alive as long as she told him stories. For a thousand and one nights the slave girl told stories, always keeping the endings a surprise until the next evening. By the time the stories were finished, the caliph was so entranced that he freed his prisoner. Two of the most popular stories from *The Arabian Nights* are 'Sindbad the Sailor' and 'Ali Baba and the Forty Thieves'. Do you know of any others?

Science and medicine

Modern science and medicine owe a lot to the scholars of the Islamic empire in the tenth and eleventh centuries. They read and studied the books of ancient Greek scholars such as Galen and Hippocrates and added to their works what they themselves learned about the way the world and human beings worked. As a result, the Islamic scholars knew much more about almost every aspect of science than other people in the world at that time.

Medicine was one area in which the Moslems excelled. Razi was the first great Islamic doctor. He lived from 865 until 925, during which time he wrote more than 200 books. He worked out how to cure smallpox, a killer disease of the time. Although he knew nothing about germs and the importance of hygiene, Razi had a 'feel' for medicine. When he was asked to suggest the

Fig. 6.22 An Islamic doctor at work.

best place for a hospital in Baghdad, he left pieces of meat out throughout the city. The place where the meat went bad most slowly he knew was the healthiest place (although he could not explain why) and it was here that he suggested the hospital should be built. Before he died, Razi had put together an encyclopaedia which set down all he knew of Greek, Syrian, Arabic, Hindu and Persian medicine. Doctors throughout Europe used his encyclopaedia of medicine for many hundreds of years.

Islamic doctors had to study and pass exams just as doctors do today. During the 800s hospitals were built in the main cities of the empire and doctors did some of their work in them. The larger hospitals had outpatients departments, medical libraries and dispensaries where patients could get drugs that were prescribed for their sicknesses. Some doctors travelled around from place to place, setting up clinics when they stopped and treating patients in tents.

Medicine was not the only branch of science in which the early Moslems excelled. Other scientists studied chemistry and alchemy—the search for a way to turn ordinary metals into gold. Some studied mathematics. From them have come the system of numbers that we used today (called the Arabic system, but actually borrowed from India), the decimal system and the idea of nothing, or zero.

Time to understand

What are proverbs? Can you think of and explain three or four proverbs in the English language?

The following proverbs have come to us from Islamic countries. Can you explain the meaning of each one?

from Morocco
'The tar of my country is better than the honey of others.'
'If you are a peg, endure the knocking; if you are a mallet, strike.'
'Among walnuts only the empty ones speak.'
from Lebanon
'He who has money can eat sherbert in hell.'
'His brains hang at the top of his fez.'
'If life is hard on you, dwell in cities.'
from Persia
'Trust in God, but tie your camel.'
'Walls have mice and mice have ears.'
'The drowning man is not troubled by rain.'

How do we know?

Have you ever wondered where the name 'tabby cat' comes from? In the city of Baghdad, the area where the weavers worked and had their shops was called *Attabiya*. The weavers of Baghdad were known for their rich fabrics, particularly a silk with a wavy stripe in different colours. This part of Baghdad gave its name to *attabi*, a word which described the silk made in the city. Later it was changed into a French word and, from there, became an English word, *attaby*. Our word 'tabby' comes from this old English word because the kind of cat it describes, with its brown wavy stripes, resembled the material being made in the city of Baghdad by Moslem weavers.

What does the word 'assassin' mean? This word comes from an Arabic word, *hashshashin*, which was used for a band of religious fanatics in Persia. At one time they numbered 50 000 people and terrified those who had to fight against them. In order to make themselves braver and overcome fear before a battle, the members of this band drank a mixture made largely of the drug hashish. It is from this word that our modern word 'assassin' has come. The original assassins lasted from 1090 until about 1272, when they were finally defeated by a sultan.

These are just two examples of the way words from one language come into another language, sometimes with a different but related meaning. The English language has borrowed words from many different people, including Australian Aborigines who have given us words like billabong, budgerigar, corroboree and kangaroo.

The Arabic language, the language of Mohammed and the first Moslems, has provided quite a number of words for the English language. It is interesting to notice that many of these words begin with the letters *al* because so many of them came from Arabic phrases which began with *al*, the Arabic word for 'the'. If you remember that Islamic scientists and mathematicians were more advanced than those from other parts of the world, it is not hard to understand why so many of the words that have come to us from Islam are linked with mathematics and science today.

The list below gives some of the words that have come into English from the Arabic language. Can you explain the meaning of each word? If you need help, look up the word in a dictionary.

alchemy	carat
alcohol	cipher
algebra	elixir
alkali	nadir
almanac	saraband
amalgam	syrup
apricot	zenith
borax	zero

7

East meets west: the crusades

APRIL 1095. A huge shower of meteorites falls from the skies over part of Europe. People are frightened. They do not understand such things and fear that it is a sign from God. Churchmen believe that the meteorites show God's anger with Christians. Why are they allowing the Islamic religion to spread so widely, its followers even attacking and capturing the holy city of Jerusalem? Surely Christian leaders can stop this growing menace to Christendom?

November 1095. It is a cold wintry day in Clermont, a town in south-east France. Yet thousands of people from many parts of Europe have gathered here to listen to the Pope speak to them of their duty as Christians. Cardinals and bishops, knights and barons, peasants and pilgrims wait in the fields outside the towns as Pope Urban II, a thin, robed figure, mounts a makeshift stage. They listen as he tells them of their stupidity in fighting each other when there are much bigger battles to be fought and won. They become angry as he recounts the horrible deeds of the Moslems who have taken the holiest of cities. They become thoughtful when Urban reminds them that those who go to fight for God will have their sins forgiven and that if they die in this noble cause they will undoubtedly go to heaven. They become impatient as he describes the treasures they will find in the east when they defeat the Moslems—the infidels, or unbelievers—and capture their cities.

As Urban II finishes his speech, the crowd erupts in hysterical screaming: 'God wills it!' they cry together, and fall on their knees. They

Fig. 7.1 Pope Urban II preaches the crusade at Clermont, France.

113

rip their cloaks to find material to make a cross, the symbol and badge of those who will go to the rescue of their religion. From the Latin word, *cruciare*, meaning 'to mark with a cross' comes the word 'crusader'. The expedition to the Holy Land—the crusade—was arranged to begin in the following August. This would allow knights time to gather their men together and prepare them and also give farmers time to harvest the next year's crops.

Those who had listened to and been moved by the meeting at Clermont went back to their homes in France, England, Scotland, Denmark and other parts of Europe, determined to add their support to the crusades. Why were they so enthusiastic? Why were the crusades needed? What happened to the excitement and religious fervour that were evident at Clermont? Did the crusaders rescue Jerusalem from the infidels? What happened when these two armies of determined fighting men met? These are some of the questions we shall be examining in this chapter.

Before the crusades

In the last chapter you read about Mohammed, the religion called Islam and the expansion of the Moslem empire.

In 638 the Arabs moved into what Christians had always called the Holy Land. Palestine (present-day Israel) was the country in which Jesus Christ was born, lived and died. Born in the town of Bethlehem, he was crucified in Jerusalem, eleven kilometres to the north. Ever since the death of Jesus, Christians had travelled to the Holy Land so that they could bathe in the Jordan River and wash away their sins, see the places that were once known by Jesus, touch the relics that were kept there, worship in the churches that had been built and know that they had done their duty as good Christians. These people were called pilgrims; their once-in-a-lifetime journey was a pilgrimage.

Jerusalem was the most holy place in the Holy Land for Christians, for it was there that Jesus died. It was also a holy place for Moslems, for it was in Jerusalem that Allah had once appeared to Mohammed. When the Moslem Arabs

conquered Jerusalem, they did not stop Christian pilgrims from visiting the city. For many years the two groups lived and prayed in an uneasy peace. The caliph Harun Al Rashid and emperor Charlemagne came to an arrangement in the 800s that Christians would not be attacked or hindered in Jerusalem as long as they paid the city's taxes and obeyed its laws.

All this changed in 1076. In this year another group of Moslems, much more warlike and lawless than the Arabs, captured Jerusalem and became its rulers. These were the Seljuk Turks, whom Europeans called *Saracens*, or easterners. The Saracens drove Christians out of the city, killed them or sold them as slaves. They believed that Christians were the enemies of Islam and that they had no right to worship in a Moslem city.

News of these events gradually passed back to Europe. It worried Christians who were anxious about the loss of their holiest city, and it worried rulers who were concerned about the expansion of the Moslem empire. Most particularly, the conquests of the Seljuk Turks worried the Byzantine emperor because he knew that his lands

Fig. 7.2 The Dome of the Rock, a mosque built in Jerusalem by Arabs in 691. It was probably built to rival the Christian Church of the Holy Sepulchre.

were next in line for invasion. You will remember that by this time there were two separate branches of the Christian church: the Catholic church, based in Rome, and the Byzantine church, based in Constantinople.

As the Seljuk Turks moved closer to Constantinople, the Byzantine emperor appealed to the Pope for help in defeating them. In 1093 the emperor asked that Christians, despite their differences, band together to fight the Moslems. It was this appeal that prompted Urban II to call the meeting at Clermont two years later in 1095.

Time to understand

An observer called Robert the Monk left the following record of Urban II's speech at Clermont. Read it carefully and answer the questions that follow.

> From the confines of Jerusalem and the city of Constantinople a horrible tale has gone forth and very frequently has been brought to our ears, namely, that a race from the kingdom of the Persians, an accursed race, a race utterly alienated from God, a generation . . . which has not directed its heart and has not entrusted its spirit to God has invaded the lands of those Christians and has depopulated them by the sword, pillage and fire; it has led away a part of the captives into its own country, and a part it has destroyed by cruel tortures; it has either entirely destroyed the churches of God or appropriated them for the rites of its own religion. When they wish to torture people by a base death, they perforate their navels, and dragging forth the extremity of the intestines, bind it to a stake; then with flogging they lead the victim around until the viscera having gushed forth the victim falls prostrate upon the ground. Others they bind to a post and pierce with arrows. Others they compel to extend their necks and then, attacking them with swords, attempt to cut through the neck with a single blow. . .
>
> Let the deeds of your ancestors move you and incite your minds to manly achievements; the glory and greatness of King Charles the Great, and of his son Louis, and of your other kings, who have destroyed the kingdoms of the pagans, and have extended in these lands the territory of

the holy church. Let the holy sepulchre of the Lord our Saviour, which is possessed by unclean nations, especially incite you, and the holy places which are now treated with ignominy and irreverently polluted with their filthiness.

1 How do you think news of what was happening in Jerusalem and Constantinople was spread to western Europe? Do you think this would be accurate by the time it reached Rome, Paris or London?
2 Was Urban II correct in blaming the attack on Jerusalem on 'a race from the kingdom of the Persians'? (*clue*: Look back to Chapter Six).
3 Both Christians and Moslems believed in one supreme god. Why, then, were they such enemies?
4 According to this record, how were the invaders of Jerusalem making life difficult for the Christians in the city?
5 Why did Urban II mention King Charles the Great who had 'destroyed the kingdom of the pagans'? Who were the pagans whom Charlemagne destroyed? Were they Moslems?
6 What did the Pope mean by the 'holy sepulchre of the Lord our Saviour' which was 'possessed by unclean nations'? What sort of people would have been stirred by this to fight in the crusades?
7 Do you think Urban II's speech was effective? Do you think it would have affected you if you had been standing in the crowd at Clermont that day in November 1095? Why?
8 Can you think of any other occasions when religious leaders have addressed large crowds? What sort of things have they been talking about? How have the crowds responded?

Why did people go crusading?

Many men became crusaders because they sincerely believed that they had a duty to rescue the Holy Land from the infidels. Others went for very different reasons. The diagram in Fig. 7.3 on the next page shows the main reasons that people went crusading.

What do you think? Can you imagine living in Europe so many years ago? Do you think you

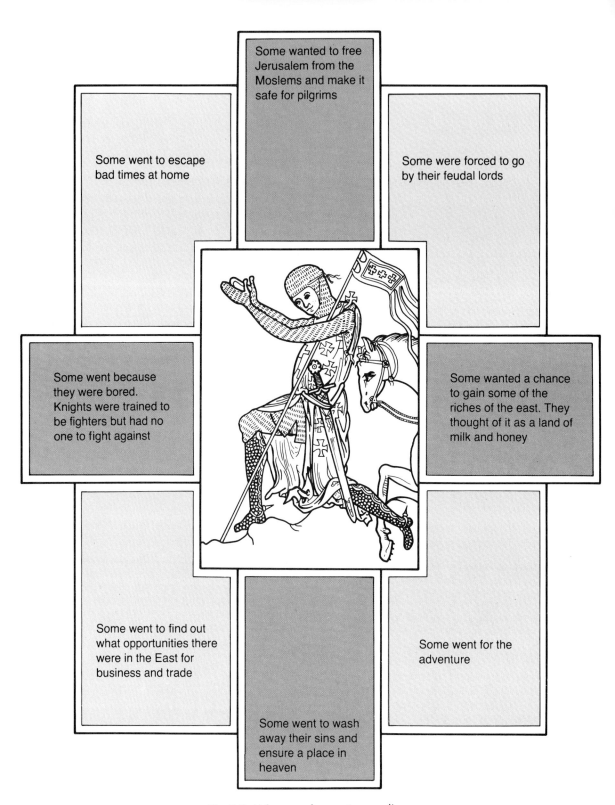

Some wanted to free Jerusalem from the Moslems and make it safe for pilgrims

Some went to escape bad times at home

Some were forced to go by their feudal lords

Some went because they were bored. Knights were trained to be fighters but had no one to fight against

Some wanted a chance to gain some of the riches of the east. They thought of it as a land of milk and honey

Some went to find out what opportunities there were in the East for business and trade

Some went for the adventure

Some went to wash away their sins and ensure a place in heaven

Fig. 7.3 Why people went crusading.

would have decided to go crusading? What do you think might have happened to the women and children the crusaders left behind? Would they have led an easy life?

Peter the Hermit and the people's crusade

The crusades got off to a bad start. As the knights prepared their armies for the crusade that Urban had set down to begin on 15 August 1096, a preacher known as Peter the Hermit moved around France, calling on peasants to sell their goods and join him in a 'people's crusade'. Peter was a religious fanatic, a man whose wild hair, rolling eyes and powerful words stirred those who heard him to believe that he was chosen by God to lead them to victory.

Thousands gathered around Peter the Hermit and a knight called Walter the Penniless. Others, joined them as they moved east. One observer recorded their departure from Cologne in Germany:

> You might see a marvellous and most laughable sight, a troop of poor folk with two-wheeled carts drawn by oxen whom they had shod after the fashion of horses, bearing their few possessions in these little carts, while their very children, as soon as they came to some walled town, would ask again and again if this were Jerusalem.

This ragged and undisciplined band of people knew little of fighting and had only a few simple weapons between them. Almost all were on foot with only a handful of knights on horseback to lead and discipline them. As they moved through Europe they attacked and ransacked the towns they came to, believing that they were entitled to everything they wanted in return for going to Jerusalem.

Further east, in Hungary, the crusaders rioted and went on orgies of looting and murder. When the gates of one town were closed against them, they broke through and slaughtered 4000 people. In revenge the Bulgar tribespeople killed the peasants by night and poisoned the wells along the roadside by throwing dead and rotting sheep into them. Combined with the thousands of deaths caused by sickness, hunger and exhaustion, it is little wonder that the number who straggled into Constantinople at the end of the first stage of the journey was just a fraction of the thousands who had set out so hopefully many months earlier.

Even Constantinople was not spared from the attacks of the so-called crusaders who had supposedly come to save the city from the infidels. Palaces were burnt, churches stripped and those who tried to stop them were murdered. The Byzantine emperor ordered the crusaders to cross into Asia—he even provided ships for them—to attack the Turks. Peter the Hermit gave up trying to discipline the unruly mob and turned back. The crusaders were ambushed by the Turks and mown down. To celebrate their victory the Turks built a monument, a 'mountain of bones, most conspicuous in height and breadth and depth'. So ended the first attempt by European Christians to free the Holy City.

Time to understand

1 Do you think the people's crusade had any chance at all of success? Can you explain why it was not successful?
2 Why do you think this crusade was so violent?

Getting ready

In Chapter Three of this book you read about the feudal system. You will remember that near the top of the feudal pyramid were noblemen and princes, feudal lords who held a great deal of power. They were served by knights who, in turn, controlled bands of men who could, in time of war, be turned into an instant army. Unlike modern armies, the armies that went crusading were not controlled from a few central headquarters. Instead, each feudal lord organised his knights as commanders of a particular band of men. The richer feudal lords were able to call upon more knights who were also able to attract more soldiers to join them.

Fig. 7.4 A well-armed and well-protected crusader knight.

Each leader had to equip the men who served under his command. Many had to sell their land and property to find the money they needed to set up an army. The costs were enormous. The noblemen and knights had to provide horses and wagons, weapons and armour, tents and equipment of all kinds. They also needed to raise enough money to pay for food along the way. Often they ran out of funds and their men simply took for themselves what they wanted.

While rich and powerful noblemen were able to arrange large, well-equipped armies which could be disciplined and kept under control, many smaller nobles and knights found themselves leading small, poorly equipped and sometimes rag-tag groups of followers. Remember that not all the crusaders were interested in spreading Christianity. So it was that the crusading armies that set off for Jerusalem in 1096 included knights and their servants, priests and pilgrims, criminals and drifters, farmers and merchants, women and children.

Time to understand

As you can see from the picture in Fig. 7.4, knights wore quite a lot of protective clothing. One of the most vital pieces of their armour was their shield. These varied in shape and design but a common shape is shown in Fig. 7.4. Medieval shields were about 55 centimetres from top to bottom and about 35 centimetres wide. They were made of wood and covered with leather. At the back was a handgrip with which the knight held the shield.

As armour became more elaborate and knights began to wear helmets that completely covered their faces, they had to identify themselves in some way. To do this the knight had his personal design—his coat of arms—painted onto his shield. Each knight had a distinct coat of arms by which other knights could recognise him.

You can make a medieval shield from a piece of strong cardboard 55 centimetres long and 35 centimetres wide. Draw a curved line on one side, as shown in Fig. 7.5 opposite, and use tracing paper to transfer the pattern to the other side. By doing this you can draw a neat shield shape. Cut out the shield and paint a design on the front. The diagrams in Fig. 7.5 will give you some ideas but you can make up any design that you like to become your personal coat of arms. If you then glue a strip of cardboard to the back of the shield as a handgrip, you will have a shield that resembles those used by the crusaders.

The first crusade

By modern standards the crusaders moved slowly. Limited as they were to the speed of walking or, if they were lucky, horses, they did well to manage thirty kilometres a day. They camped at night in a rough and ready camp and either bought food from villagers as they went or stole what they wanted in the belief that they deserved anything they needed in return for their crusade against the Saracens.

When they reached Constantinople the crusaders were amazed at what they saw. Here

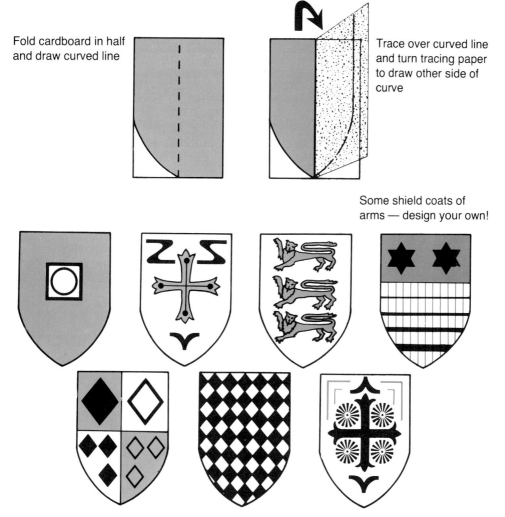

Fold cardboard in half and draw curved line

Trace over curved line and turn tracing paper to draw other side of curve

Some shield coats of arms — design your own!

Fig. 7.5 Making a crusader shield.

was a large and well-planned city with paved streets, streetlights, shops and theatres, parks and gardens, magnificent churches and luxurious palaces. The crusaders could not resist the urge to loot and rampage through this city whose people they did not trust.

From Constantinople they pushed on to the Holy Land. The going was tough. They passed through barren desert, climbed mountains and put up with hunger, thirst and heat they had never known before. Along the way they had to fight groups of Moslems who tried to stop them reaching Jerusalem. The crusaders took nine months to seize the city of Antioch. In 1099,

after fifteen days of fighting, they captured the city of Jerusalem, the most holy of cities and their destination. Their victory was celebrated by an orgy of destruction as crusaders stormed through the city killing anyone who seemed to be an enemy, destroying whatever they came upon and behaving like the barbarians the Moslems believed them to be. At the end of it all they folded their bloodied hands and prayed to God in the Temple of the Holy Sepulchre, the church they had come all this way to save.

When the shouting died and the crusaders settled down, four new kingdoms were set up in Palestine. The most important of these 'crusader

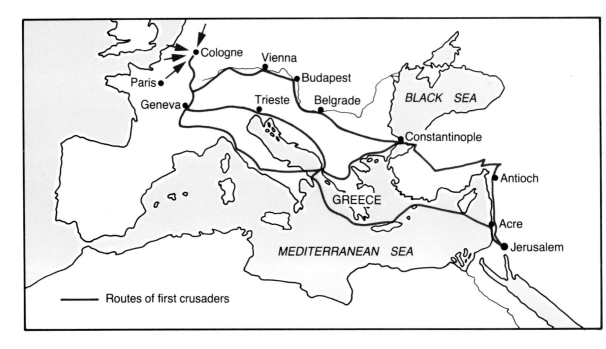

Fig. 7.6 The first crusade.

states' was the Kingdom of Jerusalem, established on Christmas Day 1100. The other kingdoms were those of Edessa, Antioch and Tripoli. Together the four kingdoms were known as *Outremer*, 'the land beyond the seas'.

The noblemen who ruled the kingdoms of Outremer set up their new lands as if they were feudal territories at home in Europe. The Moslem peasants kept working on the land but now their masters were Christian knights and barons rather than Moslem overlords. Yet, though the new rulers tried to set up systems they knew and understood, they found that their lives in the east were very different from their earlier lives in Europe. The climate was hotter and drier so they began to wear Arabian-style clothes for comfort. They enjoyed luxuries they had never known before: beautiful furniture, delicate and plentiful food, Persian carpets and wall-hangings, soft cushions and warm water for washing the whole body.

Despite all these pleasures, the crusaders who stayed in Outremer never felt secure. Their world was always threatened by the very real risk of being ambushed or assassinated, murdered by strangers or even by those who seemed to be friends. There was always the fear that the Moslems would unite and strike against them. Many knights came for a year or two, took what they could from Outremer and went back home richer and grander. Others quarrelled among themselves, making up reasons for battles and behaving in the same petty way as they had in Europe.

Time to understand

1 One crusader described the journey to the Holy Land in these words:

We pursued those abominable Turks through a land which was deserted, waterless and uninhabitable, from which we barely emerged or escaped alive. We suffered greatly from hunger and thirst and found nothing to eat except prickly plants. On such food we survived, wretchedly enough, but we lost most of our horses, so that many of our knights had to go as foot soldiers. We also had to use oxen as mounts and were compelled to use goats, sheep and dogs as beasts of burden.

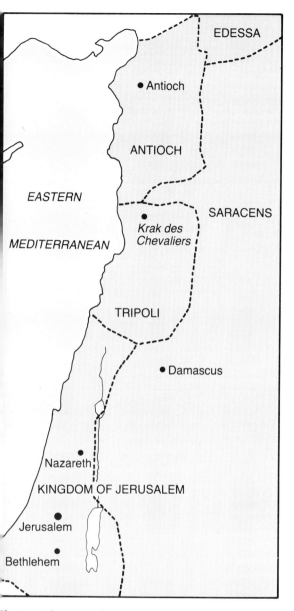

Fig. 7.7 The crusader states.

Fig. 7.8 The crusaders attack Nicosia, 1097.

Warrior monks and castles

As we have seen, many of those who went crusading were only interested in getting what they could for themselves. There were some, however, who were genuinely concerned with protecting the holy places of Jerusalem and making sure that pilgrims could visit them in safety. These knights formed what were called 'military orders'—they lived both as soldiers and as monks. In battle they were courageous and reckless; otherwise they helped and protected Christians in many ways.

The two main military orders were the Knights Templar and the Knights Hospitaller. The first took its name from the ruined Temple of Solomon near its headquarters; the second order was named because of its work in setting up and running hospitals and hostels for pilgrims and crusaders. A thousand-bed hospital was built in Jerusalem by the Knights of St John of Jerusalem, whose symbol, the eight-pointed Maltese cross, can still be seen on the uniforms of the St John's Ambulance Brigade.

The military orders helped to rebuild the Church of the Holy Sepulchre after it was attacked by Saracens. They patrolled the roads along which pilgrims and crusaders passed and

Use this description to draw a picture of the first crusaders travelling to Jerusalem.

2 Fig. 7.8 shows the first crusaders attacking the city of Nicosia in 1097 on their way to Jerusalem. They are using human heads as ammunition. Write a paragraph explaining what is happening in the picture.

Fig. 7.9 A Knight Templar (left) and a Knight Hospitaller (right).

helped to keep them safe. Their hostels gave shelter to many who travelled the long dusty journey to the Holy Land. They built many of the castles that guarded Christian territory in the Holy Land. The mightiest of these castles, *Krak des Chevaliers*, still stands in Lebanon. It could hold a garrison of more than a thousand men and withstood a dozen sieges. It was not captured by the Saracens until 1271. Even then, it was captured by a trick. The knights inside the castle were delivered a letter, supposedly from the grand master, ordering them to surrender. Only when they had marched away did they learn that the letter was a forgery.

Time to understand

1 What kind of work is done by the St John's Ambulance Brigade? In what ways is it similar to the work done by the Knights of St John, who gave the organisation its name?

2 The crusaders took the idea of concentric castles back to Europe. *Krak des Chevaliers* is one of the finest examples of this type of castle. Use a reference book to find out the main features of concentric castles. Try to find pictures of some concentric castles built in Europe after the crusades. Where were they built?

The second crusade

In 1144, a Saracen chief called Zenghi took advantage of the squabbling between the European rulers of the four crusader states and led his army to Edessa, the most northerly outpost of European rule. He took the city easily. The

Fig. 7.10 *Krak des Chevaliers*, Castle of the Knights. It was built by the Hospitallers in the twelfth century.

Moslem counter-attack had begun.

When news of Zenghi's victory reached Europe, people were shocked that the Moslems could win such an easy victory so soon after the crusaders had established their control over the Holy Land. It was time for another crusade, one led by Europe's kings, to shatter the power of Islam and to make Christianity safe in Jerusalem once and for all.

Abbot Bernard of Clairvaux preached to the people of Europe and, like Urban II and Peter the Hermit before him, fired them with the determination to march to the Holy Land. King Louis VII of France and emperor Conrad III of Germany agreed to lead the crusade, which set out from Europe in 1147.

The second crusade was a miserable failure. It really had no chance of succeeding. Too many people joined it in order to get for themselves some of the 'good life' they had heard about in the east. Many took their wives and children with them, using the crusade as an excuse for moving house. Louis was a poor leader and tried to discipline men along the way by cutting off their feet, noses and ears. This did nothing to build up loyalty! The French and Germans could not agree about tactics; in fact many crusaders went on side-expeditions and made war on other people along the way.

These crusaders never reached Jerusalem. When they were attacked by Turks near Damascus, they gave up and turned for home. Zenghi may well have used this moment to launch a full-scale attack on Jerusalem. But one night he awoke to find a servant in his tent stealing wine. The terrified thief stabbed Zenghi and killed him and the Moslems had to wait another forty years for a leader strong enough to recapture Jerusalem.

SALADINVS SVLTANVS.

Fig. 7.11 Saladin, the greatest Saracen military leader.

The third crusade

The third crusade, which lasted from 1190 until 1192, was called by the Pope as a direct result of the victories of Saladin, one of the world's greatest fighting men and an inspired leader. Saladin became sultan of Egypt in 1171. Just as the Christians believed they had a duty to rid Palestine of Moslems, so Saladin believed it was his responsibility to wage a holy war against the Christians who had set themselves up in Jerusalem.

Even with the threat of Saladin looming over them, the European rulers in Outremer could not co-operate. There was no one strong enough to lead them into battle. In September 1187 Saladin's army surrounded Jerusalem; it took them only two weeks to break down the walls and enter the city as conquerors. Once again the Holy City was in Moslem hands.

The Pope called for another crusade and convinced three European rulers to lead it. They were Philip II of France, Frederick Barbarossa ('Redbeard') of Germany and Richard I of England. Once again crusading fever spread throughout the lands of Europe. Once again men gathered to make the long journey to Jerusalem to defend their faith. By this time some lessons

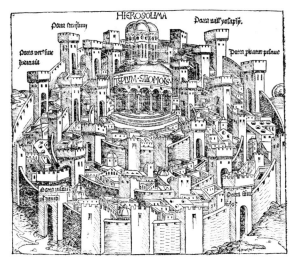

Fig. 7.12 A medieval drawing of Jerusalem. Can you see the Temple of Solomon?

had been learned from the earlier crusades and the third crusade was better disciplined and more thoroughly prepared than the first two.

The crusaders and their leaders set off with high hopes. The plan was for Frederick's army to travel by land and the troops of Richard and Philip to make the crossing by sea through the Mediterranean. In fact, Frederick did not survive long enough to reach Jerusalem. He drowned in a river on the way. His armies broke up: some men were taken as slaves by the Turks, others turned for home, many were killed by plague in Antioch.

Quarrelling all the time about the spoils of war, the English and French crusaders pushed on to the city of Acre in 1191. After five weeks of heavy fighting, the crusaders broke through and captured the city. The Moslems inside Acre were brutally assaulted and killed in another orgy of bloodshed and destruction. Richard, known to history as the 'lionheart', was a skilled commander and a courageous fighter. But his word could not be trusted (as Saladin found when he tried to make treaties with him) and he was cruel, brutal and arrogant. He cared nothing for the hardship his wars caused to those who were forced to pay for them, nor for the suffering he and his soldiers caused to those he conquered.

By September 1191 Richard's forces had taken the city of Jaffa. A year later they were still trying to reach Jerusalem. During this time there had been many battles in the hot and dusty land. Thousands had been killed; many had deserted and turned back for home. Saladin and Richard had met several times to try to make a truce: Saladin small and dark, Richard big and burly, both excellent leaders and each committed to his cause.

The truce was made in September 1192. Both Christians and Moslems were to be allowed to

Fig. 7.13 A statue of Richard I, 'the lionheart', outside the Houses of Parliament in London.

pray in Jerusalem undisturbed. The Christians were allowed to keep seven cities, including four important ports. The city of Jerusalem itself remained in the hands of the Moslems.

Saladin died of fever in 1193, never having had time to make a pilgrimage to Mecca, despite the great service he had given to the Moslem cause. He had been an honest and thoughtful man whose compassion in peace was matched by his ferocity in war and his determination to expel the Christian foreigners. Richard was killed in France in 1199 when an archer fired an arrow into his shoulder in a skirmish with a French baron.

Later crusades

Europeans made five more attempts to rid Jerusalem of Moslems. None was successful, although at times treaties were made that seemed to give Christians greater freedom and security. Most of these later crusades came nowhere near the Holy Land, for the old problems of poor leadership, quarrelling, greed and brutality continued to get in the way of a really determined effort to free Jerusalem.

The fourth crusade (1201–1204) ended in horror when the crusaders attacked and ransacked the Christian city of Constantinople, whose emperor, you will remember, first asked for help from European Christians in 1093. Blood flowed in the streets as the so-called crusaders tried to destroy one of the world's finest cities. This disgraceful conduct made it impossible for the eastern and western branches of the Christian church ever to unite to form a single religion.

The next crusade, an unofficial one, was perhaps the most tragic of all. A French teenager, 12-year-old Stephen of Cloyes, believed that he had a letter from Christ commanding him to organise a crusade of children. Their innocence and honesty, he believed, would put the adults of Europe to shame and win back the Holy Land. Stephen was under the spell of religion; he believed that God had told him that the seas would part and allow his crusaders to walk to the

Holy Land just as the waters had parted for Moses in Old Testament times.

Stephen was very persuasive and children flocked to him from all over France. Perhaps 30 000 gathered to begin what has become known as the 'children's crusade'. They left in high summer, full of enthusiasm but lacking maps, food, weapons and common sense. Many died along the way; others turned back when the reality of what they were doing struck them. When they reached Marseilles and the Mediterranean did not roll back to let them pass, the children did not know what to do. Two men—Hugh the Iron and William the Pig—offered to ferry them across the sea to Palestine in seven ships.

Stephen accepted what he thought to be a generous offer. A few days out, however, two of the ships were completely wrecked in a wild storm. The others sailed on, not to Jerusalem but south to Algeria where all the children were sold to the Saracens as slaves. Several hundred were

Fig. 7.14 The beginning of the children's crusade, 1212.

later bought by the emperor of Egypt; others ended up in Baghdad in Persia. Very few ever saw their homes again.

The last crusade set out in 1270. Like the others, it was a failure. In the following year Moslems captured *Krak des Chevaliers*, the most impressive of all crusader castles. In 1291 the Saracens took Acre, the last Christian city in the Holy Land. This was a hundred years after Richard had first captured it for the Christians and almost two hundred years after the founding of the kingdom of Jerusalem. By this time the crusading spirit which had once driven men to fight had died out, although many battles between Christians and Moslems were still to be fought. In 1453 Moslem Turks captured the city of Constantinople; in 1492 Christian armies defeated the Moslems (known as Moors) in Spain; and in the eastern part of the Mediterranean the Turks remained in control until 1571. Jerusalem itself was controlled by Moslems until 1917 when, towards the end of the First World War, it was captured by a combined British and French army.

Time to understand

When the crusaders entered Constantinople in 1204, they attacked the magnificent Byzantine church of Santa Sophia, which you read about in Chapter One. Here is an eye-witness account of what happened:

> The sacred altar, formed of all kinds of precious materials and admired by the whole world, was broken into bits and distributed among the soldiers, as was all the other sacred wealth of so great and infinite splendor.
>
> When the sacred vases and utensils of unsurpassable art and grace and rare material, and the fine silver, wrought with gold, which encircled the screen of the tribunal and the ambo, of admirable workmanship, and the door and many other ornaments, were to be borne away as booty, mules and saddled horses were led to the very sanctuary of the temple. Some of these which were unable to keep their footing on the splendid and slippery pavement, were stabbed when they fell, so that the sacred pavement was polluted with blood and filth.

Constantinople was a Christian city. Can you suggest why this church was ransacked by the invading crusaders? What do you think they would have done with all the booty they took from the church?

After the crusades

The struggle between Christianity and Islam was not resolved during the crusades; indeed it has continued until today. The crusades were violent and cruel, brutal and bloodthirsty. There was treachery, torture, greed and inhumanity on both sides. Few of those who fought came out of the crusades with honour.

For all this, the crusades were important. They brought together people from Europe and the Middle East and brought their cultures into violent contact with each other. To Europeans just emerging from the Dark Ages, the east was a revelation. The crusaders took home ideas and inventions never before known in Europe. The Saracens, in contrast, learned little from the Europeans, whose society was so much more primitive than their own.

The crusades encouraged travel beyond Europe. Europe was put in touch with the science and medicine, the art and literature, the mathematics and culture of other, more advanced societies. In Constantinople, for example, Europeans found art and architecture from ancient Greece.

Through the Arabs, who had traded with the people of China, Europeans learned about paper, herbs, spices and foods they could never have imagined. They also learned about shipbuilding and castle building, navigation and architecture. Cotton came to Europe from the crusades, as did sugar cane and apricots, slippers and glass mirrors.

The demand in Europe for goods from the east strengthened trade. Trading cities like Venice and Genoa grew rapidly. Trade brought new goods to Europe. It also encouraged the spread of ideas and an interest in societies in other parts of the world. Trade needed ships and European knowledge of shipbuilding grew quickly. Because of this, Europeans were able to travel further and extend their influence in other parts of the world.

The crusades contributed to the decline of the feudal system. To raise money to go crusading, many barons and knights had sold land to freemen and peasants. People who had never before been really free became independent; having tasted freedom they were not prepared to return to the old ways. Kings realised that full-time paid armies were more reliable than the armies provided by barons and knights. As well,

merchants became richer and more powerful with the increase of trade. There was no place for merchants in the old feudal system, so the system had to change to make room for them.

Both Moslems and Christians saw the crusades as holy wars: they were fought to spread the word of Jesus Christ or the word of Allah. The crusades caused death, suffering and hardship for many thousands of people on both sides. Yet they were partly the cause of great changes in Europe—changes that you can read about in the next chapter of this book.

How do we know?

Chronicles and illustrations

Much of our information about the crusades comes from two sources: *chronicles* and *illustrations*. The chronicles were accounts of the crusades, written by people who were involved in them or by others who recorded what they had heard of the crusades. As you can imagine, some were more accurate than others. The most reliable were those written by people who wanted to set down a record of what happened to them at the time. The least reliable were those that were made up from bits and pieces of information, rumours and stories that were told after the crusades had ended.

Some of the illustrations in this chapter were drawn at the time of the crusades or soon after. You can tell this because they are in the style of the Middle Ages. Others were drawn very much later; they are in a completely different style. Look again at the pictures in this chapter. Which ones do you think were drawn at the time of the crusades? Why do you think so? Which ones were drawn later? How can you tell? Which kind of illustrations are more useful as sources of information?

The description of Saracen fighters on page 129 was written by a crusader. The illustrations in

Figs 7.15–7.17 date from the time of the crusades. Read the extract and look carefully at the pictures. Then write down what you have learned about the difference in clothes, weapons and fighting styles between crusaders and Saracens.

Fig. 7.15 Knights and Saracens, painted on the window of a French abbey in the 1100s.

Fig. 7.16 A Saracen warrior, from an Arabian manuscript.

The Turks were not loaded with armour like our men, and their ease of movement was very disconcerting to us. For the most part they were lightly armed, carrying only a bow, or a mace bristling with sharp teeth, a scimitar, a light spear with an iron head, and a dagger. When put to flight by a greater force, they fled away on horseback with the utmost rapidity. Their agility is unequalled throughout the world. If they see their pursuers stop, they will usually turn round and come back—like the fly which, if you drive it away, will go, but the minute it sees you stop will return.

Historical fiction

Historical fiction is a story based on history. Many writers use historical events as the background for an exciting story. Good historical fiction writers spend a great deal of time researching the period they are writing about. They need to know as much as possible about what happened in the period and they also need to get an understanding of the 'feel' of the period so they can convey this to their readers.

Two excellent books of historical fiction about the crusading years are:

The Children's Crusade by Henry Treece (London, Bodley Head, 1958)

Knight Crusader by Ronald Welch (London, Oxford University Press, 1971)

Find one of these books in your school or public library and read it. Ask the librarian if there are any other books of historical fiction set in the crusades. Reading them will help you to gain an impression of what life was like during the crusades.

Fig. 7.17 Saracens approaching a crusaders' camp, from a French manuscript of the 1300s.

8

The Renaissance

RENAISSANCE is a French word meaning 're-birth'. When historians use the term Renaissance they are referring to a period of time from about 1400 to about 1600. Why has it been called the rebirth? What was reborn? When had it died? Where did this take place?

The Middle Ages, which you studied in Chapter Three, was a period of time which began with the fall of the western half of the Roman empire and lasted until the early 1400s. The early years of this period have sometimes been referred to as the Dark Ages, when the knowledge and learning of the ancient Greeks and Romans were largely forgotten. Knowledge was thought to shed light on people's understanding of the world, so when this knowledge was forgotten, the world was said to be dark.

Yet the light did not go out completely. In western Europe, monks still studied the surviving ancient books, copying them laboriously and illuminating their manuscripts with gold and vibrant colours. In eastern Europe the Byzantine empire flourished, preserving much of the Greek and Roman culture lost to western Europe.

The Renaissance of the 1500s and 1600s refers to a 'rebirth' of knowledge and a new spirit of inquiry, or desire for understanding and learning, in western Europe. The 'rebirth', or rediscovery of the knowledge of ancient Greece and Rome

began in Italy, in a prosperous city called Florence.

What happened as a result of this rebirth? Marsilio Ficino, one of the most important Florentines, who actively helped the rebirth, said:

> For this century, like a golden age, has returned to light the liberal arts which were almost extinct: grammar, poetry, rhetoric, painting, sculpture, architecture, music . . .

What happens to something when it becomes extinct? What do you think he meant?

The city of Florence

Throughout the Middle Ages, trade and commerce developed slowly. Florence became one of the leading cities in Europe in the production and trade of woollen cloth. The production of wool was of such importance that in 1338 Giovanni Villani estimated that out of a population of 90 000, approximately 30 000 people were involved in the production of 75 000 bolts of cloth annually. This not only brought wealth to Florence but also made it possible for a large group of traders and merchants to become rich and powerful.

Banks were privately owned by the wealthy families. Four of these families were the Medici, the Strozzi, the Pitti and the Pozzi. By the end of the

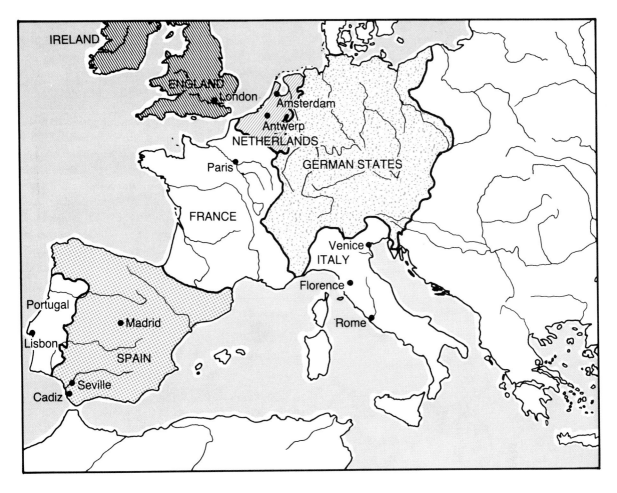

Fig. 8.1 Europe in the fifteenth century.

fifteenth century the Medici family had established branches of its bank in important cities throughout Italy and Europe.

The wealth brought to the middle class by these activities enabled them not only to become interested in the rediscovery of Greek and Roman culture but also to become actively involved in promoting it. Many wealthy families built up libraries of manuscripts and employed copyists to reproduce these valuable works.

The study of the 'humanities', that is, subjects associated with human culture such as Greek, Latin, history and literature, became fashionable. Teachers of the humanities were first known as 'humanists'. Later, anyone who was interested in the study of these subjects was known as a 'humanist'.

In Chapter One, you read that the Byzantine

empire in eastern Europe had preserved much Greek and Roman culture. In 1453, Constantinople, the capital of the Byzantine empire, was captured by the Turks. As a result of this, many scholars left the city. In Italy, especially in Florence, there was a growing demand for teachers of Greek, which was thought to be an essential part of a good education. Many Greek scholars found work in Italy. They also brought with them many manuscripts of ancient Greek books which had been lost to western Europe.

Florence became the leading city of the Renaissance. Many great artists, architects, writers, craftsmen, philosophers and scholars were either born in Florence or worked there. Artists or writers were patronised by a member of a wealthy family or a ruler. The patron supported the artist financially, usually by commissioning works of art or buildings. Other wealthy families and rulers in other cities followed the lead of Florence.

Fig. 8.3 The Mona Lisa.

Time to understand

Look closely at the two paintings in Figs 8.2 and 8.3. Write a list of the differences in the way each artist has painted the figure of a woman.

Although the artists were trying to achieve different aims, we can see what Marsilio Ficino means by a rebirth in the art of painting when we compare the two. The painter of the Virgin and Child (Fig. 8.2) aimed to show the holiness of the infant Jesus and his mother, whereas Leonardo's aim was to paint a naturalistic portrait. The Mona Lisa (Fig. 8.3) appears to be almost flesh and blood, whereas by comparison the Virgin and Child is flat and unrealistic.

Fig. 8.2 A medieval painting of the Virgin and Child.

The Medici family

The great families of Florence also ran the government. Of the many families which became powerful and wealthy, the Medici family was the most important. The head of the Medici family was virtually the ruler of Florence.

By 1430 Cosimo de Medici had established many banks in Italy. In 1433 he was banished from Florence by other members of the government who were jealous of his wealth and power. A year later Cosimo returned, as his valuable advice was missed by many people. After his return Cosimo gradually became the 'silent ruler' of Florence.

Cosimo became very interested in the humanities and the arts. He felt that some of his wealth, which came from the Medici banks, should be used to promote the new learning and to foster the arts. Cosimo supported artists by commissioning them to paint works of art.

Fig. 8.4a Botticelli's 'Adoration of the Magi'.

Time to understand

Alessandro Botticelli was a young Florentine artist supported by the Medici family. In his painting *Adoration of the Magi*, shown in Fig. 8.4a, he has included portraits of a number of Florentine men, including himself. With the help of an encyclopaedia or the index of a book about the Renaissance, see if you can discover why he included the following people.

(1) Lorenzo the Magnificent; (2) Agnolo Poliziano; (3) Pico della Mirandola; (4) Cosimo de Medici; (5) Piero de Medici; (6) Giuliano de Medici; (7) Alessandro Botticelli (the artist). (The numbers in brackets correspond with the numbers in Fig. 8.4b.)

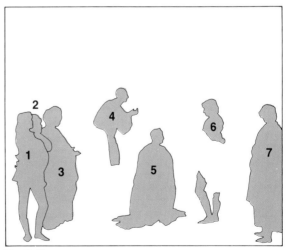

Fig. 8.4b

How are artists and writers paid today? Do they have patrons who support them? How do they make a living?

Cosimo was so impressed by Gemistus Plethon, a Greek scholar from Constantinople, that he founded the Platonic Academy to make the great teaching of the ancient Greeks available to more people.

After Cosimo's death, his son Piero carried on his father's work. Piero was head of the family until his death, only five years after Cosimo. Piero's son Lorenzo then became the ruler of Florence.

Lorenzo the Magnificent, as he has been called, was not only a patron of artists and scholars, but also a scholar and poet himself. In 1478, members of the rival Pazzi family plotted to murder Lorenzo and his brother Giuliano. On Easter Sunday, during a service in the cathedral, the assassins struck. Giuliano was killed but Lorenzo, surrounded by friends and supporters, managed to escape. The people of Florence were so angry that they rounded up all those who had anything to do with the murder and executed them.

Fig. 8.5 A woodcut showing a Florentine bank.

Time to understand

The engraving in Fig. 8.6 shows activities thought to be sacred to the god Mercury. We can tell by the dome on the left that the city depicted is meant to be Florence. Florence was the first city to put a dome over its cathedral during the Renaissance.

Find the following activities or occupations within the engraving: clock-maker, scribe, musician, sculptor, goldsmith, philosopher, painter.

Fig. 8.6 A Florentine street scene, 1465.

The invention of the printing press

Many of the great families who became patrons of artists and writers also collected books, in order to build up libraries in which scholars could study. In the Medici library the books were chained to the desks. This gives us an important clue about the value of books in the early days of the Renaissance. Books were very rare and very expensive. This was because of the way they were produced.

There were two main techniques. One was to carve out letters and drawings on a block of wood, then press it into an ink pad before printing it onto paper. This method was extremely slow. Fig. 4.13 on page 69 shows how the Chinese had developed this.

Another method was to copy out the entire book by hand. The manuscripts were very beautiful and great care was taken with miniature illustrations, but there were many disadvantages. Apart from the long hours of work involved in copying, the copyist was also likely to make mistakes while copying. He could also add whatever he liked to the text!

In Germany in 1439 Johann Gutenberg was working on a 'secret process' which was to cause great changes in the production and distribution of books. He discovered a way of making a movable metal type. The letters were formed by pouring liquid metal into moulds. This meant that the letters always turned out the same shape and size, and as they were made of metal they lasted for a long period of time. These letters could be assembled to form words, sentences, paragraphs and whole pages. When the page was printed, the letters could be reassembled to print another page. This was far easier than carving each entire page into a block of wood.

By 1477 William Caxton in England was using the same process to print books in English. He published approximately 100 books in fifteen years. When Caxton began printing, the English language varied from town to town, and region to region. These variations in language are called dialects. Caxton's books, which used one dialect of English, helped to bring about a change in the English language. As the printed books were cheaper to produce, more people were able to read them. This meant that people began to read the same dialect of English and eventually to speak it as well.

In Italy, Aldus Manutius established a printing press in the late fifteenth century. The first dated book from his press was 1494. The Aldine Press, as it was named, still publishes books today.

The use of the printing press helped to spread the ideas of the Renaissance more quickly throughout Europe. Books ceased to be rare and expensive items bought only by the wealthy.

Time to understand

1 Fig. 8.7 shows a monk copying a manuscript.
   a Describe the equipment used by the monk.
   b What are the disadvantages of producing a book in this way?
   c Are there any advantages?
2 a What do the people on the left-hand side of the picture in Fig. 8.8 on the next page appear to be doing? Note the pieces of paper above them in each case. What do you think these are?

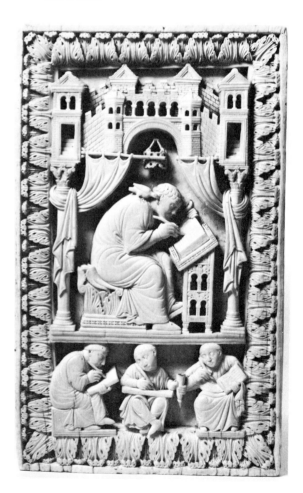

Fig. 8.7 A monk copying a manuscript.

Fig. 8.8 Printing in the sixteenth century.

b On the right-hand side of the picture two men are involved in the next stage of hand printing. Describe this stage as accurately as possible.

c What advantages did hand printing have over hand copying?

3 What was the importance of the changes caused by the invention of the printing press?

The ideal of the universal man

With the rediscovery of Greek and Roman knowledge came the idea that human beings were God's finest piece of work. There was a belief that everyone should try to develop whatever talents God had given him or her. The ideal Renaissance man excelled in whatever he attempted. Michelangelo Buonarroti, Lorenzo de Medici, Marsilio Ficino and Leonardo da Vinci are some of the most famous 'universal' men, as they were called.

Marsilio Ficino

Marsilio Ficino was a doctor, musician, writer, scholar, priest and philosopher. The Medici family supported, or patronised, Ficino. He was Lorenzo's private tutor and was chosen to run the Platonic Academy. The house in which Ficino lived was given to him by Cosimo de Medici. This became the headquarters of the Platonic Academy.

Many of the artists, writers and scholars of Florence attended the Platonic Academy. They respected Ficino not only for his scholarship but also for his understanding. He is said to have influenced the painting of Botticelli, as well as the decisions made by the Medici family about the government of Florence.

Leonardo da Vinci

Leonardo da Vinci is often remembered for his work as a painter. Yet when Leonardo wrote to the Duke of Milan in 1482 asking for a job, he mentioned painting as the last of his talents. Leonardo could design bridges, cannons, catapults, guns, ships and buildings. He thought these talents would interest a duke who had to defend his city against attackers. The duke employed Leonardo until 1499 when Milan was taken over by French invaders. From his childhood Leonardo had wanted to know and understand everything. Leonardo thought that an understanding of how the human body worked and moved would add more depth to his painting. To achieve this he dissected thirty human corpses, over a period of years, making detailed sketches of the internal structure of the human body.

Leonardo felt that the talent of seeing, or observing, was something everyone could develop. Through observation, people would begin to ask questions, and eventually find the answers, about Nature which surrounded them. For years, Leonardo observed birds in flight to try to discover a way in which people could fly. It was not until hundreds of years after Leonardo's death that the answer to this problem was discovered.

Time to understand

Fig. 8.9 shows one of a number of designs by Leonardo for a large catapult.
1 For what purpose would this device have been used?
2 What material would be used to build it?
3 What would it be likely to fire?
4 Would there be any difficulty in using it?
5 What would be the main disadvantage in using such a weapon?

Fig. 8.9 Leonardo's design for a catapult.

The spread of the Renaissance

The Renaissance which developed in Italy eventually spread throughout Europe. This was partly because Italian cities traded with other cities of Europe. Merchants and traders were not the only travellers in Europe at this time. Printed books and engravings from Italy whetted the appetite of scholars, artists, scientists and writers. Many of them travelled to Italy itself in order to understand more of the new learning.

In some cases princes invited artists to their courts to work. Francis I, king of France from 1515 to 1547, supported the sculptor Benvenuto Cellini for a number of years. Eventually Cellini returned to his native Florence where he cast in bronze his most significant piece of work, a statue of Perseus. Another artist patronised by Francis I was Leonardo da Vinci. The last few years of Leonardo's life were spent as 'First Royal Painter, Architect and Engineer' of France, although he produced none of his major works in that time.

In England a small group of scholars brought the new learning home from Italy as well. Amongst these John Colet, the son of a wealthy London merchant, returned from Italy in 1496. He decided to use his newly acquired knowledge of Greek to revive study of the New Testament, most of which was written originally in Greek. He became a priest in 1496. By 1505 he had become Dean of St Paul's Cathedral in London. When he inherited his father's fortune four years later he decided to re-establish St Paul's school. He modelled the new form of the school on the humanist schools he had seen in Italy. Before the Renaissance, many people believed that education, which sometimes had to be 'beaten' into children, corrected what they thought was a child's natural tendency to develop bad ways. John Colet and other humanists felt that education developed children's natural tendency to goodness and virtue.

Time to understand

Look at the painting in Fig. 8.10.
1 Who is the schoolmaster in this painting?
2 What is happening to the boy on the left?
3 To whom was this advertisement likely to appeal?

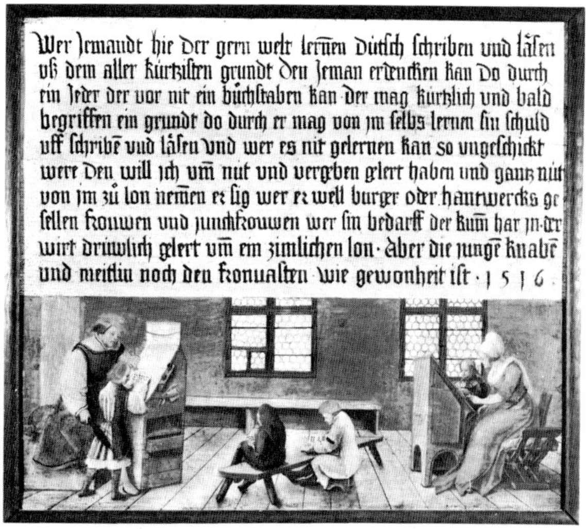

Fig. 8.10 An advertisement for the schoolmaster Oswald Myconius. The advertisement hung outside his school in about 1516.

The craftsman's life

Florence was the home of artists such as Leonardo and Michelangelo. It was also the home of many craftsmen who helped to build the reputation of Florence as being a city of fine arts and crafts.

The workshops of wool-workers, woodcarvers, stonemasons and leather-workers lined the streets of Florence. There were so many of these workshops that to prevent overcrowding, a limit was set regulating the minimum width of buildings which faced the street.

Workshops usually opened out onto the street. Sometimes work benches were even taken out onto the street where work was continued under a kind of awning. Next to the workshop there was usually a doorway leading to a narrow and often steep staircase which led to the upper storeys of the building. Here the craftsman and his family lived a simple and cheap life.

The whole family rose early. The heavy wooden shutters which had protected the house during the night were thrown open. As the pale light of early morning filtered through the oiled linen windows a frugal meal of wine and bread would be taken before the work of the day commenced.

Downstairs the craftsman and his apprentices opened the doors of the workshop. Often the workshop was the only room on the ground floor. Extra light came from a courtyard at the back.

Upstairs the women of the family would tidy the house, wash and repair clothes, spin wool and sometimes weave cloth. There were two other meals of the day to prepare: dinner, which was eaten before midday, and supper, which was eaten at sunset. Food was simple: wheat bread, beans, salad, macaroni and wine. There was little entertainment in the evening, except in the homes of the wealthy, so people usually went to bed early.

Developments in science

The Renaissance spirit of inquiry led people to question old and accepted ways of thinking.

138

There was more confidence in the individual's power to observe things for himself or herself. However, scientists who introduced new theories or ideas often had to face criticism and opposition from groups such as the Church, which wished to preserve established beliefs.

During the Middle Ages people believed that the Earth was the centre of the universe and that all the other planets and stars moved around the Earth. The planets and stars were thought to be embedded in clear 'crystalline spheres' which rotated at different speeds around the Earth. To us this may sound ridiculous. But the Church supported the idea and not many people dared to question it. The Church said that beyond all the spheres was Heaven. Everybody wanted to go to Heaven when they died. So the idea went unchallenged for hundreds of years.

In about 1500 a young Polish university student was studying medicine, law and astronomy in Italy. He was fascinated by the discussions with other students and tutors who suggested that the Sun, not the Earth, was the centre of the universe.

Many years later the Polish student, Nicholas Copernicus, wrote a book about the idea of a sun-centred universe. He felt that other scientists would not accept his theory and so the book was not published until just before his death in 1543.

The work of later scientists such as Galileo Galilei helped to prove that Copernicus' theory was correct. Galileo is best remembered for his development of the telescope. In 1610 he wrote about the possibilities of the new instrument with great excitement:

> . . . I betook myself to observations of the heavenly bodies; and first of all I viewed the moon as near as if it was scarcely two semi diameters of the earth distant. After the moon, I frequently observed other heavenly bodies, both fixed stars and planets, with incredible delight . . .

Later, Galileo defended the theory of Copernicus against opposition from the Pope and other church leaders who wanted the old beliefs about the universe to remain. After a long and drawn-out battle for acceptance of the theory, Galileo was finally put under house arrest in 1633. He died in 1642, having been confined by law to his home for nine years. During this time he conducted many experiments, including studies of motion.

Time to understand

1 Draw a diagram using concentric circles to illustrate the order of the 'crystalline spheres' of the universe thought to exist by medieval scientists. Earth was said to be at the centre. The spheres were supposed to enclose each other in the following order: the Moon, Mercury, Venus, the Sun, Mars, Jupiter, Saturn, the stars, the two other spheres containing no planets or stars. Outside the spheres was Heaven where God lived with the angels and the souls of good people. You may care to add small illustrations to each sphere as they did in the Middle Ages.
2 Compare this diagram with a diagram of the solar system as we now know it. Which planets had not been discovered? Why? What holds the planets on course? Do you think that the medieval idea of crystalline spheres was a reasonable explanation at that time? Why? Could you think of another explanation?

The fading of the Renaissance in Florence: Savonarola

During the Renaissance, Florence had become a centre of culture and learning. This was reflected in the lifestyle of the people, particularly the wealthy. People enjoyed pageants and carnivals, and wore colourful clothes.

By 1494 Florence had changed. Lorenzo the Magnificent had died in 1492 and his son Piero had become unpopular. A priest by the name of Girolamo Savonarola had become the most popular preacher in Florence. He told people that they were leading sinful lives and that love of beauty had changed to love of luxury and idleness. He also said that a great disaster would occur if people did not become more religious.

Fig. 8.11 Savonarola preaching.

At the same time French troops under Charles VIII were invading Italy and marching towards Florence. Savonarola convinced Charles that he would not gain any more victories if he overran Florence. Florence was saved by Savonarola! You can imagine that he must have been at the peak of his popularity. At this point Piero de Medici was driven from Florence and sixty years of Medici family rule in Florence came to an end. A new government was set up.

People thought of Savonarola as a prophet and many took his advice and became less interested in the richness and wealth of Florentine life. They held a bonfire to burn all their luxury goods:

> They went about during the carnival gathering up dice, playing cards, cosmetics, indecent pictures and books, and burned them publicly in the piazza of the Signoria . . .

In 1498 Savonarola was excommunicated by the Pope, partly because of his preaching. He was accused of being a false prophet. To prove his special powers he was asked to walk through fire. He refused and after a trial he was condemned to be burnt at the stake in 1498. Savonarola had been a great influence on Florentine society, but that was quickly forgotten.

When French troops had been invading Italy some years earlier, Florence had made an agreement with France which protected the city from the war. By 1509 the French were very strong in

Italy. Three years later the tide turned and French power in Italy collapsed. In Florence the Medici family returned to rule. Yet things were never quite the same again. As the sixteenth century wore on Rome became the artistic centre of Italy instead of Florence. Artists and architects were brought to Rome to serve the Church.

Time to understand

Francesco Guicciardini wrote a history of Florence in 1509. His description of the death of Savonarola (called Brother Jerome in this extract) reveals some interesting details.

> About twenty citizens were assigned to examine Brother Jerome and his colleagues, all of them his fierce enemies. Without the Pope's permission, they gave him a taste of the rack; and then after a few days they ordered a trial. They reported to the Great Council the statement they said they had got out of him . . . . In brief, the most important conclusions were these: that the things he had predicted were not from God, revelation, or any divine source, but were of his own invention, . . . that he had done it out of pride and ambition, and that it had been his intention to have a council of the Christian princes called to depose the Pope and reform the Church; that if he had been offered the papacy he would have accepted . . .
>
> When these proceedings were published, sentence was put off for several days, for the Pope, having heard with glee of his arrest and confession, first sent his absolution not only to the citizens who had examined him without ecclesiastical permission, but also to the citizens who had listened to his sermons . . . . The Pope then appointed the general of the Dominican Order and a Spaniard named Messer Romolino, to come to Florence to examine Brother Jerome and his colleagues . . .
>
> The commissaries arrived from Rome, again examined Brother Jerome and the others, and finally condemned all three to be burned at the stake. On the (twenty-third) of May, they were hanged and burned in the Piazza della Signoria, in the presence of far more people than were generally at his sermons. It was deemed an astonishing thing that none of them, not even

Brother Jerome, should have used the occasion to make a public statement, either to accuse or excuse himself.

1 What accusations were made of Savonarola?

2 Were these crimes?
3 What was unusual about Savonarola's trial?
4 Was his sentence justified?

How do we know?

The revival of Greek and Roman culture

Historians have often described the Renaissance as not only a revival of Greek and Roman culture but as a flowering of western European culture as well. Ascanio Condivi wrote a description of Michelangelo and his work in 1553 which seems to agree with this assessment. Much of the work of Michelangelo can still be seen today. Read the description on the next page and look closely at the two illustrations in Figs 8.12 and 8.13 below.

Fig. 8.12 Michelangelo's 'Pieta'.

Fig. 8.13 Greek statue of the goddess Tyche.

It seems to me that nature has endowed Michelangelo so largely with all her riches in these arts of painting and sculpture, that I am not to be reproached for saying that his figures are almost inimitable. Nor does it appear that I have allowed myself to be too much carried away, for until now he alone has worthily taken up both chisel and brush . . . Of the ancients . . . to whom does he yield in their sculpture? . . . In the judgment of men learned in the art, to no one . . .

1 What does Ascanio Condivi mean by the phrase 'nature has endowed'?
2 What does he mean when he describes his figures as 'inimitable'?
3 Why does Condivi compare the sculpture of Michelangelo, working during the Renaissance, to the sculpture of the 'ancients'?
4 Why does he say that Michelangelo 'yields to no one'?
5 Do you think Condivi has made an accurate assessment of Michelangelo's work or is he simply expressing an opinion?

The prosperity of Florence

You read earlier in this chapter that Florence became a leading city in the Renaissance because of its wealth and the patronage of artists. Some of the best sources for finding out about life in Renaissance Florence are the letters written by its inhabitants. This extract from a letter written in 1472 by Benedetto Dei to a friend in Venice, tells us much about the industries of Renaissance Florence.

Our beautiful Florence contains within the city in this present year two hundred and seventy shops belonging to the wool merchants' guild . . . It contains also eighty-three rich and splendid warehouses of the silk merchants' guild, and furnishes gold and silver stuffs, velvet, brocade, damask, taffeta, and satin to Rome, Naples, Catalonia, and the whole of Spain, especially Seville, and to Turkey and Barbary . . . . The number of banks amounts to thirty-three; the shops of the cabinet-makers, whose business is carving and inlaid work, to eighty-four; and the workshops of the stonecutters and marble workers in the city and its immediate neighbourhood, to fifty-four. There are forty-four goldsmiths' and jewellers' shops, thirty gold-beaters, silver-wire-drawers, and a wax-figure maker . . .

Sixty-six is the number of apothecaries' and grocer shops; seventy that of the butchers, besides eight large shops in which are sold fowls of all kinds, as well as game and also the native wine called Trebbiano.

Benedetto's description of Florence lists many of the activities and industries of the city in the 1400s.
1 What are the first three?
2 Why do you think he has placed these first?
3 What other activities has he mentioned?

9

Venturing into unknown seas

THIS CHAPTER is about a period of time during which a number of different forces inspired Europeans to venture forth into the unknown, to discover new trade routes, new lands, new groups of people—that is, new to the people of Europe. Obviously, these lands and

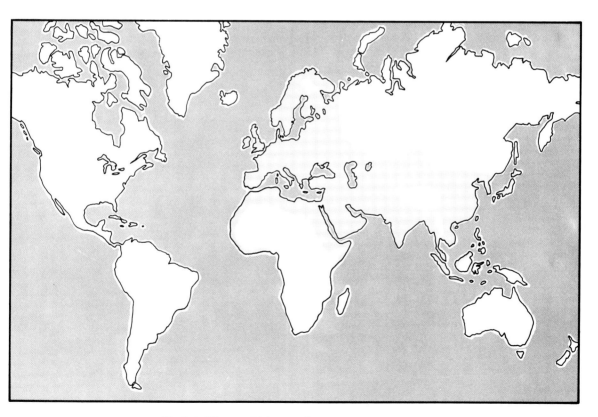

Fig. 9.1 The world known by Europeans in 1400.

groups of people already existed. European explorers simply discovered these lands and people for themselves.

An example of this is the 'discovery' of America in 1492 by Christopher Columbus. Columbus called the native inhabitants Indians because he thought he was in the East Indies. Many accounts were written about the strange 'new' people and, in fact, the Americas were later called the 'New World'.

What motivated Europeans to go on voyages of discovery? You can see from the map in Fig. 9.1 that in 1400 Europeans knew little of the world outside Europe. There were a number of reasons for this. The first section of this chapter will help you understand why European knowledge of world geography was so limited at this time.

The expansion of European knowledge of the world

Europeans of the early Middle Ages lived an insecure life. The western Roman empire had collapsed and barbarian tribes had conquered most of it. Some of these tribes settled in the territory they conquered. These territories gradually grew into European states that we know today. It was a very slow process. You will recall from Chapter Three that most people at that time lived by subsistence farming. They knew very little of the world outside their own village. The rulers of these territories spent a great deal of time defending their kingdoms against the attacks of other rulers who wanted more land. Gradually the borders of the different territories became more established and life was a little more peaceful. During these more peaceful times, knowledge and learning developed. An example of this is the reign of Charlemagne (see pages 36–41).

By the year 1100 most European countries were reasonably settled. Trade between European countries began to flourish.

In the eleventh century, a group of Moslems, the Seljuk Turks, conquered Palestine and would not allow Christians to visit the Holy Land. As a result, the Pope launched a series of crusades

to regain the Holy Land. As you read in Chapter Seven, the crusades did not succeed in doing this. However, they were very important to Europe for other reasons. The Moslems were highly civilised. European crusaders brought back to Europe Arabic knowledge of science, geography, medicine and mathematics. Arab explorers had travelled as far as China by 850 and had established trading contacts with both India and China. After the crusades, European merchants also travelled to places like Constantinople to buy goods from the Far East from Arab merchants. These goods included spices, silks, sugar, precious stones, dyes for cloth and exotic carpets.

Most goods from the Far East were considered luxuries, as the cost and risk of obtaining them meant merchants charged high prices for them. Spices, in particular, were in great demand, as they covered up the unpleasant taste of meat which had been poorly preserved by salt. Meat was salted to preserve it during the cold winter months or in times of war or famine.

At first European merchants relied on Arab traders to bring goods from the East. However, by 1200, European merchants were making their

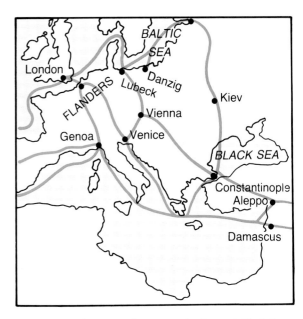

Fig. 9.2 Trade routes between Arabs and Christian Europe.

own way to China. This was possible because China had recently been conquered by the Mongols. The Mongol leader, Genghis Khan, encouraged merchants from other countries to trade and travel within the Mongols' large empire. He protected the merchants and kept the trade routes safe from robbers and other hazards.

The most famous traveller to China was Marco Polo. On his return to Venice after almost twenty years in China serving Kublai Khan, Marco Polo told of all he had seen in the East in his book *The Travels of Marco Polo*. People at first did not believe all he said as it seemed too marvellous and lavish. However, the tales of other travellers supported Marco Polo's claims. Travellers' tales encouraged some people to travel to the Far East. Some were simply curious; others wanted to make their own trading contacts.

Sometimes travellers' tales were exaggerated and gave Europeans a strange picture of life in other lands. For example, the natives of the Andaman Islands in the Indian Ocean were described as having heads like those of dogs.

As a result of far-fetched stories like these, unexplored territory was often thought to be inhabited by horrible monsters and hideous forms of human life. Uncharted seas were said to be full of huge sea dragons which devoured whole ships. It was also believed that the seas near the equator boiled and that the sun could burn men black. Sailors were, in general, reluctant to travel beyond the Mediterranean Sea or the coastline of inhabited lands such as Britain or Spain. In fact, for many years the Straits of Gibraltar, called the Pillars of Hercules, were thought to be the furthest western point fit for human beings to live in. Many ordi-

Fig. 9.3 Spices such as these fetched high prices in European markets.

Fig. 9.4 The 'dog-headed' traders of the Andaman Islands bartering with one another.

nary seamen believed the far-fetched stories, or superstitions, and so refused to sail into unknown territory or out of sight of land.

The trade routes to the East by land were very busy and profitable. The Indies was a name given by Marco Polo to all land between Zanzibar in Africa and Japan. The luxuries of the Far East and the Indies, such as spices and silk, were exchanged for the iron, timber and woollen cloth of western Europe. So there was no need for Europeans to venture into unknown seas.

European knowledge of the world in 1400 had been expanded by Arab knowledge of geography and the tales of various merchants and travellers, but it was still very limited. It was thought that the Indies could be reached by sea but the route from western Europe was unknown. Europeans did not have enough navigational knowledge to make such a voyage. Nor did they know how to build suitable ships.

This situation changed in the mid-1400s. Firstly, the Mongol empire collapsed, making travel on the overland route unsafe once again. Secondly, Constantinople was finally captured by a group of Moslems called the Ottoman Turks. The empire of the Ottoman Turks, based on the former Byzantine empire, now stood in the way of trade to the Far East. Any trading concessions granted to merchants from western Europe were in favour of the Ottomans. Christians were also horrified that Moslems infidels had conquered so much former Christian territory.

The solution to the problem of closed trade routes was obvious. A sea route to the Indies had to be found from western Europe, and suitable ships had to be designed and built for the voyage.

Time to understand

Here are some extracts from a book of travellers' tales by Sir John de Mandeville. Read his descriptions carefully and look for any exaggerations or inaccuracies he may have included.

India
In India there are many different kingdoms; it is called India from a river called the Indus which runs through the country. In that river they find eels thirty feet long or more. The people who live near the country are a nasty colour, green and yellow. Around India are five thousand inhabited islands . . . In that country are snakes and vermin because of the great heat of the country and of the pepper. And when any man dies they burn his body and his wife with him if she has no child . . .

What mistaken impressions does the author create about the people and country of India? Would you say he had been to India himself? Why would he write such a description?

Islands of the East
In one of these islands are giants, hideous to look on, and they have only one eye in the middle of the forehead, they eat nothing but raw flesh and fish. In another isle to the south live a small, evil tribe who have no heads and their eyes are in their shoulders . . . In another isle there are people with lips so big that they can cover their faces with them as they sleep in the sun. In another isle there are people with ears which hang down to their knees.

Imagine you have been asked to illustrate Sir John de Mandeville's book. Draw two or three creatures from this description.

Portugal's search for a sea route to the Indies

By the mid-1400s, with the fall of the Mongol empire and the capture of Constantinople, the need for a new trade route to the Indies was pressing. The old trade routes to the East were closed to western Europe, yet spices from the East had become a basic necessity for both preserving and flavouring food. The lead in the search for a new route was taken by Portugal.

Portugal was ideally situated for coastal exploration. Africa, a land which seemed to contain great riches, was just to the south of Portugal. Portuguese sailors were used to the rough waters of the Atlantic Ocean off the Portuguese coast, whereas most European sailors had only experienced the calm waters of the Mediterranean, and were not prepared to sail out of sight of land.

The Portuguese had learned of Africa's riches after capturing the town of Ceuta in North Africa in 1415. Ceuta was a centre of trade. One of the main articles of trade was gold, brought across the Sahara desert by Arab traders.

The Portuguese wanted to find other sources of food, as their own country contained little fertile land. Portugal's location on the edge of Europe also meant that it had not taken part in many of the wars involving other rival states of Europe. Although a poor country, Portugal was secure and peaceful.

Prince Henry the Navigator

Prince Henry, the third son of John I of Portugal, began to support, encourage and finance sailors, map-makers, geographers, shipbuilders and anyone else who had anything to contribute to his aim: to find, through exploration, the source of the gold supply in Africa. Another strong motive was to convert the native people of Africa to Christianity. Henry and his brother Pedro, who also patronised exploration, wanted to prevent the spread of the religion of Islam in Africa. They also dreamed of finding the legendary kingdom of a Christian ruler, Prester John.

Prester John's mythical kingdom was at first thought to be somewhere in Asia. By the fifteenth century, people believed it was in Africa. Not only was Prester John's kingdom said to be full of Christians, it was also said to be full of gold. Prince Henry thought that Prester John would be a powerful ally and that together they would oppose the spread of Islam.

From Sagres in southern Portugal, many voyages of exploration were planned. Henry's great interest in exploration earned him the title 'Prince Henry the Navigator'. However, he did not travel on any voyages of exploration himself.

The ships from Portugal gradually travelled further and further down the coast of Africa, taking care not to sail out of sight of land. Many seamen were still superstitious and believed that to the far south there was a 'Green Sea of Darkness' from which ships never returned.

In 1434 the furthest known point to the south was reached: Cape Bojador. To round this cape sailors had to brave stormy, foggy conditions. They must have felt that they were really sailing into the Green Sea of Darkness. The rounding of Cape Bojador was a breakthrough in Portuguese exploration. For the first time, seamen could travel southwards with more confidence.

Islands off the coast of Africa were also charted and explored. To prevent rivalry from other countries, these islands were occupied by Portuguese settlers.

After Prince Henry's death King John II continued the patronage of exploration. By 1482 the mouth of the Congo River in Africa had been reached. The aim of further Portuguese exploration was to find a sea route to India to obtain spices. As Portuguese explorers came closer and closer to the tip of Africa, another country had begun to take a greater interest in exploration. This country was Spain. The quest for a sea route to India became more important when it was realised that the Spanish had the same aim.

Bartholomew Diaz

In 1487 Bartholomew Diaz sailed far down the coast of Africa. His ships were suddenly hit by a violent storm which lasted thirteen days. When it subsided Diaz sailed east towards, as he thought, the coast of Africa. He found that there was nothing ahead but open sea! Diaz realised that his ships had rounded the tip of Africa which he named the Cape of Storms. Diaz could not continue his exploration as the crew would sail no further. They were plagued by the old superstitions and wanted to return before it was too late. King John II renamed the tip of Africa the Cape of Good Hope. What do you think he meant by this?

Bartholomew Diaz had not found the sea route to India but he had overcome the main obstacle by rounding the southern tip of Africa. The route to India was established by Vasco da Gama, who led the best equipped expedition that had ever sailed from Lisbon.

Vasco da Gama

Vasco da Gama sailed as far south as the Cape Verde Islands and then sailed out into the Atlan-

Fig. 9.5 Prince Henry the Navigator.

dressed in clothes which clearly showed the influence of Arab traders. In fact, some of them even spoke Arabic.

At Malindi, da Gama managed to hire an Arab pilot to guide him through the final stages of the journey to India. Finally, in May 1498, the expedition arrived in Calicut. On meeting the ruler of this wealthy trading city da Gama is reported to have said: 'We have come to look for Christians and spices.'

The Portuguese had finally found the sea route to India. They had won a prize coveted by Spain. This prize was the future control of the spice trade with India. It brought great wealth to Portugal.

The Spanish, in the meantime, had made a discovery which was to change European life dramatically. Six years earlier, in 1492, Christopher Columbus had sailed west. He believed he could find another route to the Indies by sailing west across the Atlantic Ocean. Instead he discovered America.

Time to understand

1 In order to explore safely and successfully by sea, explorers had to travel in suitable ships. The traders who sailed the calm waters of the Mediterranean had used either an oared galley or a lateen-rigged coaster. Neither of these ships was suitable for the rough waters of the Atlantic. The caravel was developed by the Portuguese for coastal navigation. It had large lateen (triangular) sails and sometimes a square mainsail or foresail. Often cannons were carried on board. Look at the pictures of these ships in Figs 9.7–9.9 on page 150.
 a What obvious advantage does a caravel have over an oared galley or a lateen-rigged coaster?
 b Galleys often had a single sail to supplement the power of the rowers. Why would rowers be unnecessary on a caravel? What could happen to a caravel that could not happen to a galley?
 c Why do you think cannons were taken on board during voyages of exploration?

tic to bypass many of the coastal currents which he thought would slow down the expedition. This meant, however, that the crew did not see land for three months. That was the longest time ships had ever spent on the open sea. You can see on the map in Fig. 9.6 that da Gama's expedition sailed south in a huge arc.

After rounding the Cape of Good Hope, da Gama sailed northwards up the east coast of Africa. The captain and crew took note of all they saw and what happened when they dropped anchor. The further north they sailed the more evidence they found of African contacts with the East, usually through Arab traders. According to reports, Africans in the very south wore animal skins or no clothing at all. Much further north at Mozambique they were surprised to see negroes

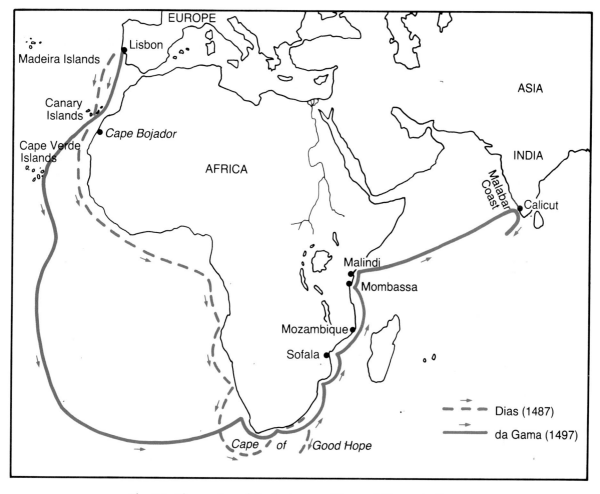

Fig. 9.6 The routes of Bartholomew Diaz and Vasco da Gama.

2 Imagine you are a sailor on the expedition which rounded Cape Bojador. Describe your experience as you approached the Cape and what you felt lay beyond it.

Christopher Columbus and the discovery of America

While the Portuguese were exploring the coast of Africa, an Italian seaman was at the court of King Ferdinand and Queen Isabella of Spain, presenting his own scheme of a route to the Indies. This seaman was convinced it was pos-sible to reach the Indies by sailing west rather than east around Africa. Finally, after six years of debate, the Spanish monarchs decided to support the Italian. His name was Christopher Columbus.

Columbus had been working on his scheme for years. He had read *The Travels of Marco Polo* and dreamed of sailing to the gold- and spice-rich Indies. Columbus believed that the earth was round, and calculated the size of the earth using the calculations of the ancient Greeks. He thought the world was about one-fifth of its actual size. When he claimed that by sailing west one would reach the eastern side of the Indies, he thought it would be a short trip.

King Ferdinand and Queen Isabella hoped

Fig. 9.7 An oared galley.

Fig. 9.9 A caravel.

Fig. 9.8 A lateen-rigged coaster.

secretly to find a route to the Indies before Portugal did. Even though Bartholomew Diaz had rounded the Cape of Good Hope in 1487, the remainder of the route to India was yet to be discovered. The Spanish monarchs were also keen to convert the 'heathens' of the Indies.

On 3 August 1492, Columbus set sail from Palos in Spain with three ships: the *Santa Maria*, his flagship, plus two small caravels, the *Nina* and the *Pinta*. The little fleet sailed across the Atlantic with steady, good winds behind it. After thirty days at sea they had not sighted land. The crews of the three ships became frightened and wanted to return home. Columbus persuaded them to sail for two or three more days. Fortunately land was sighted two days later.

Columbus thought he had reached islands off the coast of the Indies. He called the natives he saw there Indians. We now know that he had landed on an island in the Bahamas, off the American coast. Overjoyed at reaching what he thought was the edge of the Indies, he sailed

Fig. 9.10 Christopher Columbus.

further until he reached what he believed to be *Cipango* or Japan. It was, in fact, Cuba. Columbus returned to Spain declaring the success of his voyage. On later voyages he discovered more islands, including Jamaica, and part of the coast of Central America. Columbus never admitted that he had not discovered the western route to the Indies. When he died in 1505 he still believed in the success of his voyages despite the fact that other explorers had proved him wrong.

The name America comes from the name of another explorer, Amerigo Vespucci. Vespucci accompanied Columbus on his second voyage. Later he made voyages of his own and claimed that his discoveries showed that the new land was in fact a continent previously unknown to Europeans.

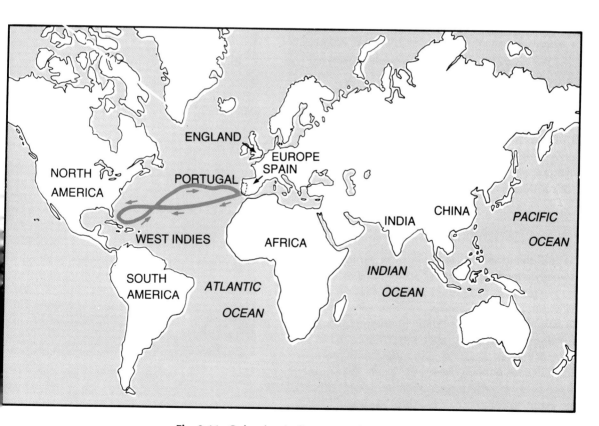

Fig. 9.11 Columbus's discovery of America.

Time to understand

1 Columbus was a skilful navigator. He sailed across the Atlantic and back to Spain without the sophisticated navigational aids sailors use today. Look at the navigational instruments shown below. Some were used for finding the latitude (distance north or south of the equator) and some were used for estimating the longitude (distance east or west of a standard line running north to south) or distance from the original point of departure.

a The *astrolabe* was used to measure latitude. The outer edge was marked in degrees. The centre had movable hands. It was held vertically and the mariner sighted along the centre, moving the hands until they aimed at the sun. The angle marked on the outer edge was the latitude at that particular point. What would have been the disadvantages of using an astrolabe on board ship? Where would be the best place to use it?

Fig. 9.12 An astrolabe.

b The *quadrant* was used to measure the height above the horizon of the Pole Star (which was directly above the North Pole). The arc of the quadrant was one quarter of the circumference of a circle. There were two sets of markings. On the outer edge were the degrees showing the height of the star. On the inner circle were the degrees of latitude. The star was sighted along the edge of the quadrant. A weighted cord pointing straight to the earth's surface gave the measurement. What was the advantage of using a weighted cord? (*clue*: remember the force of gravity.) Do you think a quadrant would be more reliable than an astrolabe? Give reasons for your answer.

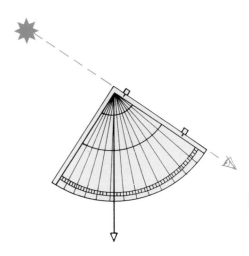

Fig. 9.13 A quadrant.

c The *hour glass* was used to measure the passage of time so that a seaman could estimate the speed at which a ship was travelling. Upon what did the use of an hour glass depend? What could happen to calculations?

d To calculate the speed of a ship a wood chip was sometimes thrown off the bow and timed until it was at the stern. Then the chip was tied to a line knotted at regular intervals and thrown overboard. The time was then measured in 'knots' as they passed overboard. What could upset the accuracy of this method? How is the speed of a ship recorded today?

Fig. 9.14 A scene on board Columbus's ship, showing various navigational aids.

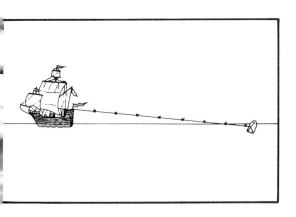

Fig. 9.15 Measuring a ship's speed in knots.

2 Christopher Columbus had on board a simple compass, a number of maps and charts (some of which were inaccurate), a pair of dividers, a straight edge, an hour glass, an astrolabe and a quadrant. He could not make accurate readings of latitude with the quadrant or astrolabe so he used some of the other instruments to estimate the distance travelled each day by 'dead reckoning'. Only an experienced mariner could do this with confidence. He did this by calculating the speed in a particular direction over a certain period of time. Which instruments would he have used if he was plotting his route on a map? Explain your choice of instruments.

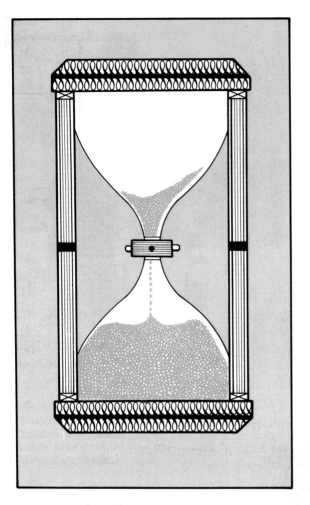

Fig. 9.16 An hourglass.

Further Spanish exploration

Columbus did not recognise the importance of his actual discovery, nor did the Spanish monarchs. This was because Spain was still trying to outdo Portugal by finding a western route to the Indies and the Spice Islands (the Moluccas). Portugal commanded the eastern route via Africa and so had control of the spice trade. The rivalry was so intense that in 1493 the Pope drew an imaginary line through the Atlantic Ocean from north to south. He then declared that all land discovered west of the line belonged to Spain; all land discovered east of the line belonged to Portugal. The line passed through the eastern side of South America.

In 1513 a Spanish explorer called Balboa crossed the Isthmus of Darien between North and South America. Balboa sighted the vast ocean which lay beyond but no sea route to it had yet been discovered. This would have to wait another six years.

Ferdinand Magellan

In 1519, Ferdinand Magellan sailed from San Lucar in southern Spain with a fleet of five small ships. He was a Portuguese seaman working for the new Spanish king, Charles V. Sailing south as far as the Cape Verde Islands, Magellan then turned the fleet westwards to the coast of South America. His plan was to follow the coast of South America as Diaz and da Gama had followed the coast of Africa.

The fleet sailed south to Patagonia where they stopped until the winter was over. The name Patogonia comes from the Spanish word *patagones* which means 'big feet'. When Magellan and his crew first landed at present-day Port St Julian they did not see any natives. After two months, the first of the natives appeared. The natives were almost twice as tall as the Europeans! Their feet were wrapped in skins which had been packed with dry grass. The giant natives were called *Patagones* by the sailors and soon the country was known as Patagonia. Later, an Englishman on a similar voyage reported that the size of the natives had been exaggerated. The Patagones, if they ever existed, have now disappeared.

In the spring Magellan's expedition continued southwards. When the fleet arrived at the mouth of the straits, or passage, at the tip of South America the crew of one ship mutinied and returned to Spain. A second ship was wrecked in the stormy weather. It was not a promising start to a dangerous part of the voyage.

All Saints' Straits (later renamed after Magellan) varied in width. There were many reefs as well as misleading bays and small channels. On both sides of the straits were high, ice-covered cliffs and mountains.

After 38 days the ships emerged from the straits. The ocean in front of the fleet was so calm that Magellan named it the Pacific.

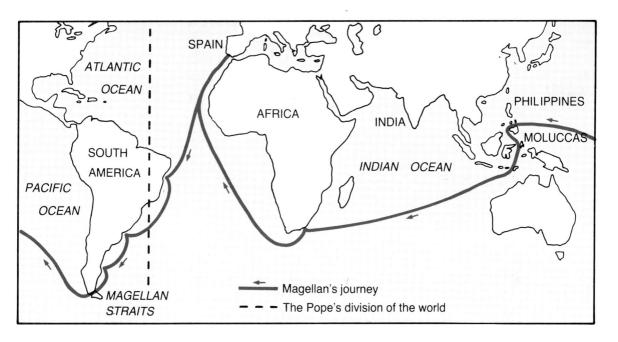

Fig. 9.17 The Pope's line of division and Magellan's circumnavigation of the world.

Magellan then spent four months crossing the Pacific. Many of the crew died of a disease called scurvy or of starvation as supplies ran out. Scurvy was caused by the lack of fresh fruit and vegetables in a seaman's diet. It caused the gums to swell, making the teeth fall out. Also, the joints became very weak, eventually making it impossible for the victim to stand.

In March 1521, the fleet discovered a group of islands which Magellan named the Philippines after Prince Philip of Spain. Magellan established friendly relations with the rulers of the island of Cebu. He also converted the islanders to Christianity. However, Magellan was never to leave the Philippines. On the island of Mactan he was killed by another more hostile group of natives.

Sebastian del Cano took command of the fleet for the rest of the voyage. The fleet of three ships eventually arrived in the Moluccas, where a cargo of spices was purchased. Del Cano then decided to complete the voyage with two ships only, and so the third was burnt. One of the two remaining ships soon became unseaworthy and so was left behind. It was later captured by the Portuguese.

The remaining ship returned to Spain via the Cape of Good Hope. Many of the crew died of scurvy in the final stages of the journey. Only 13 of the original crew of 230 stumbled ashore in September 1522. The world had been circumnavigated.

Meanwhile other Spaniards had been exploring Central and South America. These men soon realised the importance to Spain of Columbus' discovery. They discovered the rich empires of the Aztecs and the Incas.

Time to understand

1 Imagine you are standing on shore in Spain watching the last ship of the Magellan fleet arrive after a three-year voyage. What questions would you ask the sailors on board?

2 The food supplies on a voyage of discovery often had to last for long periods of time. Usually food rotted, weevils destroyed flour, rats ate ships' biscuits and water became putrid. As supplies became low a captain

155

usually hoped for a landfall so that the ship could be restocked with such things as coconuts, salted penguin meat, breadfruit and fresh water. Below is a typical list of food supplies for a three-month voyage, followed by a list of the captain's special food supplies.

8000 pounds salt meat
2800 pounds salt pork
600 pounds salt cod
20 000 biscuits
30 bushels oatmeal
40 bushels dried peas
1½ bushels mustard seed
1 barrel salt
100 pounds suet
1 barrel flour
1 large cask vinegar
10 500 gallons beer
3500 gallons water

captain's stores: cheese, pepper, currants, cloves, sugar, ginger, bacon, wine, rice, cinnamon.

a What is a landfall?
b Why were the meat and fish salted?
c From what disease did sailors often suffer due to the lack of fresh food?
d The captain's stores included spices but the crew's did not. Why was this?
e What other items are listed in the captain's stores which may have been considered delicacies? Why?
f Why is there a greater quantity of beer than of drinking water?
g Why were biscuits included but not bread?

The search for a northern passage

Neither the French nor the English accepted the Pope's division of the world between Spain and Portugal. Portugal controlled the spice trade to the Indies, having set up trading posts and settlements along the route to the south-east (around Africa). Spain was gradually shipping the riches of the Aztec and Inca civilisations out of Central and South America. Spain had also begun to colonise the Philippines and to develop the Pacific as a trade route.

The English and the French felt that an alternative route to the spices of the East had to be discovered. It was believed that such a passage could be found by sailing north-east above Russia or north-west above North America. No one anticipated the danger of pack ice and frozen seas.

To the north-west

In 1497 John Cabot, an Italian serving Henry VII of England, sailed west from England to find a passage to the Indies. He landed on the coast of North America, at Newfoundland. In fact, Cabot was only rediscovering North America. The Vikings had discovered and colonised it as early as the ninth century, and the Indians had lived there for many thousands of years. However, this was not known by most of the countries of northern Europe. Cabot made two voyages to North America without achieving his aim of discovering a north-west passage. His son Sebastian continued the search after Cabot's death.

The French king, Francis I, sent Giovanni Verranzano to attempt to discover a north-west passage to the East in 1524. Verranzano explored much of the east coast of North America without success. Instead, his voyages proved that America was a continuous land mass.

Three years later Jacques Cartier, a French explorer, sailed north from Newfoundland and explored the Gulf of St Lawrence. In 1536 he returned with a larger expedition and explored the St Lawrence river as far as the modern sites of Quebec and Montreal. Cartier hoped that the rapids of the St Lawrence River beyond Montreal would become a passage to the East, but he was forced to give up the search.

Meanwhile English seamen had not given up hope of finding the elusive passage which had been named the Strait of Anian by Sir Humphrey Gilbert in his book *A Discourse to prove a Passage by the North-west to Cathaia and the East Indies*, published in 1576. ('Cathaia' or 'Cathay' was a name for China.)

Martin Frobisher went in search of the Strait of Anian in 1576. He sailed as far as 63° north,

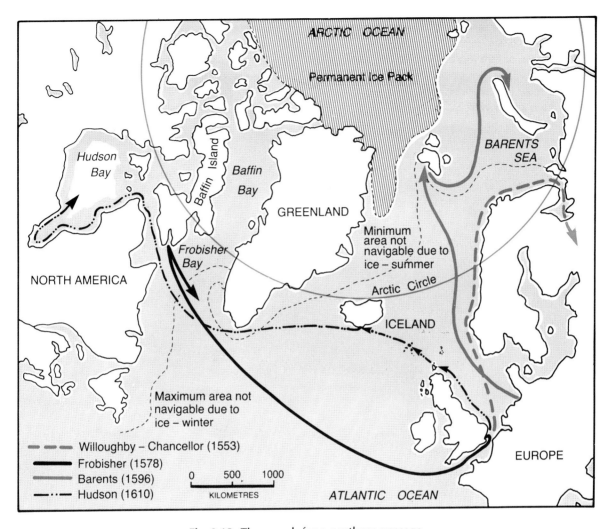

Fig. 9.18 The search for a northern passage.

past Greenland, returning to England with some black rock that he thought contained gold. His second and third voyages were financed by the newly formed Cathay Company which consisted of a group of merchants who hoped to become wealthy either after the passage to the East was discovered or from the new source of gold. The expeditions were failures. The three shiploads of rock which were brought to England contained iron pyrites or 'fool's gold' and the passage remained undiscovered.

The most tragic voyage was that of Henry Hudson in 1610. Hudson had explored much of North America on three earlier voyages. After sailing into the bay which now bears his name, his ship became icebound and the crew were forced to spend the winter there. In the spring when the ship was freed, half the crew mutinied. Hudson, his young son and the rest of the crew were set adrift in a longboat. The mutinous half of the crew sailed home, claiming that Hudson had deprived them of their due rations during a long and difficult winter.

Despite many attempts, the passage to the north-west was never discovered, due to the difficulty of the permanent pack ice within the Arctic circle. It was not until the twentieth century that an icebreaker ship managed to get through.

Fig. 9.19 John Cabot leaves Bristol, England.

To the north-east

In 1553 Sir Hugh Willoughby and Richard Chancellor attempted to find the route to the Indies to the north-east, above Russia. They encountered difficulties similar to those faced by explorers looking for the north-west passage. A violent storm separated the ship commanded by Chancellor from the other two ships of the expedition. Chancellor was driven eastwards and finally successfully found his way to Archangel in Russia. The two ships under Willoughby became ice-bound and the crews died slowly from cold and starvation.

During the remainder of the sixteenth century, other English explorers tried without success to discover a north-east passage. So too did two Dutch explorers, Olivier Brunel and Willem Barents. The voyage of Barents is of particular interest as a journal of the voyage was kept by a crew member. The passage to the north-east was not discovered until the nineteenth century.

Time to understand

The extracts quoted below are from the journal recording the voyage of the explorer Willem Barents in 1596.

> The 27 of August the ice drove round about the ship, and yet it was good weather; at which time we went on land, and being there, it began to blow south-east with a reasonable gale, and then the ice came with great force before the bow, and drove the ship up four foot high before, and behind it seemed as if the keel lay on the ground, so that it seemed that the ship would be overthrown in the place.
>
> The 28 of August we got some of the ice from it, and the ship began to sit upright again; but before it was fully upright, as Willem Barents and the other pilot went forward to the bow, to see how the ship lay, and how much it was risen, and while they were busy upon their knees and elbows to measure how much it was, the ship burst out of the ice with such a noise and so great

158

Fig. 9.20 Barents' ship stuck in ice. Three men have attempted to free it using axes.

a crack, that they thought verily that they were all cast away, knowing not how to save themselves.

The 30 of August the ice began to drive together with greater force than before, with a boisterous south-west wind and a great snow, so that all the whole ship was borne up and enclosed, whereby all that was both about and in it began to crack, so that it seemed to burst in a hundred pieces, which was most fearful both to see and hear, and made all the hair of our heads to rise upright with fear; and after that, the ship (by the ice on both sides, that joined and got under the same) was driven so upright, in such sort as if it had been lifted up with a wrench or vice.

1 What did the crew do when their ship was lifted out of the ice?
2 How did they try to free the ship?
3 What eventually happened?
4 How could the ship have been destroyed?

How do we know?

Magellan's circumnavigation of the world

During a voyage of exploration a number of different records were kept. The commander of the expedition would keep a journal, as would the captain of each ship in the fleet. Masters and pilots (senior crew members) would keep logs recording navigational data about winds, courses, distances and positions. Sometimes other members of the crew would also keep journals.

Very few records from Ferdinand Magellan's expedition have survived. Earlier in this chapter, you read that only one ship of the five which sailed returned to Spain. The logs and journals of the commander, captains, masters and pilots may have been on board those ships which never returned.

One outstanding account survived all the mishaps. It is the work of Antonio Pigafetta who volunteered to join the expedition even though he was not a professional seaman. His account lacks accurate navigational details but gives a vivid account of the geography and people of the Pacific.

1 The weeks in the Pacific Ocean.

On Wednesday the twenty-eighth of November, 1520, we issued forth from the said strait and entered the Pacific Sea, where we remained three months and twenty days without taking on board provisions or any other refreshments, and we ate only old biscuit turned to powder, all full of worms and stinking of the urine which the rats had made on it, having eaten the good. And we drank water impure and yellow. We ate also ox hides which were very hard because of the sun, rain and wind. And we left them four or five days in the sea, then laid them for a short time on embers, and so we ate them. And of the rats, which were sold for half an écu apiece, some of us could not get enough. Besides the aforesaid troubles, this malady was the worst, namely that

the gums of most part of our men swelled above and below so that they could not eat. And in this way they died, inasmuch as twenty-nine of us died . . .

But besides those who died, twenty-five or thirty fell sick with various diseases . . . Yet by the grace of our Lord I had no illness.

During these three months and twenty days, we sailed in a gulf where we made a good four thousand leagues across the Pacific Sea, which was rightly so named. For during this time we had no storm, and we saw no land except two small uninhabited islands, where we found only birds and trees. Wherefore we called them the Isles of Misfortune.

a What is the name of the 'said strait'?
b What were the crew forced to eat and drink? Why?
c What happened as a result of the poor rations?

2 The battle on the island of Mactan, in the Philippines.

Those people had formed three divisions, of more than one thousand and fifty persons. And immediately they perceived us, they came about us with loud voices and cries, two divisions on our flanks, and one around and before us. When the captain saw this he divided us in two and thus we began to fight. The hackbutmen and crossbowmen fired at long range for nearly half an hour but in vain, they fired at us so many arrows, and lances of bamboo tipped with iron, and pointed stakes hardened by fire, and stones, that we could hardly defend ourselves . . .

Then they came so furiously against us that they sent a poisoned arrow through the captain's leg. Wherefore he ordered us to withdraw slowly, but the men fled while six or eight of us remained with the captain. And those people shot at no other place but our legs, for the latter were bare. Thus for the great number of lances and stones that they threw and discharged at us we could not resist.

Our large pieces of artillery which were in the ships could not help us, because they were firing at too long range, so that we continued to retreat for more than a good crossbow flight from the shore, still fighting, and in water up to our knees. And they followed us, hurling poisoned arrows four or six times; while, recognizing the captain, they turned toward him inasmuch as twice they hurled arrows very close to his head. But as a good captain and a knight he still stood fast with some others, fighting thus for more than an hour. And as he refused to retire further, an Indian threw a bamboo lance in his face, and the captain immediately killed him with his lance, leaving it in his body. Then, trying to lay hand on his sword, he could draw it out but halfway because of a wound from a bamboo lance that he had in his arm. Which seeing, all those people threw themselves on him, and one of them thrust a large javelin into his left leg, whereby he fell face downward. On this all at once rushed upon him with lances of iron and of bamboo and with these javelins, so that they slew our mirror, our light, our comfort and our true guide.

a Make a list of the weapons of each side. How does Pigafetta account for the victory of the islanders?
b How was Magellan killed?
c Why would Pigafetta describe Magellan as 'our mirror, our light, our comfort and our true guide'?

10

The Spanish conquistadors in the New World

INDIAN TRIBES had lived in the New World (North and South America) for many thousands of years before the arrival of Europeans. By the time Columbus reached America in 1492 these tribes had developed sophisticated cultures and societies. In Central and South America some of the rulers of various tribes had amassed priceless treasures of gold, silver and precious stones.

When the Spanish learned of the wealth of these civilisations in the New World, ambitious explorers known as *conquistadors* set out to conquer them. (*Conquistador* means 'conqueror'.) They took the treasures of the conquered civilisations back to Spain. The wealth acquired by the Spanish from these treasures was used to pay for wars against other countries of Europe. Spain became one of the most powerful countries in Europe.

In this chapter you will learn about two tribes conquered by the Spanish conquistadors: the Aztecs and the Incas. Both were conquered by small groups of Spaniards through determination, clever leadership and superior weapons. Often the Spaniards had to endure great hardship to reach their goal, climbing rugged mountains or hacking through steaming jungle.

For the Aztecs and the Incas, the coming of the conquistadors was a catastrophe. Very little of the Aztec civilisation remains today as it was brutally and ruthlessly destroyed. There is more surviving evidence of the Inca civilisation.

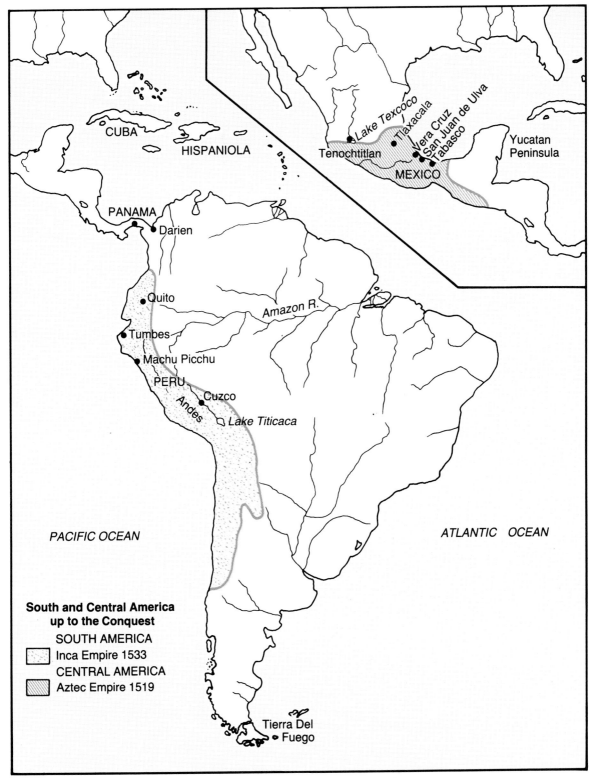

Fig. 10.1 The Aztec and the Inca empires.

Hernando Cortes and the conquest of the Aztecs

The arrival of Cortes in Mexico

In 1519 a Spanish soldier commanding a small expedition landed on the coast of Mexico at Vera Cruz. He had come to conquer the Indians of Mexico in order to obtain gold and other treasure and to convert them to Christianity. His name was Hernando Cortes.

Cortes had gone to the Spanish settlement of Hispaniola at the age of nineteen. He later fought with the Spanish forces in the conquest of Cuba and was secretary to the Spanish governor when a settlement was established there.

In 1517 the governor of Cuba sent out an expedition to search for treasure on the mainland to the west of Cuba. When land was sighted the seamen were surprised to see stone houses and elaborate temples on the Yucatan peninsula. These showed that the Indians who had built them were much more civilised than those on the island of Cuba.

The Spaniards were unable to explore the peninsula because of hostile Indians.

A second expedition in 1518 managed to establish contact with Indians at Tabasco. From them the Spaniards learnt of the wealth in Mexico. The Spaniards were unaware that the expedition was being watched very carefully by spies sent to Tabasco by Montezuma, ruler of the Aztecs of Mexico. Montezuma was waiting in his palace for the report. It finally came:

> . . . in the middle of the water [we saw] a house from which appeared white men, their faces white and their hands likewise. They have long, thick beards and their clothing is of all colours: white, yellow, red, green, blue and purple. On their heads, they wear round coverings . . .

This report convinced Montezuma that an ancient prophecy (a statement about the future) was about to come true. This prophecy stated that a fair-skinned and bearded god would one day come to the land of the Aztecs. Montezuma sent his messengers back with lavish gifts: gold, precious stones, featherwork and exotic food such as chocolate and turkey (neither had ever been tasted by Europeans before).

The Spaniards were surprised when they met Montezuma's messengers. They did not understand why the ruler of the Aztecs had sent such wonderful gifts. The Spaniards took the messengers on board ship and offered them some of their ship's provisions and wine. When the Aztecs left the Spaniards gave them a necklace of glass beads to present to Montezuma. The Spaniards also indicated, through sign language, that they would return.

Hernando Cortes was chosen to lead the next expedition in 1519. When Cortes' expedition landed at Tabasco it was not welcomed as the earlier expedition had been. Instead the members of the expedition were faced with 12 000 hostile Indians. After a fierce battle the Spaniards were victorious. The Indians gave them treasures, food and women. One of these

Fig. 10.2 Dona Marina became Cortes' interpreter. Why was her role important?

women, called Dona Marina by the Spaniards, became Cortes' adviser and interpreter.

Cortes then sailed further south along the coast near the island of San Juan de Ulva. He founded a coastal settlement called Vera Cruz in the name of the king of Spain. Cortes declared himself in charge of the colony, from which he planned to attack the Aztec capital, Tenochtitlan. So that none of his men would desert him and return to Spain, he sank all the ships of the fleet. Only one ship was sent back to Spain to inform the king of the new colony.

Time to understand

1 Fig. 10.3 shows a series of Aztec drawings

Fig. 10.3 The first meeting between the Aztecs and the Spanish.

showing the first meeting between the Spanish and the Aztec messengers. Reconstruct the story using these pictures as your evidence.

2 The Aztec who first saw the Spanish ship described it as a 'house' which stood in the water. Why would he have thought this? Other Indians thought that the Spanish mounted on horseback were strange creatures, which we would call centaurs. What is a centaur? Why would the Indians have thought this? Draw a picture of a Spanish 'centaur'.

A meeting of two worlds: Montezuma and Cortes

Cortes had landed on 22 April 1519. To Montezuma, emperor of the Aztec empire, this meant that his suspicions about the newcomers were correct. Montezuma sent gifts fit for a god. This was because he believed Cortes was a god. The story below explains why.

Most of the Indian tribes of Mexico believed in the same gods. Sometimes one god was more important to a particular tribe than any of the other gods. The main god of the Aztecs was Huitzilopochtli, known to other tribes as Tezcatlipoca. He was a warrior-god whom the Aztecs believed had helped them defeat many of the other tribes of Mexico and establish the Aztec empire.

The Toltecs had ruled in Mexico before the Aztecs. The main god of the Toltecs was Quetzalcoatl. Legends said that Quetzalcoatl had been a god sent to rule on earth. He was tricked by the god, Tezcatlipoca, into disgracing himself. Quetzalcoatl had to leave Mexico. When he did so he ascended to join the rising sun. The legends said he would return one day to regain his kingdom.

The Toltec rulers said that Quetzalcoatl was their ancestor. Each ruler called himself Quetzalcoatl, although each also had a personal name. The first Aztec ruler married a descendent of the Toltec rulers so that the Aztec rulers could also claim to be descended from Quetzalcoatl. Montezuma was even born on the same day Quetzalcoatl was said to have been born.

Fig. 10.4 The god, Tezcatlipoca, recognisable by his missing foot.

Fig. 10.5 Quetzalcoatl, the god who was driven out of Mexico.

There was a prophecy that a fair-skinned Quetzalcoatl with a long beard would return to claim his kingdom. Do you remember the first report given to Montezuma about the Spaniards? He thought that Cortes was Quetzalcoatl returning to claim his kindgom. This is why Montezuma sent lavish gifts. Perhaps he hoped that the god would not take away his kingdom, which included most of Mexico.

According to the Mexican calendar the day on which Quetzalcoatl was supposed to arrive was, by chance, the day on which Cortes arrived.

Cortes left a small garrison of soldiers in charge of Vera Cruz, then set out for Tenochtitlan. Cortes judged that the Aztecs were very wealthy from the gifts Montezuma had sent him. On the way to Tenochtitlan, Cortes' small army was joined by Indians of other tribes that resented Aztec rule. Some Indian tribes, such as the Tlaxacalans, that had not been conquered by the Aztecs, had to be defeated by Cortes so that the Spaniards could pass through their territory.

When Cortes and his men first sighted their goal they were struck with wonder and awe. After climbing over snow-capped mountains they saw the Valley of Mexico dotted with towns and cities. The finest sight of all was the city of Tenochtitlan, built on an island in the middle of sparkling Lake Texcoco. It could be reached only by causeways or ramps.

Montezuma, richly dressed, came to meet the Spaniards as they approached the city. He was carried in a golden litter over which was a green canopy decorated with jewels and feathers.

When Montezuma met Cortes he rose and bowed his head. Remember that he thought Cortes was Quetzalcoatl and so offered no resistance to the newcomers. Rather than lose his kingdom, Montezuma invited the Spaniards back to rest and refresh themselves in Tenochtitlan.

Time to understand

The painting in Fig. 10.6 shows the meeting between Montezuma and Cortes. Notice that cloth is placed under Montezuma's feet as he walks to meet Cortes. This was because he was considered so holy that his feet could not touch the ground. Montezuma thought Cortes was a god. Describe the meeting as if you were Montezuma and then as if you were Cortes. You need to remember that Montezuma had never seen white Europeans before, and that Cortes was planning to conquer the Aztecs without knowing exactly how wealthy or how powerful they were.

Fig. 10.6 Montezuma meets Cortes.

The fall of the Aztec empire

The Spaniards stayed in a magnificent palace in the centre of the city. The temple was nearby and here the Spaniards learned why the Aztecs were feared and resented by the Indian tribes they had conquered. Each day the Aztecs sacrificed human beings to the sun god so that the sun would rise. The victims were prisoners of war from other Indian tribes. After visiting the temple, one of the soldiers wrote: 'Every wall of the chapel and the whole floor had become almost black with human blood and the stench was abominable.'

Cortes worried that Montezuma would change his mind. So he boldly captured Montezuma and kept him prisoner in the palace where the Spaniards were staying. This meant that Cortes was now in control of the city and the Aztecs. The Spaniards often went in search of gold in Tenochtitlan and in other towns of Mexico.

Soon after, Cortes heard that a new Spanish fleet had arrived on the coast. It had been sent by the governor of Cuba with orders to arrest Cortes. Cortes decided to leave one of his men, Alvarado, in charge of Tenochtitlan, so that he could march to the coast. He there succeeded in defeating the Cuban force sent against him. Some of the new force even joined Cortes and marched back to Tenochtitlan with him.

While Cortes had been away, Alvarado had made the mistake of killing a large number of

Fig. 10.7 A Spanish version of the temple in the centre of Tenochtitlan.

Aztec warriors who had been taking part in a religious festival. The palace where the Spaniards were staying had been surrounded by angry Aztecs. However, when Cortes and his men marched back into the city all was silent.

The silence did not last. Cortes and the Spaniards were beseiged in the palace. Cortes forced Montezuma to appeal to the Aztecs from the walls of the palace.

The crowd responded with stones and arrows. Montezuma himself was hit and died some days later.

The Spaniards tried to escape one moonless night across one of the causeways, but were discovered. In a terrible battle Cortes lost two-thirds of his men, some of whom were carried off to be sacrificial victims. The remaining Spanish force retreated to Tlaxacala.

When Cortes returned to Tenochtitlan in May 1521 he was well prepared for the attack. As well as gaining more men from the Tlaxacalans, he had built a small fleet of ships with which to control the lake and prevent escape.

Gradually the Spaniards advanced across the causeways and penetrated into the city. The Aztecs fought fiercely to defend their city. As the Spaniards moved into the city they destroyed houses and other buildings until Tenochtitlan was in ruins and only the temple remained. Finally the new emperor was captured, which meant defeat for the Aztecs.

The remaining parts of the city were destroyed. The masterpieces of gold and silver were melted down and sent back to Spain. Six months later the mounds of rubble were levelled and a new Spanish city was founded there—Mexico City. Cortes was made governor of New Spain, the Spanish name for what had been the Aztec empire. Cortes destroyed the Aztec civilisation so completely that only one small Aztec temple remains today. He had not hesitated to destroy a civilisation he felt was wrong in the eyes of God.

Time to understand

1 *Tribute* means money or goods paid to a ruler or government 'in acknowledgement of submission or as a price of peace or protection'. The tribes conquered by the Aztecs in Mexico paid tribute to the Aztec rulers. Fig. 10.18 on page 177 shows some of the goods paid as tribute. How many of the goods can you name? How would these goods have been used?
2 The legend about the god Tezcatlipoca in Fig. 10.4 on page 164 tells of how he lost his foot in a struggle with the Earth Monster. In the beginning the Earth Monster lay beneath the waters, so Tezcatlipoca tempted it to the surface with his foot. The Earth Monster snapped off his foot but in the process its lower jaw was ripped off. As a result of this the Earth Monster could not sink beneath the waters and the Earth was created from its body.

Whenever Aztecs saw a picture of a god with a missing foot they knew it was Tezcatlipoca. Write your own legend about a god of nature and illustrate it showing the distinctive feature of the god.

The city of Tenochtitlan

When the Spaniards first saw Tenochtitlan they were impressed with its spectacular beauty. It was situated on an island in a lake, overlooked by snow-capped mountains. Legends tell us that the first Aztecs built their city on the island because of a special message given to them by the god Huitzilopochtli.

The Aztecs may have migrated to Mexico to escape a drought in North America. Huitzilopochtli told them to build a city where they saw an eagle eating a snake while perched on a cactus. According to the legend, this was seen on the island in Lake Texcoco.

When the Spaniards arrived there were about 300 000 people living in the city. There were other towns on nearby islands and on the shores of the lake. The walls of the buildings were mostly covered in stucco, a kind of plaster. They must have been dazzlingly white in the sunlight. In the middle of the city was the temple where human sacrifices were performed. It is possible to guess what the temple looked like from Mexican and Spanish drawings of the time.

On the lake were 'floating islands' or *chinampas*. These were rectangular rafts filled with the fertile silt of the lake as well as rushes and reeds. Trees were planted in the corners of the

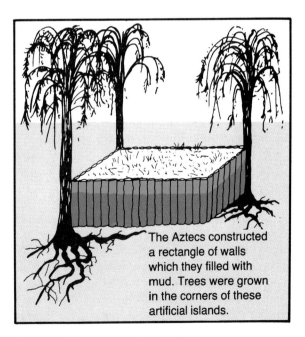

The Aztecs constructed a rectangle of walls which they filled with mud. Trees were grown in the corners of these artificial islands.

Fig. 10.8 The construction of a *chinampa*.

chinampas to prevent them floating away. Fruit, flowers and vegetables were grown on the *chinampas* for the people of Tenochtitlan.

In the northern sector of the city was a market where the produce of the *chinampas* could be bought, as well as other more exotic goods such as jaguar and deer skins, jewellery, dyes for cloth, birds' feathers, precious stones and tobacco. Many goods were brought in from the empire.

The Spaniards were not interested in the articles made of gold and precious stones. They were only interested in the gold and precious stones of which they were made. Many beautiful pieces of Aztec craftsmanship were melted down or dismantled before being shipped back to Spain. Only a small proportion has survived to

give us some idea of the degree of skill of Aztec goldsmiths. Copper was also valued by the Aztecs. Copper bells were used as money.

Time to understand

The map in Fig. 10.9 shows the position of Tenochtitlan on Lake Texcoco. Why would the causeways have been built in the positions indicated on the map? Can you think of any other suitable positions? Why did the Aztecs choose that island and not one of the many others in the lake?

Francisco Pizarro and the conquest of Peru

Pizarro's arrival in Peru

Francisco Pizarro was the illegitimate son of a Spanish army officer. In 1502, at the age of twenty-four, he went to the Spanish settlement of Hispaniola. (Two years later Cortes arrived in the same settlement.)

By 1521 Pizarro had moved to the colony of Darien on the isthmus of Panama, where he made a living from farming and mining. There he heard talk of a southern kingdom, more wealthy and sophisticated than that of the recently conquered Aztecs. Pizarro dreamed of making his fortune by leading an expedition to the south. There had been some exploration south of the new city of Panama on the isthmus but no fabulous hoards of gold had been found. There were reports from Indian traders of an empire ruled by the Incas.

With the support of the Spanish governor of Darien, Pizarro led a small expedition to the

south in 1524. This expedition achieved little. A second, with the support of the mayor of Panama, was a little more successful. Pizarro landed on the coast of present-day Columbia. A smaller group of the expedition sailed further south. They returned with the news Pizarro had longed to hear. The towns further south were well developed and sophisticated. A party of Indians on board a raft told the Spaniards of the Incas' wealth. These Indians themselves were richly dressed in colourful clothes and wore gold and silver jewellery.

After sending back to Panama for more supplies and men Pizarro sailed further south to see for himself. By the time he returned to Panama, after over two years absence, the expedition had been given up as shipwrecked or dead.

Pizarro returned with gold, silver, llamas and tales of a temple sheathed in gold that he had

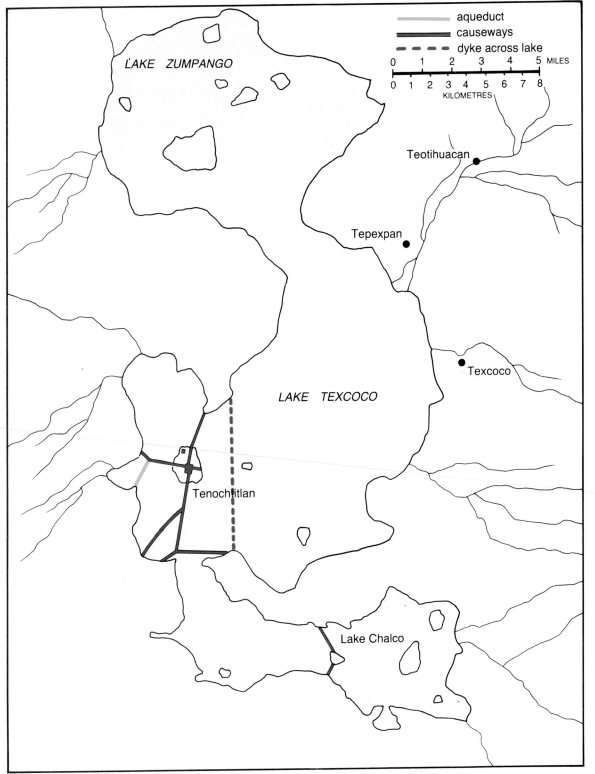

Fig. 10.9 Lake Texcoco.

seen in the Inca city of Tumbes, on the coast of Peru.

Pizarro could gain no financial support in Panama for another expedition, so he decided to ask the king of Spain. In July 1529 the king agreed to send Pizarro on the expedition and to make him governor of any lands he conquered. In 1531 Pizarro set off accompanied by his three brothers Hernando, Juan and Gonzalo. At Tumbes Pizarro learned that a great war had been fought between two Inca brothers over the throne. The Inca empire was weak and disorganised because of this war.

Time to understand

Make a list of the similarities between the motives for exploration of Hernando Cortes and Francisco Pizarro. What conclusions could you draw about Spanish exploration and conquest of South America from these motives?

The rule of the Incas

The Inca civilisation was more sophisticated and wealthy than that of the Aztecs. The Incas ruled Peru, which had been inhabited by a number of different tribes for centuries.

The story of how the Incas became the rulers of Peru is shrouded in legend. In about 1100 three brothers and a sister, who claimed to be children of the sun, came down from the Andes mountains to the town of Cuzco. By trickery and perhaps some magic one of the brothers and his sister became rulers of part of Cuzco. What happened to the other two brothers is not known. The legend says that they were turned into sacred rocks. The people of Cuzco must have believed their claim to being children of the sun. The brother and the sister were called Incas.

From that time on, the eldest son of the Inca family married the eldest daughter. They did this because of their claim to being descended from the sun. No one else could claim the throne,

because only the pure descendants of the sun could rule. Other people who descended from the original Inca marriage were nobles.

After about a century the Incas took over the whole town of Cuzco. Then they began to conquer the other tribes of the Andes. Gradually they extended the territory they controlled. By about 1500 the Inca empire extended as far as

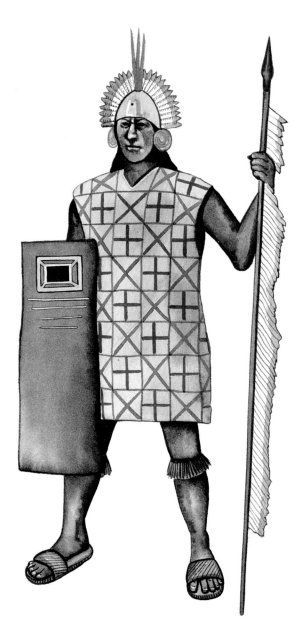

Fig. 10.10 An Inca general.

Ecuador in the north and Chile in the south, from the Andes to the Pacific Ocean.

The Inca army was very well organised. This helped it to conquer other tribes. Some tribes asked to become part of the empire, to avoid the pains of conquest and also to share in the benefits and protection of a well-organised society.

Often the captives of a conquered tribe were skilled craftsmen. The Incas wisely used such people as either workmen or teachers. The Inca way of recording was learned from the Chimu tribe in the south of Peru. The Incas did not develop a system of writing so this method was a great help. This was called the *quipu* method and consisted of tying knots in lengths of string hanging from a main piece of string.

The Inca empire became very strong. The Supreme Inca was respected and obeyed by all his subjects. When Supreme Incas died their

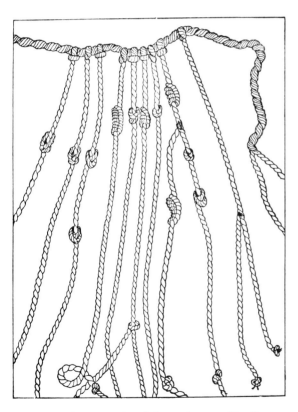

Fig. 10.11 An example of the *quipu* used by the Incas to keep accounts, record events and relay messages.

bodies were mummified and kept in their palaces. The mummies were carried on golden biers to the Great Sun Temple once a year for a big festival.

The people of the empire were completely dependent on the Incas for leadership. In turn, the Incas depended on the Supreme Inca. Within the Inca empire everybody had a particular task to perform and everybody had enough food and possessions. After tribute was collected, it was redistributed, as needed, by the Incas. Law and order were strictly kept. Punishment for crimes was very severe. A liar could be flogged, beaten with a club or nailed to a board by the tongue, depending on the number of offences.

In 1493, just a year after Columbus discovered America, a new Supreme Inca, Huayna Ccapac, came to the throne. He was, of course, married to his sister. He also married a princess of the Cara tribe in the north of Peru. She bore him a son who was named Atahualpa.

When Huayna Ccapac died he divided his empire into two halves. This had never been done before. The northern half was to be ruled from Quito by the half-Inca, half-Cara, Atahualpa. The southern half was to be ruled from Cuzco by his other son, the full-blooded and legitimate Supreme Inca, Huascar.

Atahualpa wanted to rule the whole empire. His army attacked Cuzco and defeated the army of Huascar, after a five-year struggle. During this time the empire became disorganised and weak. The Incas no longer collected tribute.

Atahualpa became the Supreme Inca. He had to reorganise his empire after the long war. Gradually the tribute began to come into the capital of Cuzco once again.

Time to understand

Fig. 10.12 is a photograph of a body mummified during Inca times. People were often buried with their personal possessions, such as basic utensils, and also some food. Sometimes when an Inca noble died his wife and servants were killed and buried with him. This evidence may be interpreted in a number of ways.

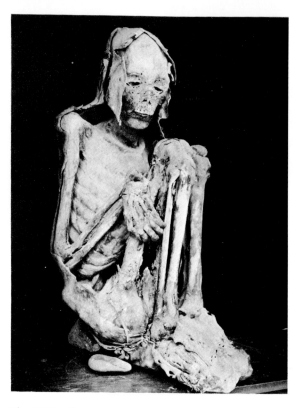

Fig. 10.12 An Inca mummy.

1 Do you think that the body was carefully prepared and dressed for a particular reason?
2 Why would personal possessions, utensils and food be buried with the body?
3 Why would an Inca noble's wife and servants be buried with him?
4 Do you think that the Incas believed in reincarnation? Why or why not?
5 Do you think that the Incas believed in an afterlife?

The capture of Atahualpa

At Tumbes Pizarro learned that Atahualpa had just defeated his half-brother Huascar. While recovering from a wound Atahualpa was staying at the town of Cajamarca high in the Andes. Pizarro calculated that the town was only twelve days march away. He decided to go at once.

After marching across the Sechura desert and then up the icy Andes mountains, Pizarro and his men arrived at the town. Atahualpa's army of between thirty and forty thousand men was camped on the slopes above the town. Pizarro's force numbered approximately eighty. It was a bold attempt on Pizarro's part. Perhaps he thought he would be received as Cortes had been by the Aztecs.

Two of Pizarro's men arranged a meeting between the two leaders for the following day. Atahualpa did not seem to fear the Spaniards at all. He promised that he and his attendants would come unarmed to the meeting. Pizarro decided that his men would abduct the Supreme Inca, killing all the attendants if necessary.

When Atahualpa and his nobles arrived at the agreed meeting place they were greeted by a friar carrying a cross and a Bible. The friar tried to convert Atahualpa to Christianity. This seemed to irritate the Supreme Inca who threw the Bible to the ground, according to Spanish reports. At this point, Pizarro gave the signal and his men rushed from their hiding places. All the defenceless Inca nobles were killed and Atahualpa was taken captive.

Atahualpa offered to fill a large room with gold if Pizarro would set him free. For two months, golden ornaments came in from all over the empire. Atahualpa also promised he did not intend to attack the Spaniards if he was set free. Pizarro's men were very few in number and did not trust the Supreme Inca. Eventually the Spaniards decided to put Atahualpa on trial for worshipping idols (gods other than the Christian god), and a number of other offences such as incest (marriage to his sister). Atahualpa was found guilty and sentenced to death by burning at the stake. At the last moment his sentence was changed to death by strangulation.

After the death of the Supreme Inca, the Incas offered no resistance. They were completely confused by the change in the situation. The Spaniards took advantage of this. They marched on to the capital of Cuzco, where they stripped the city completely of anything of value. In the process, many of the inhabitants were killed.

Pizarro then established order in the city. He

Fig. 10.13 The ruins of Machu Picchu, an Inca fortress high in the Andes mountains.

Fig. 10.14 Gold being brought in from the Inca empire for Atahualpa's ransom.

appointed a new Supreme Inca, although a council of Spaniards really controlled the city. On the coast he established a new 'City of the Kings' which became the main Spanish city in South America over the next two hundred years.

Much of South America was explored by Spanish conquistadors in search of gold. Some of them survived to tell stories of miraculous escapes. One expedition was swept down the full length of the Amazon River by the force of the current. Unable to return, the Spaniards had to spend their nights almost totally unprotected in the wild, unexplored Amazon jungle, which was full of jaguars and huge ants. When the expedition finally reached open sea they made a rough sail and sailed many hundreds of kilometres north to a Spanish settlement.

How do we know?

The codices

There are a number of books which have survived from ancient Mexico. These books are known as *codices*. There are no words written in them. Each page contains pictures which tell a story about one of the gods or an incident from history. The ancient Mexicans, including the Aztecs, had no form of writing.

The pages of each codex are all joined together. The codex is then folded up, as shown in Fig. 10.16. The pages were made of deer skin which was specially prepared. Both sides of the page were used.

Historians would not have been able to interpret the codices if it were not for the work of Father Bernardino de Sahagun, a priest who was living in Mexico City just after the Aztec empire had fallen. As a priest, Father de Sahagun was responsible for the education of young Mexicans. He asked his pupils, whose fathers and grandfathers were Aztecs, to find out whatever they could about Aztec life. He then wrote down their

accounts. Historians were able to use his book to help them interpret the codices.

The pictures on these pages shows some examples of panels from the codices. Look carefully at them before attempting to solve the following problems.

1 Fig. 10.15 shows one of the many gods worshipped by the Aztecs. He is a 'planetary' god which means he was connected with one

Fig. 10.15 Aztec 'planetary' god.

Fig. 10.16 An Aztec codex.

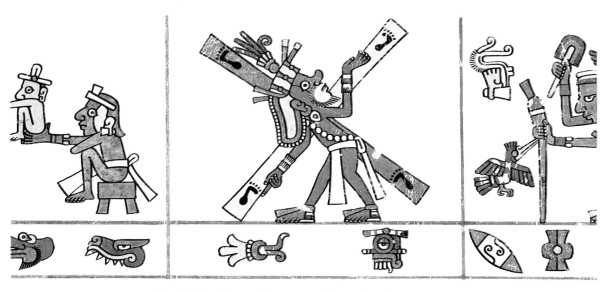

Fig. 10.17 The god Yacatecuhtli (centre) and merchants.

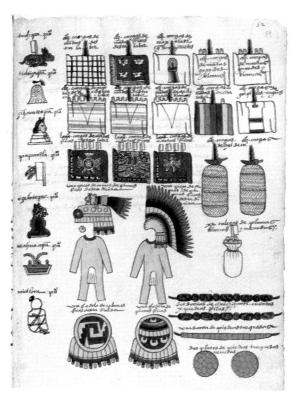

Fig. 10.18 Goods given as tribute to the Aztecs by conquered tribes.

of the planets visible to the Aztecs. Beneath the god are a number of dots and bars. These are part of the number system used by the Aztecs. Each bar is worth five units and each dot is worth one unit. How many different numbers could the dots and bars represent? Which number do you think it could be? Why? If this is a 'planetary' god, what could the number possibly mean? What other kind of information would you need to work out what the number means?

2 At the centre of Fig. 10.17 is the god Yacatecuhtli, Lord Nose, the patron god of merchants. His red nose helped Aztecs to recognise who he was. He is carrying a cross which represents crossroads and is marked with merchants' footprints. Why would the patron god of merchants be shown with crossroads? Were roads important to merchants? Why?

On either side are merchants with their goods. What kind of goods are they carrying? What would these be used for? Where might they be going?

3 Fig. 10.18 shows some of the goods given to the Aztecs by other tribes as tribute. It is not part of an Aztec codex. It was commissioned by the first Spanish viceroy of Mexico, or New Spain, to explain Aztec life to the Spanish king. How can we tell it is not an Aztec codex? Why would the style of painting be similar to that on the Aztec codices?

11

The Reformation

BY 1500 a number of changes had taken place in Europe. The Renaissance had produced a new generation of writers and philosophers who questioned the teaching of the Church. Geographical and scientific discoveries also challenged established ideas. The invention of the printing press meant that these new ideas spread quickly.

During the Middle Ages life had changed little. Most people earned a hard living, either from the land or perhaps as a craftsman in a town, with little to relieve the daily routine. Their main hope was some reward for their hard work. This was the reward of Heaven. The Church gave them this hope. Because of this the Church occupied an important place in people's lives and in society in general.

In western Europe and Great Britain there was one religion only, known as the Roman Catholic Church. In this chapter you will learn how events of the 1500s seriously threatened the position of the Church and its teaching.

The Church in the 1500s

The Church played a very important role in people's lives almost from the moment they were born. There were several important stages or events in life which were acknowledged with special ceremonies conducted by the Church.

These were called 'sacraments' and included such things as baptism and marriage. Another sacrament was the Mass, during which Christians remembered the Last Supper where Christ had blessed the bread and wine. When bread and wine were taken during Mass they were thought of as the body and blood of Christ. In other words, Mass was celebrated to remind Christians that Christ had died on the cross for their sins.

The Church taught that people who had committed too many or very bad sins would suffer everlasting punishment in hell; those whose sins were not so severe would have to spend time in purgatory before they would be allowed to enter heaven.

People went regularly to the local priest to confess their sins and be forgiven. Often people would also perform penances such as fasting, or going on a pilgrimage to a holy place, or paying money to the Church. Penances were done in the hope that the time one would have to spend in purgatory would be shorter. It was believed that by paying money to the Church, people could buy forgiveness for their sins. These pardons for sins became known as 'indulgences' which were sold regularly to add to the wealth of the Church.

People began to believe they could buy indulgences not only for their own sins, but also for those committed by dead relatives already in purgatory. The sale of indulgences was criticised very strongly by writers and philosophers. They said that people were simply buying these indulgences and continuing to lead sinful lives instead of performing good deeds and following the teaching of the Bible.

As today, the head of the Roman Catholic Church was the Pope. Beneath him were cardinals, archbishops, bishops and priests. This system is called a *hierarchy*. The Pope at the top had the most authority and power, the local priest at the bottom had the least. Men tried to gain high positions in the Church. Often their reasons for doing so were to gain wealth and power. They were not necessarily concerned with religion. How did high positions in the Church help some people to become wealthy?

Each position in the Church gained some share in the Church's wealth. The Church gained wealth through the sale of indulgences and also special taxes which every Christian had to pay. Over the years the amount paid and the number of different taxes had increased. People resented these increases.

The archbishops and bishops would be given a share of the taxes for their part in collecting them. Often they had themselves bought the position of bishop from the Church authorities. This shows us that the position of bishop must have had some advantages.

The organisation of the Church became bigger and more complicated. It needed more and more people to make sure everything ran smoothly. Church leaders were criticised for being more interested in worldly affairs, for example, making money, than they were in religion. Look back to Fig. 3.14 in Chapter Three (p. 47) which shows the organisation of the Church.

The average peasant or town labourer would not have been aware of the corruption within the hierarchy of the Church organisation. However, he or she may have been aware that often the local priests no longer set an example of holiness. Many of the local priests were poorly educated and did not understand the services which they spoke in Latin.

The rulers of the different countries and kingdoms of western Christendom had to make sure that their subjects obeyed the laws of the Church. The Pope could punish rulers, or anyone else who did not obey Church rules. The main punishment used by the Pope was called 'excommunication'. A Christian who was excommunicated was expelled from the Church and therefore could not take part in the Mass or be forgiven for his or her sins. This was understood to mean that he or she would suffer forever in hell.

As a result of the control of rulers by the Pope, archbishops and bishops were often allowed to advise rulers on important decisions. Even though Church leaders sometimes interfered in the government of a country, rulers could not interfere in the affairs of the Church. The Church had its own courts in which priests and other churchmen who may have broken a law were tried and sometimes convicted.

Many of the people who criticised the Church in the 1500s felt that much of the corruption was due to its wealth and power. They wanted a return to the teachings and the simplicity of the early days of Christianity. Some said that this simplicity could be found in the Bible.

Fig. 11.1 A late fifteenth century engraving predicting the 'wreck' of the Church, shown here as a ship tossed by rough seas. What do the rough seas represent?

Time to understand

The following document was written by a critic of clergymen. Read the document and then answer the questions.

> The office of curate is ordained of God; few do it well and many full evil . . . They are more busy about worldly goods than virtues and good keeping of men's souls . . . They run fast . . . to get rich benefices; but they will not knowingly go a mile to preach the gospel, though christened men are running to hell for want of knowing and keeping of God's law . . . They . . . much love worldly riches, and labour for them night and day, in thought and deed, and labour little for God's worship and the saving of Christian souls . . . They are angels of Satan to lead men to hell; for, instead of truly teaching Christ's gospel, they are dumb . . . Instead of example of good life, they hurt their parishioners in many ways . . . they teach idleness, gluttony, drunkenness . . . and maintaining of these sins, and many more . . . these curates . . . are not angels of God, but of the fiend.

Vocabulary
  curate: clergyman
  benefice: property held by clergymen
  parishioner: member of a church or parish

1 What does the writer claim the curates are doing?
2 What does the writer feel they should be doing?
3 Who is the 'fiend' of whom the writer speaks?

Fig. 11.2 A monk shown as a wolf devouring the innocent.

Martin Luther and the Reformation in Germany

As the son of a prosperous German copper miner born in 1483, Martin Luther was given a good education and later left his home town of Mansfield in Saxony to study law at Erfurt University. There was nothing unusual about Luther's background or the career his parents had planned for him. Yet several events changed the course of his life and turned him into one of the most influential men of the 1500s.

At the age of fourteen he saw a prince who had given away all his wealth and possessions to lead the life of a begging friar. Friars were a common sight as they wandered from place to place preaching. Luther later wrote that he felt ashamed of his own life when he saw the prince, who was so devoted to spreading the word of God.

As a student at Erfurt University he was travelling home to visit his parents when he was caught in a violent storm. He was almost killed by a flash of lightning. He fell on his knees and vowed: 'Help me, dear St Anne and I will become a monk.' The storm cleared and he continued his journey safely.

Just over two weeks later he left university and joined an Augustinian monastery. He was twenty-two years old at the time and so did not have to seek permission from his parents. When Luther wrote home to tell them of his decision, his father was angry and disappointed. He felt that he had worked hard to give his son a good education so that he could become a lawyer. His son had now decided to become a monk.

Luther was a very devoted and hard-working monk yet he felt he was a sinner. He could not be happy even though he had kept his vow. Being an educated man he was able to read the Bible itself which was written only in Latin. Many people were poorly educated and so could not read the Bible. They relied on the priests to teach them.

Luther's study of the Bible led him to believe that the only way he could be saved from his sins was through confession and faith in God's mercy. This idea conflicted with the teaching of the Church at the time. The Church taught that salvation was available through confession and the purchase of indulgences.

Luther was made a professor at Wittenberg University. He lectured to students on the Bible and was a thorough teacher. He was also still a monk. While he was in this position a Dominican friar visited the nearby town of Brandenberg. He had come to sell indulgences.

The Pope needed money to rebuild the church of St Peter in Rome. He sent an experienced indulgence-seller, a Dominican friar named Tetzel, to sell indulgences in Germany.

Luther disagreed with the selling of indulgences as he thought it encouraged people to believe they could commit sins and still be forgiven. Luther wanted to point out that instead they should be leading Christian lives and performing good deeds. The arrival of Tetzel prompted him to nail a list of ninety-five points or *theses*, criticising the Church, to the cathedral door in Wittenberg. This was the usual way in which a scholar of the time would publish his views. Other scholars would then agree or disagree with them. Luther especially criticised the sale of indulgences.

Time to understand

Fig. 11.5 on the next page is an illustration from Luther's time of Tetzel arriving to sell indulgences to the German people. Part of the ditty on the left hand side translates:

When the coin in the coffer sings
Then the soul to Heaven springs.

1 What is a 'coffer'?
2 Explain why people would have given money to Tetzel.
3 Why did Luther object so much to this practice?

Fig. 11.3 Martin Luther.

Fig. 11.4 An illustration showing the Great Flood from the first edition of Luther's Bible.

181

4 What kind of people do the two men on the left appear to be?

5 Do you think they would have given money to Tetzel if they did not believe that 'the soul to Heaven springs'?

Fig. 11.5 Tetzel arrives in Germany to sell indulgences.

The effect of Luther's ninety-five theses

Luther did not anticipate the effect of his criticisms. The Pope immediately summoned him to Rome. Luther refused to go. He knew that he would probably be excommunicated but became determined to make his views known.

The news of the challenge spread quickly throughout Germany and Luther gained much support. Some German princes who felt discontented about the dealings of the Church in Germany, which was then part of the Holy Roman Empire, were stirred by Luther's 'Address to the German Nobility'.

Attacks on Luther from Rome became more and more intense. Finally, Luther agreed to meet the Pope's representatives at the city of Worms in 1521. He was given a final chance to repent of his attack on the Church. He is reported to have said, 'I cannot and I will not recant anything, for to go against conscience is neither right nor safe. God help me. Amen'.

Luther was excommunicated from the Church. He had gained much support from both rich and poor. Duke Frederick of Saxony offered Luther shelter in his castle. Whilst there, Luther translated the Bible from Latin into German so that everyone could read it. He also continued to write pamphlets and books on what he called the 'abuses' of the Church.

People who protested against the Church became known as Protestants. In Germany the movement begun by Luther gained momentum. In 1546 civil war broke out in Germany between the princes who had become Protestant and those who remained Catholic. The war lasted until 1555 when a treaty known as the Peace of Augsberg was signed. The emperor Charles V, who was head of all the German princes, agreed that each prince should be able to decide on the religion practised by his subjects. The form of Protestantism practised in Germany was, and still is, known as Lutheranism.

The influence of Luther spread throughout Europe and other men set up Protestant churches. John Knox began the Presbyterian Church in Scotland. John Calvin in Switzerland endeavoured to make Geneva a model Christian city. His supporters were called Calvinists.

Time to understand

The following extract, written by a historian of the time, describes the immediate effect of Luther's ninety-five theses.

Though he had these propositions printed, he merely wanted to enter into a debate with the faculty of the University of Wittenberg concerning the nature, effect, foundation, and significance of indulgences. But hardly fourteen days had passed when these propositions were known throughout Germany and within four weeks almost all of Christendom was familiar with them. It almost appeared as if the angels themselves had been their messengers and brought them before the eyes of all the people. One can hardly believe how much they were talked about. They were quickly translated into German and everyone was highly sympathetic, with the exception, of course, of the Dominicans and the Bishop of Halle, and all those who daily benefited from the Pope.

1 What is a faculty in a university? Do faculties exist today?
2 What is the writer suggesting was Luther's aim in writing the ninety-five theses?
3 Does the writer give any explanation for the popularity of the theses?
4 How do scholars publicise their ideas today?

Fig. 11.6 Two Protestant soldiers of the German civil war.

The Counter-Reformation

As Protestantism spread in its varied forms throughout Europe the weaknesses of the Catholic Church became more and more clear. Finally, in 1537 Pope Paul III took the initiative of beginning a reformation within the Catholic Church. This is often called the Counter-Reformation, because it was a movement *against* Protestantism.

Firstly, the Pope corrected some of the abuses of the higher members of the clergy. He made it clear that using high positions in the Church to obtain wealth was illegal. This was a bold step because it reduced the income of the Church. It also meant that the Pope himself had to set an example for all the other clergymen to follow.

In 1545 he assembled a general council of the Church at Trent in Austria. Many important and influential churchmen were present. The Council of Trent met several times over a period of twenty-two years to reorganise the Catholic Church. There were long intervals when the Council did not meet at all. The three main sessions, however, involved many heated discussions.

There were some very important changes as a result of these discussions. Firstly, the Catholic Church had taken a stand which showed there was no possibility of a reconciliation with the Protestant churches. From this point on there were two distinct churches recognised in western Europe: Catholic and Protestant. Some countries, such as Spain and Italy, remained wholly Catholic. In other countries, such as Germany and France, there were both Catholics and Protestants. Wars were fought over which form of Christianity was correct. Many people suffered persecution if they believed in a form of Christianity which differed from that favoured by the ruler of the country. This happened in France where the *Huguenots*, or French Protestants, were ruthlessly attacked by a succession of French kings who remained Catholic.

Secondly, the teaching of the Catholic Chursh was redefined and clearly set out. The Pope remained the supreme head of the Church.

In 1480 King Ferdinand and Queen Isabella

Fig. 11.7 This engraving from the eighteenth century shows the various kinds of torture which the Inquisition was suspected of using.

had set up the Inquisition in Spain. This was a group of men whose work was to discover anybody who was opposed to Catholicism. The Inquisition was very active in the 1500s and many people were tried in its courts. Heretics were people who did not practise or believe in the teaching of the Catholic Church. Although at first the Inquisition was sanctioned by the Pope it was never controlled by him.

In 1543 the Pope decreed that no book might be published without the consent of the Catholic Church. This was an attempt to prevent Catholics from reading Protestant or anti-Catholic books. Another step was later taken by Pope Paul IV in 1559 when a list of books Catholics were forbidden to read was published.

These various activities during the 1500s helped to reform the Catholic Church. There was also a revival of the religious orders. They sought not only to help restore the Catholic religion but

also to help the poor. Many monks and nuns established and ran hospitals, schools and orphanages.

Time to understand

The Inquisition in Spain aimed to uncover any heretics in order to force them to confess. 'Heretics' also included Jews and Moslems who were living in Spain at that time. These people were forced to convert to Catholicism but were often accused of still practising their old religions.

A heretic was usually discovered after an informer had told the Inquisitors of the heretic's suspicious behavior. Many extreme accounts have been written of the tortures used to extract confessions and of the sometimes horrifying trials. Read the following document, which, although a primary source, needs to be considered carefully. It was written by an Englishman in 1599.

> Not far from the cathedral and next to the episcopal palace is the palace of the Inquisition. It is an enormous building and very high, with a facade ornamented with large beautiful windows. Each time that I passed this building my thoughts turned to the cruelties which are committed there, and which and described in the great Book of Martyrs. Any man who is suspected by his conduct or his speech of . . . not finding everything perfect that is Catholic, is at once denounced to the Jesuit inquisitors and promptly incarcerated in this palace, charged with heresy. After a few days, or a few months, as the fathers think fit, one of them comes to interrogate him on the reasons for his detention, or to acquaint him with them, if he does not know. If he says that he is a Catholic, they ask him his age and where he was born, and where he made his last confession and his last communion, and his answers are at once checked by the spies whom the Jesuits have everywhere. If the prisoner has lied, or if he contradicts himself during the inquiry, without further ado he is burned alive as a heretic, for having misled the Holy Office.

1 How does the writer know about the Inquisition? Do you think the book would speak favourably of the Inquisition? Why? (*clue*: what is a 'martyr'?)
2 What happens to someone accused of heresy, according to the writer?
3 What kind of impression is the writer conveying of the Inquisition? Does he have first-hand knowledge of its methods?
4 What other kinds of evidence or primary sources could be used to find out whether the writer's impression is correct?
(Remember that heretics were tried in a court.)

Ignatius Loyola—a 'soldier of Christ'

In 1521 a young nobleman called Ignatius Loyola lay wounded on the battlefield at Pamplona. His leg was shattered by a canon ball. He had intended to pursue the career of a professional soldier. During his long and painful recovery he realised that he would be crippled for life and would have to give up his ambition of becoming a famous soldier.

He passed the time of his recovery by reading spiritual books on the lives of Christ and the saints. These made a deep impression on his mind and he decided to become a 'soldier of Christ'.

In order to do this, Loyola thought it was necessary to be disciplined and strong-willed. He worked out a series of 'spiritual exercises' and a training programme. He believed that hardship and a disciplined life strengthened the soul. The 'soldier' could then perform God's work by helping the poor and destitute and by converting others to Christianity.

In 1523 Loyola went to Jerusalem with the aim of converting the Moslems. There he realised that he needed a better religious education and so decided to study to become a priest. During his studies in Spain and France Loyola joined forces with a few men who felt the same as he. All these men became priests in order to begin their missionary work. They called themselves the Society of Jesus. They were unable to achieve their aim of converting the Moslems in Jerusalem due to a war. Instead, they offered their services to Pope Paul III.

The members of the growing Society of Jesus worked tirelessly in Italy, helping the poor and preaching to the masses. Their work helped to bring many people back to the teaching of the Catholic Church. In 1540 the Pope recognised the Society as a Holy Order. It became known as the Jesuits.

Loyola became the 'general' of the Jesuits. He was called the 'general' because the order was organised like an army. Discipline and training were strict and a good education was considered essential for every Jesuit. Gradually, the order set up training schools to educate priests and other young men. These schools gained such a high reputation that many people sought to enrol their sons, even if they did not intend to become members of the order. The Jesuits still run many schools today.

The work of the Jesuits became mainly concerned with education. This proved very successful in restoring the strength and vitality of the Catholic religion. As missionaries Jesuits worked hard in both non-Christian countries such as Japan and Protestant countries, to convert people to Catholicism. Often these missionaries were persecuted and, at times, even executed.

Henry VIII and the Reformation in England

Henry VIII was given the title by the Pope of Defender of the Faith. This was because he had written an article criticising Luther's attack on the Church. He was a great supporter of the Church even though many people in England disliked having to pay high taxes to Rome.

Henry VIII's father had established the Tudor dynasty after winning the Wars of the Roses in 1485. It was necessary for the Tudor kings to establish a strong line of succession through sons who would inherit the Crown. Henry VIII's wife Catherine of Aragon, had given birth to a daughter but not to a son, during their eighteen years of marriage. This disturbed Henry very much.

We can only guess whether Henry VIII decided to look for another wife who could bear him a son or whether he simply fell in love with Anne Boleyn and decided to divorce Catherine. Anne Boleyn was one of Catherine's ladies-in-waiting. She was young and beautiful. Henry became so infatuated with her that he asked Cardinal Wolsey, the Pope's representative in England, to arrange that his marriage with Catherine be annulled. His excuse was that Catherine had been the wife of his brother and that because of this God would not give him a son. Henry had originally been given a special papal dispensation to marry Catherine. He now felt that Pope Clement VII would not refuse his request.

Unfortunately for Henry, the Holy Roman Emperor, Charles V, was Catherine's nephew. The Pope needed Charles' support and so could not displease him by granting Henry a divorce.

Fig. 11.8 Henry VIII.

For five years Henry threatened and pleaded unsuccessfully with the Pope through his adviser, Cardinal Wolsey. Wolsey was consequently dismissed from office. Finally, Henry accepted the advice of another member of his court, Thomas Cranmer. The matter had become urgent as it was revealed in 1532 that Anne was pregnant.

Thomas Cranmer advised Henry that he did not need the permission of the Pope. Instead, Parliament could pass a series of laws which would allow the matter to be settled in England.

In 1533 the Act of Restraint of Appeals was passed. This meant that all legal cases had to be tried within England and no appeal could be made to other courts, especially that in Rome. Thomas Cranmer, who had been promoted to the position of Archbishop of Canterbury, used this Act to declare Henry's marriage to Catherine annulled and to allow him to marry Anne. A few days after his marriage to Anne, Henry was excommunicated by the Pope. This gave Henry the opportunity of using his divorce to strengthen his position as king of England.

In 1534 Parliament passed laws which ended the Pope's authority in England. Henry was given the power to make appointments in the Church and the paying of taxes (known as 'Peter's pence') to the Church in Rome was forbidden. An Act was passed which made Anne's children the successors to Henry before Mary, the only daughter of Catherine and Henry. Every subject of Henry had to take an oath of loyalty to this Act. A number of important members of his court refused and were eventually executed on charges of treason.

Finally the Act of Supremacy made Henry the head of the Church of England. The break with Rome was complete. Henry did not introduce many changes to the form of the Church and its services, except for the introduction of an English translation of the Bible.

However, he decided to dissolve the innumerable Catholic monasteries throughout England. His main motive for doing this was to increase the wealth of the Crown. His lavish court had consumed much of his private wealth. Most monasteries were very wealthy. He also needed to reclaim the land they occupied as Crown land. He intended to sell this land to increase his wealth, which had been depleted as a result of his extravagant lifestyle.

Time to understand

Life in a monastery

The English countryside was once dotted with hundreds of monasteries, until they were closed during the time of Henry VIII.

Read the following extracts from *The Rule of St Benedict* and then answer the questions.

> If it be possible let them all sleep in a common dormitory, but if their great number will not allow this they may sleep in tens or twenties, with seniors to have charge of them. Let a candle be constantly burning in the room until morning, and let the monks sleep clothed and girt with girdles

or cords. In this way the monks shall always be ready to rise quickly when the signal is given and hasten each one to come before his brother to the Divine office . . .

> None, without the leave of the abbot, shall presume to give, or receive, or keep as his own anything whatever, neither books, nor tablets, nor pens, nothing at all . . .

> Idleness is the enemy of the soul. Because this is so the brethren ought to be occupied at specific times in manual labour, and at other fixed hours in holy reading.

> Let the abbot pour water on the hands of the guests, and let him and the whole community wash their feet . . . Let special care be taken of poor people and pilgrims. Let the charge of the guest place be assigned to a brother whose soul the fear of God possesses . . . No one, unless ordered may associate with or speak to the guests . . .

> Let clothing suitable to the locality and the temperature be given to the Brethren . . . In ordinary places it will be enough for each monk to have a cowl and tunic, in winter the cowl being of thicker stuff, in summer of finer or old cloth. He should have also . . . shoes and stockings for the feet . . .

1 Look up the meanings of the following words: dormitory, girt, hasten, idleness, brethren.
2 Write an outline of a typical day in a monk's life.
3 What kind of people would want to become monks or nuns? Why?

Henry VIII and the dissolution of the monasteries

In Chapter Three you read about the monasteries of the Middle Ages. Before the time of Henry VIII the monasteries of England had become very wealthy, and were centres of learning. Many young men went to the monasteries to be educated. The libraries of most monasteries were storehouses of magnificently decorated books.

The place of monasteries in society was beginning to change by Henry VIII's time. During the Renaissance towns had become not only centres of trade and industry but also of education and

Fig. 11.9 Anne Boleyn.

leave and the wealth of the monasteries was taken by the Crown. The land the monasteries occupied was sold to the land-hungry gentry—men with wealth but no land.

How accurate were these reports? It is possible that in many cases they were completely untrue. Sometimes the commissioners did not actually visit the monasteries but simply asked certain questions of people who lived nearby. It is also probable that the answers to some of these questions were misinterpreted or taken the wrong way.

In 1538 Henry VIII dissolved the bigger monasteries as well, using his position as head of the Church to do so. The wealth of these monasteries, often called abbeys, greatly increased culture. Despite their declining position, the monasteries were still wealthy and occupied much land which Henry felt could be used more profitably by other people.

After the Act of Supremacy in 1534 Henry looked for an excuse to dissolve the smaller monasteries and nunneries. Thomas Cromwell, who had replaced Cardinal Wolsey as one of Henry's main advisers, found the excuse.

Commissioners were appointed to visit the monasteries and make detailed reports on their expenditure and incomes. They were also instructed to report of the state of 'morals' in each monastery. When the reports came in, Henry had the evidence he needed. The reports said that they found monks and nuns were often not faithful to their religious vows and that they were often immoral.

Because of this, Henry felt he could legally dissolve over 200 small monasteries and nunneries. The monks and nuns were asked to

Fig. 11.10 The ruins of Fountains Abbey centuries after its dissolution.

the resources of the treasury. Much more land was made available.

What happened to the monks and nuns who were dismissed? Reports say that many of them married and settled back into ordinary life. Others were given pensions to support them for the rest of their lives.

The land made available by the dissolution of the monasteries was used for farming and pasture land. A long-term result of this was an increase in the production of wool and later the manufacture of woollen cloth. At the time the action taken by Henry against the monasteries seemed harsh and even greedy, but the later benefits were obvious. England's wealth grew partly as a result of the greater availability of land.

How do we know?

History, as you know, is written by drawing conclusions from the available facts and evidence about particular events. A primary source may contain a bias, or present an event in a particular way. The historian must be able to detect bias in a primary source. Not only written sources but also pictorial evidence may show bias.

The following description of Luther was written after the writer had met Luther once in Wittenberg.

> I visited [Luther] toward the end of the evening meal to which he had invited some of the brothers of his order who were clad in robes of white colour, but cut according to the rule. Thus they were known as brothers, though their hair did not distinguish them from peasants. Luther stood up, self-consciously gave me his hand, and asked me to sit down. We sat down and for almost four hours talked until late at night about many things. I found him to be a man of discernment, knowledge and eloquence. Apart from words of contempt and arrogance, as well as acid comments concerning the Pope, the Emperor and several other rulers, he did not say, however, anything of significance . . . Luther conveys the same impression in his countenance as in his books. His eyes are penetrating and almost sparkle in a sinister fashion as one can observe it at times among mentally ill. His manner of speech is vehement, abounding in insinuations and ridicule. His apparel hardly distinguishes him from a courtier. When he leaves the house in which he lives—it was formerly the cloister—he wears, it is said, the robe of his order. Sitting together with him we did not merely talk but also drank beer and wine in a good mood, as is custom there. In every respect he seems to be 'a good fellow', as they say in German. The integrity of his life, which is frequently praised among us here, does not distinguish him from the rest of us.

a Look up the meaning of the following words:
   discernment, eloquence, contempt, arrogance, vehement, insinuation, ridicule.
b What does the writer mean by 'countenance' and 'apparel'? Are these words used commonly today? What words or phrase could be substituted for these words?
c After reading this extract, how would you describe Luther? Does your description resemble the person in Fig. 11.3? Which source would be more reliable, the pictorial or the written? Why?

12

Two ruling families

The Tudor dynasty

DURING the fifteenth and sixteenth centuries members of the Tudor family governed England.

Henry VII

The Tudor dynasty was established in 1485 when Henry Tudor won the Wars of the Roses at the Battle of Bosworth Field. The Wars of the Roses were fought by two powerful English families over which family should govern England. Henry Tudor belonged to the House of Lancaster which was represented by a red rose on flags and battle standards. Three months after he became king he married Elizabeth from the rival House of York, which had been represented by a white rose. The two rival families were reconciled and united by this marriage.

Henry VII, as Henry Tudor became known, laid the foundations of a prosperous and colourful era of English history. Henry and Elizabeth had four children, two sons and two daughters. Arthur, the elder of the two sons, died before his father and so when Henry VII died in 1509 his second son, Henry, succeeded him.

Henry VIII

As you can see by the Tudor family tree (Fig. 12.1), Henry VIII is best remembered for his six marriages. In the previous chapter you read about the role he played in the Reformation in England. He appears to have been a popular yet extravagant king. On occasions he seemed arrogant and unreasonable. He divorced his first wife, Catherine of Aragon, as she did not bear him a son. Anne Boleyn, his second wife, was beheaded for the same reason. Both Catherine and Anne had borne Henry daughters.

Henry's third marriage, to Jane Seymour, produced the long-desired son in 1537. The child was christened Edward. Jane never recovered from the birth of her son and within just two weeks had died. Henry seems to have genuinely mourned her death. His marriage to Anne of Cleves two years later was merely to cement an alliance between himself and the Duke of Cleves. Within six months, however, they were divorced as Henry did not love her. He then married the young Catherine Howard. For two years the aging Henry seemed to be happy once again. When it was discovered she had other lovers she was beheaded for treason. Henry was a proud man and could not tolerate behaviour he

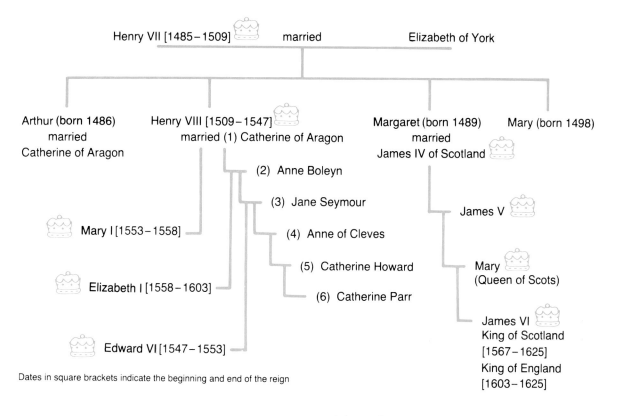

Fig. 12.1 Family tree of the Tudors.

regarded as showing such disrespect for the king. His sixth wife, Catherine Parr, outlived him.

Edward

When Henry VIII died his son Edward was only nine years old. Henry had appointed a council to govern on Edward's behalf until he came of age. The head of the council was Edward's uncle, the Duke of Somerset. He was known as the Lord Protector.

Although only young, Edward was eager to continue the religious policies of his father. During his reign the English Protestant Church became more distinct from the Roman Catholic Church. The Lord Protector introduced a new prayer book, in English instead of Latin, to be used in all services. Many churches were stripped of their ornaments and statues. Some people did not like these changes and tried to rebel against them. These rebellions were crushed ruthlessly by the Lord Protector. His way of handling other problems caused him to become unpopular. He

was finally removed from his position as Lord Protector by the Earl of Warwick, who later became the Duke of Northumberland.

Northumberland passed a number of religious reforms to please the young king. A new prayer book with greater changes was issued, and the celebration of Mass was eliminated from the English Protestant Church altogether. It was replaced by a communion service in which the Last Supper was 'remembered'. However, Northumberland was not a successful administrator and England's position in relation to other countries became weak.

In 1553 Edward died, leaving no heir to the throne. The next in line to the throne was therefore Edward's sister Mary, daughter of Henry VIII and Catherine of Aragon.

Mary

Once on the throne, Mary tried to undo the damage she thought had been done to the English Church by her father and her brother's

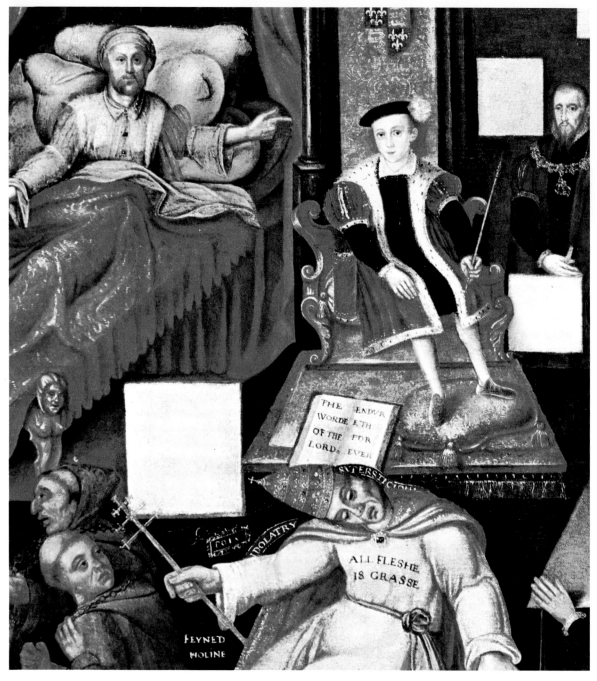

THE ENDVR
WORDE ETH
OF THE FOR
LORDs EVER

VPERSTICION

OLATRY

POIX

ALL FLESHE
IS GRASSE

FEYNED
HOLINE

Fig. 12.2 Henry VIII (in bed) bequeaths his throne to young Edward VI. Why would the Pope (figure in foreground) collapse in dismay?

ministers. Perhaps to the confusion of most English people, Mass was once again celebrated in the Church and both the new prayer books were discarded. Later in her reign, Mary ordered the execution by burning of many Protestants who would not return to the old faith. These

Fig. 12.3 Henry VIII and some of his family.

Fig. 12.4 A glittering procession of queen and courtiers, similar to the Recognition Procession.

burnings earned her the name of Bloody Mary. It was not uncommon at the time for rulers to execute people who opposed them or their policies.

Mary also faced the problem of finding a suitable husband. She was not a young woman and her future husband would be, in effect, king. To the horror of her advisers she chose Prince Philip, the son of the emperor Charles V of Spain. The marriage was unpopular not only because Philip was a foreigner but also because people feared that Spain would come to dominate England as it already dominated the Netherlands and Italy.

Mary's marriage and her later treatment of Protestants caused resentment towards both Mary and the Catholic Church. Philip became king of Spain in 1555 and eventually returned there in 1557 after having shown little interest in his wife. The child Mary had hoped would continue to restore the Catholic faith in England had never been born. Mary died in 1558 after a long illness, with little support or love from either her husband or her subjects.

On the day of her death bells rang out the news and many rejoiced. The day was called the Birthday of the Gospel. In other words, her death signified that England had once again become a Protestant country.

The heir to the throne was Elizabeth, the daughter of Henry VIII and Anne Boleyn. Elizabeth was 25 years old. She was well educated, intelligent and charming, and a Protestant. She attracted to her court men who sought to marry her, and also men who desired to serve their queen and their country.

Time to understand

1 Look carefully at Fig. 12.3. On Henry's VIII's right is his son Edward, of whom he was very proud. Who are the ladies depicted in the painting? (The following clues may help you answer this question.)
a The painting was probably finished before

Henry's death, while Edward was very young (between five and eight years old).
b At that time Henry was married to either Catherine Howard or Catherine Parr.
c Edward had two older sisters. The woman on Henry's far left seems younger than the lady on the right.

2 Study the Tudor family tree in Fig. 12.1.
a Henry VIII was married to Catherine of Aragon just after he became king. What else does the family tree tell us about Catherine of Aragon?
b Who was the eldest of Henry VIII's three children? Do you know why the youngest, Edward, inherited the throne when their father died?
c If Edward was nine years old when he became king, how old was he when he died?
d How was Henry VIII related to James IV of Scotland? How was Mary Stuart, Queen of Scots, related to Henry VIII? Does this explain why Mary Stuart was an heir to the throne of England?
e James IV of Scotland and his family were Stuarts. When the Tudor family line ended in England, the crown passed to the Stuart family. How was James VI related to Elizabeth I?

The accession of Queen Elizabeth I

The coronation of the new queen took place in January 1558. Like her father and grandfather she knew how important it was to win the confidence of the people she was to rule. To achieve this at the beginning of her reign, Elizabeth and her advisers decided to stage an extravagant and magnificent coronation over four days.

The first stage was the entrance to the Tower of London, the main fortress of England. This act showed symbolically how as queen, Elizabeth was to be responsible for the defence of her kingdom. During the reign of Mary, Elizabeth had been imprisoned in the same Tower, for plotting a rebellion against Mary. As she entered

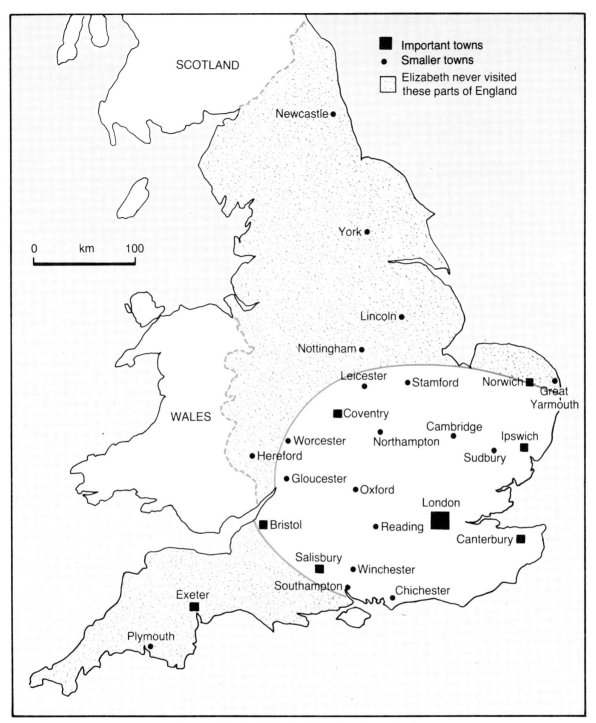

Fig. 12.5 England during the reign of Elizabeth.

195

the Tower on Thursday 12 January, she announced proudly:

> Some have fallen from being princes of this land to being prisoners in this place. I am raised from being a prisoner in this place to being a Prince of this land. That dejection was a work of God's justice; this advancement is a work of his mercy ...

The second stage of the coronation was the Recognition Procession through the streets of London to the Palace of Westminster. For this occasion the streets and houses of London were decorated with banners and tapestries made of costly silks and velvets embellished with gold and silver thread. The procession included hundreds of officials, members of the court, judges, bishops, barons, ladies-in-waiting, knights and footmen, all bedecked in their finest clothes, uniforms and jewels. The queen was carried in a golden palanquin over which hung a crimson velvet canopy. She was dressed in fine silver and gold robes. You can imagine the effect of such a glittering and colourful procession on the citizens who lined the streets in order to gain a glimpse of their queen.

At various points along the way pageants were staged, each designed to show the virtues and qualities, such as wisdom, love of religion and of her subjects, of Elizabeth. The queen frequently called the procession to a halt to receive flowers or greetings offered to her by her subjects. Throughout her reign she maintained this policy of being interested in and attentive to all her subjects. Feeling that she should be seen often by her people, she frequently toured the countryside staying in the homes of the wealthy.

The third stage of the coronation was held in the Abbey Church of St Peter where Elizabeth was actually crowned queen of England. The ceremony was much the same as that in which the present queen, Elizabeth II, was crowned. On the final day of the festivities an elaborate and sumptuous banquet was held in Westminster Hall.

Time to understand

1 Fig. 12.6 shows the portrait painted of Elizabeth I for her coronation as queen. In her right hand she holds a sceptre and in her left a ball with a cross on top. These are symbols of her power as queen. Use an encyclopaedia to find out what each symbolises. This will help you understand the way people of England saw their queen. Compare these with the symbols held by Charlemagne in Fig. 3.5 on page 39. What differences can you see? What would be a possible explanation for any difference?

2 Elizabeth I thought it was very important to be seen by the people she ruled. The map of Elizabethan England in Fig. 12.5 shows the area in which she toured frequently. The shaded areas were never visited by her. Using the scale of kilometres, estimate the furthest distance she travelled from London. Why would she not have travelled much further? (*Clue*: look at main centres of population.)

3 In 1983 Prince Charles and his wife Diana visited Australia. Do you think it was important for Australians to see the future king and queen of England? Why?

The Elizabethan court

When historians refer to the court of a particular ruler they mean not simply the palace in which the ruler lived, but the members of the royal household—the members of the council, the chief advisers, the ladies-in-waiting, the court favourites and even the court jester and servants.

The court of Elizabeth I was the centre of government and politics, of fashion and art, of high society and culture. Her court attracted ambitious young men who sought to win the favour of the queen and thus be given an important position, either in the court itself or in a foreign country. Sometimes men were content to earn the patronage or favour of one of the

Fig. 12.6 Elizabeth I: her coronation portrait.

Fig. 12.7 An Elizabethan courtier.

queen's courtiers, as the men who attended the court were called. Elizabeth's court also attracted young women hoping to catch the eye of a courtier.

Much of the queen's day was occupied with receiving foreign ambassadors or discussing state matters with her councillors and advisers. Throughout her reign Elizabeth consistently listened to the advice of William Cecil (and later his son Robert). She chose him above the others as her chief adviser. For many years, Robert Dudley, Earl of Leicester, was known to be the queen's favourite courtier. Other members of the court, including William Cecil, were worried that she may consider marrying him. Elizabeth was too shrewd to do so. Leicester had already married once. His wife had been 'accidentally' killed by falling down the stairs in their home. Elizabeth knew that she would offend not only many of her courtiers but also many of her subjects if she married Leicester after this had happened. She could not afford to lose their

support, even if it meant not marrying a man whom she obviously loved.

The problem of Elizabeth's marriage was complex. In order for the Tudor dynasty to continue, Elizabeth needed to marry. Otherwise, the next ruler would be Mary Stuart, Queen of Scots. The Tudor family tree (Fig. 12.1) shows how this was possible. If Mary Stuart, a Catholic, gained the English throne, England would once again have to return to Catholicism.

Members of the royal houses of Spain, France, Austria and Sweden proposed to Elizabeth throughout her reign. Their reasons for doing so were usually political. Elizabeth often kept them waiting for a definite answer for years.

Elizabeth never married. She was criticised for this, as people did not understand a woman choosing not to marry. Perhaps Elizabeth did not marry for the reason which she herself proclaimed, that she was devoted to being queen of England and that such a position meant she did not have time for a husband and family. Her life long service to her country seems to support her claim.

Elizabeth's influence over both the men and women of her court was strong. For example, the queen's appearance, although she was never called beautiful, set the standards of elegance and fashion. Elizabeth wore her reddish, fair hair frizzed and bedecked with jewels. So did many other ladies of the court. A pale complexion like the queen's, perhaps itself artificial, was also desirable. To achieve this, ladies at court plastered their faces with a mixture of lead and vinegar. The effect on the skin was disastrous.

Male courtiers were also very conscious of their appearance. Often a young man would spend most of his money on expensive clothes so that he could attract the attention of the queen and earn a place at court.

Elizabethan clothes

Women's clothes

The clothes worn by Elizabeth were copied by other ladies at the court. They were very expensive. To achieve the dramatic effect similar to that shown in Elizabeth's portrait (Fig. 12.10) a lady wore many different layers of clothing, none of which could be left out. Study Fig. 12.8 carefully, then number the drawings 1–7 in the order in which you think an Elizabethan lady would have dressed. The first has been numbered for you.

Men's clothes

Noblemen's clothes at court were also very stiff and probably uncomfortable. Using Fig. 12.7 and the following description of men's appearance, answer the questions.

Fig. 12.8 Stages of dress of an Elizabethan noblewoman. Can you work out the correct order?

They have great and monstrous ruffs . . . their doublets are no less monstrous than the rest . . . being so hard quilted, stuffed, bombasted . . . as they can neither work, not yet play well in them, through the excess heat thereof . . . they have cloaks also . . . of divers colours . . .

1 What part of men's clothing was the doublet? What article of clothing worn by men today is like a doublet?
2 Breeches were often padded or embroidered. Do you think those in Fig. 12.7 would have been comfortable?
3 What articles of clothing worn by the gentleman in this picture were also worn by Elizabethan women?

Children's clothes

Children wore miniature versions of their parents' clothes. Girls also wore stiff corsets and in some cases serious injury resulted from the restrictions to growth. One father reported that due to the clothes his little daughter had been wearing:

Her bodice was her pain and hindered her lungs to grow, and truth the surgeon found her breast bone pressed deeply inwards and he said two of her ribs were broken.

Fig. 12.9 A nobleman and a country man.

Fig. 12.10 Portrait of Elizabeth I standing on a map of England.

1 Why do you think children were forced to wear such uncomfortable clothing?
2 Why would the comment 'he's like a man', made about a young boy be thought a big compliment?

Farmers', labourers' and craftsmen's clothes

The clothes of other classes of society were more suitable for everyday living and working. Look back at Fig. 12.9 on page 199.

1 Why would the clothing of the farmer have been loose fitting?
2 In contrast, what does this tell us about the life of the nobleman?

Fig. 12.11 English middle class woman.

3 Make a list of the differences between the clothing of a nobleman and that of the farmer.
4 What were the most obvious features of a noblewoman's clothing not worn by the middle class woman in Fig. 12.11 below?
5 Why would the young woman in the illustration have fastened her overskirt at waist level?

The religious settlement of Elizabeth

The Reformation of Henry VIII had not actually changed the form of religion in England. It remained basically Catholic. However, Henry's defiance of the Pope over his divorce of Catherine of Aragon caused his excommunication from the Church. The king of England then became head of the Church of England.

Under Edward VI, Henry's only son, the form of the religion was changed and the Church in England became Protestant rather than Catholic. Mary reversed this and England became Catholic once more. All this happened within approximately ten years. You can imagine that many people felt confused about which religion they were practising.

Early in her reign Elizabeth decided to settle the religious question once and for all. Most of her people were quite happy to do whatever they

Fig. 12.12 Riveaulx Abbey.

were asked to do in matters of religion. It did not really affect their day-to-day lives. There were some small groups who held stronger beliefs and opinions. There were those who wanted a complete return to Catholicism and those who wanted radical changes to 'purify' the English church by ridding it of all traces of the Catholic religion. Elizabeth tried to please both these groups.

The matter of religion had become more important since Henry VIII's break with Rome. English people who remained loyal to the Pope were said to be disloyal to England and the queen. Because of this England could never again become a completely Catholic country. The Church and the State had been joined together under one person, the ruler of England.

Elizabeth's parliament quickly passed the Act of Supremacy early in 1559. This act declared that the queen was the supreme governor of England and the Church. The Act of Uniformity brought in a new prayer book based on the second one of Edward VI's reign, and ordered that all people were to attend their parish church on Sundays. If they did not they were fined. Disobedient priests were to be sacked or imprisoned.

Many wealthy Catholic families were dissatisfied with Elizabeth's settlement of the religious question. Around the countryside were the ruined abbeys and monasteries which reminded them that Catholicism had once been the only religion. Many Protestants had become wealthy after the closing of the monasteries and the distribution of their lands. You will remember that the need for more land to satisfy the rising number of wealthy men was one of the main reasons for the closing of the monasteries. The older, established Catholic families resented the fact that many Protestants, such as the Cecils, occupied key positions in Elizabeth's court.

In 1568 Mary Stuart, Queen of Scotland, arrived in northern England after losing her throne. She had been forced to give up the throne in favour of her son James VI. She had come to gain Elizabeth's support in order to defeat the Protestant government in Scotland. Mary's presence in England seemed to set off a Catholic rebellion in the north of England. The Catholics hoped to oust Elizabeth and see Catholic Mary on the throne, as she was the next legal heir. The rebellion was quickly suppressed and those involved were executed or severely punished.

Mary was then held prisoner in England. Elizabeth did not want her to be executed in case Catholic Spain or France reacted against England. Over the next nineteen years Mary was involved in a number of plots with English Catholics against Elizabeth. Finally, in 1586, enough evidence was discovered against Mary for her to be tried for plotting against the queen of England. In 1587 she was tried, found guilty and executed.

The attempted rebellions by Catholics and other resistance to the religious settlement forced Elizabeth to introduce harsh punishments for anyone found practising any form of religion other than that defined by the Acts of Parliament made earlier in her reign.

The extreme Protestants became known as the Puritans, because they wanted to 'purify' the Protestant Church. They also wanted to do away with bishops, giving their power to appoint priests to the local congregations. The Puritans were very strict and moral. They felt that people should work hard and avoid the excesses of life such as gambling, drinking, wearing extravagant clothes and going to the theatre. The Puritans of England eventually sailed to America where they were free to practise their own form of religion.

Time to understand

Amidst all the religious changes, the belief in the supernatural, in witches, wizards, ghosts, fairies and so on thrived. Most villages and towns had a resident 'cunning woman' who could be called upon for any number of things including curing toothaches or burns, recovery of stolen property or tracing missing persons. There were also usually resident 'witches' who were often accused of being responsible if an inexplicable death or illness occurred. They were sometimes tried and punished severely.

Fig. 12.13 Witches were suspected of associating with devils.

1 Here is a rhyme used by a 'cunning woman' to heal a burn:

Two angels come from the West,
One brought fire, the other frost.
Out fire! In frost!
In the name of the Father, Son and the
Holy Ghost!

a What effect were the words 'Out fire! In frost!' supposed to have on the burn?
b Why was the name of the 'Father, Son and the Holy Ghost' used?
c Do you think a 'cunning woman' would be accused of witchcraft? Why?

2 This extract comes from a sixteenth century book on witchcraft:

One sort of such as are said to be witches, are women which be commonly old, lame, bleary-eyed, pale, foul, and full of wrinkles; poor, sullen, superstitious, and papists; or such as know no religion: in whose drowsy minds the devil hath gotten a fine seat; so as, what mischief, mischance, calamity or slaughter is brought to pass, they are easily persuaded is done by themselves . . . These miserable wretches are so odious unto all their neighbours, and so feared, as few dare offend them, or deny them anything they ask . . . and sometimes think they can do such things as are beyond the ability of human nature. These go from house to house, and from door to door for a pat of milk, yeast, drink, pottage . . . without which they could hardly live . . .
It falleth out many times, that neither their necessities, nor their expectation is answered or served, in those places where they beg or borrow . . . so as sometimes she curseth one, and sometimes another; and that from the master of the house, his wife, children, cattle etc., to the little pig that lieth in the sty . . . Doubtless (at length) some of her neighbours die, or fall sick; or some of the children are visited with diseases . . . Also some of their cattle perish, either by disease or mischance. Then they, upon whom such adversities fall, weighing the fame that goeth upon this woman . . . are resolved that all mishaps are brought to pass by her only means.

a How were witches commonly supposed to look? Using the description given above, draw an Elizabethan witch.
b How did they earn a living?
c What would convince people that such a woman was a witch?
d What is the writer of this extract suggesting is the real explanation?

Town life in Elizabethan England

During the Elizabethan age most people lived in the country. Only one-fifth of the population lived in towns. Those who lived in towns usually worked as craftsmen, merchants or traders. There were also large numbers of unemployed and poverty-stricken men, women and children. These people survived by stealing food, picking pockets or other devious means. In villages the poor were cared for by the other villagers, if they were felt to be deserving. There were strict laws to prevent beggars or unemployed people leaving their own village.

Most towns were little more than villages by modern standards. As there were not yet any heavy manufacturing industries or factories, the towns often contained large open spaces and were full of trees and gardens.

Elizabeth ruled from London, which was the biggest town, almost a city. It was a mixture of wealth and poverty, elegant townhouses and filthy slums.

The most important part of London was the 'city', bounded by the original Roman and medieval walls and the river Thames. Here was the centre of business and government. London Bridge itself, spanning the Thames, was lined with shops and houses.

Most of the narrow streets of London bore the names of the traders and craftsmen who lived and worked in them. Once business began, early in the morning, the streets were crowded with shoppers, beggars and street vendors. Street vendors sold anything from ballad sheets to hot pies. Weaving carefully through the thronging crowds would ride men on horseback, or carts bearing produce and goods to the markets.

Houses were usually several storeys high, often with a shop or workroom on the ground floor. The overhanging upper storeys almost met with those across the street. This caused the streets to be dark, smelly and airless.

There were no organised drainage or sewerage systems except for an open drain which ran down the middle of the street. Scavengers were men employed to clear the rubbish from the streets. Rat-catchers were another kind of tradesman constantly in demand. Fresh drinking water was supplied to houses by water carriers from five or six pumps in London.

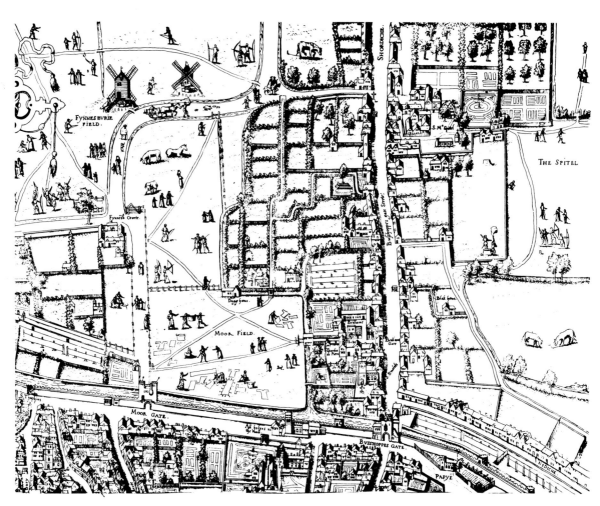

Fig. 12.14 Part of an Elizabethan map of London.

Time to understand

The section of an Elizabethan map of London shown in Fig. 12.14 helps us to understand several aspects of town life at that time. Study it carefully and answer the following questions.

1 The wall running across the lower part of the map was part of the north side of the original town wall. What has happened to London since the wall was built? What do we call the areas outside the wall? (Clue: the Latin word for city is *urbs*).

2 Note the activities in Moor Field. How was washing dried in an Elizabethan town?

3 Find Bishopsgate Street. What clue does it provide about the water supply to towns?

4 Find out where and how grain was made into flour in Elizabethan London. Are there any suitable locations on the map?

5 Bedlam prison was notorious in its time. Find it on the map and describe its location as if to a stranger in London. What does the word 'bedlam' now mean?

6 What did most houses have even though they lined both sides of a street?

Country life in Elizabethan England

During Elizabeth's reign much of England was still farmed on the open-field system which had existed for hundreds of years. The main change was that a farmer now paid rent to his landlord rather than working for him. Some land, after the dissolution of the monasteries, had been enclosed by wealthy landowners or their tenants and was cultivated separately. Farming had become a profitable business as the population of England was increasing and so the price of food was rising. People invested the profits made from farming in houses, furnishings and other possessions such as bedding and clothing. It was common for even a moderately prosperous farmer to draw up a will before his death, bequeathing all his possessions to relatives,

friends or the local church. The passing on of possessions and land through the members of a family helped to build up the family fortune.

The most prosperous kind of farmer was called a *yeoman*. He often owned the biggest and most impressive house in the village. There were also *husbandmen* who farmed on a much smaller scale yet could still make good profits from the land they rented. The farm labourer usually worked for a yeoman or a husbandman.

The growing prosperity of England could be seen in the houses and villages of the countryside. The nobility or aristocracy owned huge houses set in well-organised gardens and parkland. Glass was still expensive but was more readily available. It was possible to display one's wealth by building a house with plenty of glass windows. The nobility usually owned large estates which they either rented out or farmed for themselves. Fortunes could sometimes be made by buying and selling land.

The church was still the most important building in the village. The parson was required to preach and give services on Sundays. He also had a new duty of recording all baptisms, marriages and funerals. These are valuable records for the historian as often the only record of a labourer's life and that of his family lies in the church records. The parson was assisted by a clerk and the church wardens. The clerk kept church records and educated the local children. Churchwardens were yeomen farmers who were elected in turn to the office at the annual parish meeting. They were responsible for the maintenance and repair of the church.

The upkeep of the church was at times expensive. There were the bell-ringers to pay, new equipment such as prayer books to be purchased and the altar cloths to be laundered. Fund-raising activities and collecting from house to house supplemented the income from church lands. Special collections were taken for occasional expenses such as major repairs to the church.

There was not usually any form of schooling in a village except that offered by the parson and his clerk. Usually village children learnt a craft or farming. The children of yeomen were often sent to a grammar school in a larger town.

Fig. 12.15 A middle class home typical of the Elizabethan countryside.

Elizabethan seamen

In Elizabethan times the main product exported to Europe by England was woollen cloth. The merchants who supervised the trade were called the Company of Merchant Adventurers. A merchant who belonged to the company was allowed to trade on his own but had to follow certain rules. Also, the company had officials in the main trading centres who helped the merchant sell his goods.

Wars in Europe, particularly those of France and Holland, led to a decline in the amount of cloth bought by those countries. This led to a need for other markets. In Chapter Nine you learnt about the opening of the sea trade route to the East by Portugal and the discovery of America by Spain. Portugal and Spain dominated trade with the East and America respectively.

English merchants wanted to establish their own trading contacts with the East. English seamen made a number of attempts to find a new route to the East. Sir Hugh Willoughby and Richard Chancellor tried sailing north-east in 1555. One ship of the expedition reached the fishing village of Archangel in Russia. Chancellor then travelled to Moscow where he met the tsar, Ivan the Terrible. As a result of this voyage trading contacts were made with Russia. The Moscovy Company was later formed by a group of merchants. Woollen cloth, naturally popular in Russia's cold climate, was exchanged for furs, timber and hemp.

Although the expedition had not discovered a new route to the East the eventual success of the venture led to further attempts during the reign of Elizabeth. But expeditions led by Martin Frobisher between 1576 and 1578 exploring to the north-west were also failures.

Fig. 12.16 A Spanish galleon (left) attacked by an English ship.

Ralph Fitch succeeded in reaching India by an overland route in 1590. At Agra he met Akbar the Great, the Mughal emperor who controlled much of India. In 1591 an English expedition successfully sailed around the Cape of Good Hope and on to India. In 1600 the East India Company was formed in anticipation of trade with India. In 1601 a representative of the company met with Akbar the Great to suggest trade with England. No doubt the representative was impressed by the splendour of Akbar's court, equal to that of the English monarch. You will learn more about Akbar later in this chapter.

While the monopoly of Portugal's trade with India was being challenged, so was Spain's hold on South American treasure. Some seamen traded with existing Spanish colonies, until the Spanish government decided to forbid it. Sir John Hawkins ignored the new law and continued to sell negro slaves captured in Africa to Spanish colonists in the New World. While his small fleet was sheltering from a storm in the Mexican port of San Juan de Ulva (now Vera Cruz), it was attacked by ships of the Spanish navy. It was like a declaration of war. From then on English ships began to attack Spanish treasure ships returning to Spain from South America.

Francis Drake

'Seadogs' were English sailors who earned their name attacking Spanish treasure ships. The most famous of the English 'seadogs' was Francis Drake. In 1577 Drake commanded an expedition of 'exploration' to the Pacific Ocean. Elizabeth supported the expedition by providing one of her own ships and money for others. The real object of the expedition was to raid Spanish colonies on the Pacific coast of South America. Only Drake's ship, the *Golden Hind*, managed to reach the Pacific. The others were destroyed or forced to turn back earlier in the voyage.

In a series of daring raids Drake attacked ports in Peru and Chile. Further up the coast he attacked a Spanish galleon laden with gold, silver and precious stones. This made sure the voyage was financially successful. The *Golden Hind* returned to England by sailing across the Pacific, through the East Indies and around Africa, thus circumnavigating the world. Drake was knighted on his return to England. But the voyage was to be one of the causes of a later conflict between Spain and England.

Time to understand

Richard Hakluyt was an Elizabethan writer. He wrote about the travels and successes of explorers, merchants and 'seadogs'. In 1589 he wrote:

> At that time our merchants perceived the commodities and wares of England to be in small request with the countries and people about us, . . . and the price thereof abated, . . . certain

grave citizens . . . began to think how this mischief might be remedied . . . for seeing that the wealth of the Spaniards and the Portuguese, by the discovery and search of new trades and countries, was marvellously increased, supposing the same to be a course and means for them also to obtain the like, they thereupon resolved upon a new and strange navigation.

1 What was the main commodity exported by England? Use an encyclopaedia to find out some of the others.
2 What were the 'countries and people about us' to which Hakluyt refers?
3 What does Hakluyt mean when he says 'the price thereof abated'?
4 How was the wealth of Spain and Portugal increased?
5 Did the English learn anything from the example set by Spain and Portugal? What did they do?

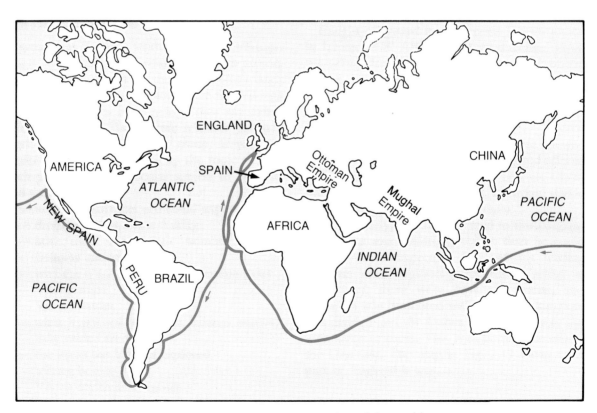

Fig. 12.17 Drake's circumnavigation of the world.

Elizabethan theatre

Theatre-going was one of the most popular forms of entertainment in Elizabethan England. Funds were supplied by noblemen who patronised groups of actors. Robert Dudley, the Earl of Leicester and the queen's favourite, formed a company of actors in 1559. Players were known by the name of the patron, such as the Earl of Leicester's Men.

At first plays were performed in inn-yards, such as the Bull in Bishopsgate Street. Later, commercial playhouses were built. The first, opened in 1576, was called simply The Theatre.

Sometime in the late 1580s a young man from the small town of Stratford-on-Avon joined one of the theatre companies in London. By 1594 he had bought a share in a new theatrical company called the Lord Chamberlain's Men, who performed at the Globe Theatre in London. Between 1594 and 1597 a number of plays written by the same young man were performed there. The titles of these plays are now well known to the English-speaking world—*Romeo and Juliet*, *A Midsummer Night's Dream* and *The Merchant of Venice*. The name of the young man was William Shakespeare.

Performances at the Globe took place in the afternoon on fine days. Fig. 12.18 shows a reconstruction of an Elizabethan theatre. The stage, which was partly covered, protruded into the open courtyard. On three sides were rows of tiered seats, usually on three levels. Around the stage people could stand and watch for a penny. These people were called the 'groundlings' and were known for their sometimes riotous behaviour. The more well-to-do paid extra to sit in a seat.

There was no curtain across the stage so all action was continuous. Behind the stage was the actors' dressing room which enabled them to make quick changes if they were playing several different roles.

The words of Shakespeare's (and other playwrights') plays not only conveyed the story or plot but also the time of day, the setting and the weather conditions. There was, of course, no stage lighting, and very little in the way of special effects. The play itself had to be both enter-

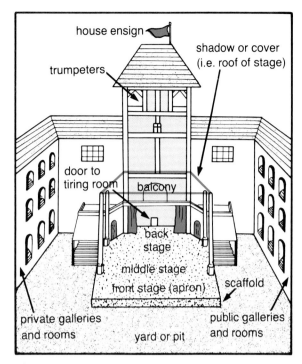

Fig. 12.18 An Elizabethan theatre.

taining and interesting to hold the attention of a sometimes restless audience. Food and drink were sold throughout the performance by people moving among the crowd.

Puritans often objected to theatre-going because of the behaviour of the audience. One critic of theatres claimed that they were places 'for vagrant persons, masterless men, thieves, horsestealers . . . and other dangerous persons to meet together'. Despite the opposition, however, the theatre continued to develop, perhaps because the queen herself supported it. In 1583 a company of actors called the Queen's Men was formed. This meant that the queen had given full royal approval to the 'evil' that Puritans felt should be banned.

Time to understand

The following extract from one of Shakespeare's plays indicates how the words were used to convey the setting.

In *The Tempest*, a party of Italians are shipwrecked on an island. A number of them survive but are scattered either in small groups or alone. The passage below is spoken by Trinculo, a jester, as he wanders alone.

> Here's neither bush nor shrub to bear off any weather at all, and another storm brewing; I hear it sing in the wind: yond same black cloud, yond huge one, looks like a foul bombard that would shed his liquor. If it should thunder, as it did before, I know not where to hide my head; yond same cloud cannot choose but fall by pailfulls.

1 What impression is conveyed about the landscape around Trinculo?
2 What are the weather conditions?
3 What do you suppose was the cause of the shipwreck?

The Mughal dynasty of India

The Mughal period in Indian history bears a striking resemblance, in some ways, to the Tudor period in English history. In both cases a powerful family established a line of hereditary monarchs. As a result a strong government centred on the ruler was set up. Beneath the ruler, in both cases, was an elaborate system of officials. Both families displayed their wealth and power to the people they ruled by building magnificent palaces and wearing costly clothes decorated with jewels.

In the early sixteenth century India was a land divided between Moslem and Hindu rulers. When the first of the Mughal rulers, Babur, invaded India in 1526 he conquered the ruler of much of northern India. Babur was a Moslem and was of Turkish descent on his father's side and Mongol descent on his mother's. It was this connection which gave the dynasty the name Mughal.

Babur had held territory north of India in Kabul. He decided to expand into India when his ambitions in other territories were thwarted by other rulers. He died in 1530, probably from the many serious wounds received in battle.

Babur's son Humayan succeeded him. He was neither as strong nor as experienced in battle as his father. He lost his position to a local chieftain, Sher Shah Sur, in 1540. Sher Shah Sur ruled until 1545. His efficient leadership and many reforms of the system of government during this time helped the Mughals when they regained power.

Fig. 12.19 Akbar directing the building of the great city of Fatepur Sikri.

210

Fig. 12.20 Akbar riding on an elephant. How did Elizabeth I travel?

Sher Shah's son Islam Shah ruled successfully for five years after his father's death. Then, due to squabbles over the succession, the Shah dynasty became weak. Meanwhile, Humayan had returned to Kabul where after a long and bitter struggle he re-established himself in the original position of his father. On the death of Islam Shah, Humayan had little trouble defeating the successor to the throne in Delhi. In 1555, after fifteen years, he regained the position he had lost.

After Humayan's death in 1556, his son Akbar inherited the throne. Akbar was not quite fourteen. The government was managed for four years on his behalf by Bairam Khan, a faithful friend of Humayan's and a capable soldier and leader. Bairam Khan became too powerful. When Akbar was eighteen he was advised by

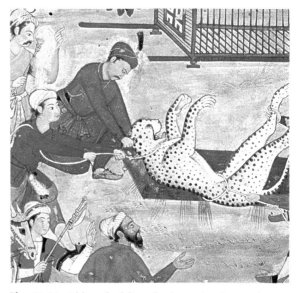

Fig. 12.21 Akbar (holding the beast by the ears) capturing a cheetah.

other members of the court to remove Bairam Khan from his position.

Akbar the Great became one of the greatest rulers of India, as Elizabeth I was of England. It is interesting to note that their reigns began and finished at almost the same time. Akbar the Great ruled from 1556 to 1605. Elizabeth I ruled from 1558 to 1603.

Under Akbar's leadership most of northern India was conquered, forming the beginning of the Mughal empire. This territory was controlled by dividing it into a number of provinces, each with a governor who carried out Akbar's orders and maintained law and order.

Time to understand

Akbar was a successful ruler even though opposition from rival local rulers and chieftains was brutal and ruthless at times. In Fig. 12.21 on the previous page Akbar is shown catching a cheetah. He is said to have had over 1000 cheetahs which were trained to hunt.

1 Do you think Akbar's enemies may have thought carefully before attacking him? Why?
2 Compare this illustration with the coronation portrait of Elizabeth I (Fig. 12.6). What kind of image is conveyed in each painting? Make a list of the words or qualities you would use to describe each.
3 Both Elizabeth I and Akbar the Great were strong rulers. Why would artists depict them in such different ways?

The reign of Akbar

Throughout his reign Akbar showed that he was a wise ruler. Like Elizabethan England, India was divided over the matter of religion. The Mughals were Moslems although most Indians were Hindus. In the tradition of Islam, tolerance of other religions was not permitted. In the past, when Moslem rulers had dominated northern India many Hindus had converted to Islam, especially if they wished to be involved in the government service. Akbar, however, followed

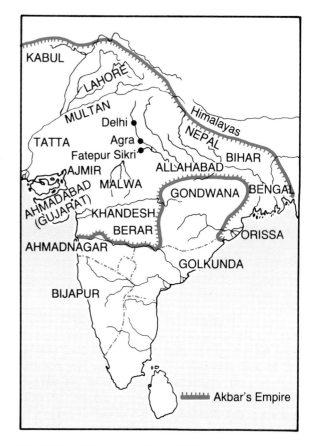

Fig. 12.22 Akbar's empire in 1605.

a policy of 'universal tolerance', by which people were allowed to practise their own religions.

It was common for Moslem men to have a number of wives. Some of Akbar's wives were Hindus. He allowed them to practise their religion within the palace. Hindus were given responsible jobs within the government. Akbar encouraged classical Hindu artists, musicians, poets and dancers to continue to develop their arts.

Akbar also introduced many reforms both to strengthen his government and to change some aspects of Indian society. He was opposed to child marriage and marriage between near relations. He also passed a law to prevent a Hindu widow being burnt alive on her husband's funeral pyre without her consent. (This was a common practice among Hindus.)

On his death Akbar's only son, Jahangir, succeeded to the throne.

Time to understand

Akbar, although uneducated himself, encouraged writers, scholars and artists. One of Akbar's closest friends, Abul Fazl, wrote the following about the duties of a Mughal king:

> A paternal love toward the subjects. Thousands find rest in the love of the king and sectarian differences do not raise the dust of strife. In his wisdom, the king will understand the spirit of the age and shape his plans accordingly.

1 What does he mean by a 'paternal love toward the subjects'? Would you say that Akbar loved his subjects in this way? Why?
2 Did Akbar seem to understand the 'spirit of his age'? How would you be able to tell?

How do we know?

The defeat of the Spanish Armada, 1588

Historical accounts of battles or other major events often show bias or prejudice. Sometimes this may be deliberate on the part of the writer, such as when a particular case is being argued, as in a debate. Sometimes this may be unintentional and due to such things as the nationality of the writer. The extracts given below will give you some experience in spotting bias or prejudice.

The Spanish Armada was a fleet of 130 ships sent by Philip II of Spain to attack England and defeat the English navy. His motives for doing so were mixed. Firstly, he wished that England had remained a Catholic country. As king of the most powerful Catholic country in Europe he was one of the leading figures, at the time, in the Catholic Reformation. Secondly, Elizabeth I, who had succeeded Philip's Catholic wife Mary to the throne of England, had sent help to Protestant rebels in the Netherlands who were trying to shake off the dominance of Spain. And thirdly, English ships had been raiding Spanish treasure ships returning from the New World.

The Armada sailed in a strict crescent formation right up the English Channel. The English navy was unable to break this formation as powerful warships were at each tip. If the English tried to attack the weaker ships in the centre they risked being surrounded. Several attempts at battle proved fruitless.

The Spanish fleet dropped anchor near Calais on the French coast. Here the Spanish were to pick up badly needed supplies and extra men. But Dutch ships came along the coast to Calais in support of the English, cutting the Spaniards off from their supplies.

The English admirals decided to send in 'fire ships' (ships which had been set alight, after being filled with tar and gunpowder). Although the Spanish had been expecting this to happen, the 'fire ships' were much bigger than usual. The Spanish commanders ordered anchors to be raised. The crescent formation was broken. Not a single Spanish ship caught fire, yet they were almost defenceless as their supplies of ammunition were very low. The Spanish Armada was badly defeated in the battle that followed. The surviving ships fled northward around Scotland to return home.

Here are two accounts of the battle.

An English account

> Certainly he that will happily perform at sea must be skilful in making choice of weapons to fight in . . . The Spaniards had an army aboard their ships and he (Hawkins) had none; they had more ships than he had and of a higher building and charging. So that, had he entangled himself with

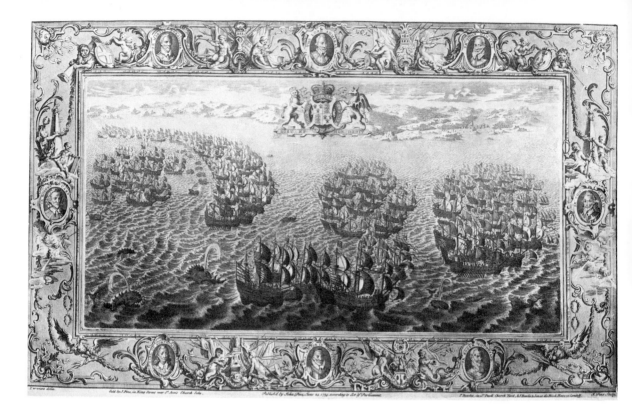

Fig. 12.23 The crescent formation of the Spanish Armada.

those great weapons, he would have greatly endangered this kingdom.

But our admiral knew his advantage and held it . . . for a fleet of twenty ships, all good sailors and good ships, have the advantage on an open sea, over a hundred as good ships but of slower sailing.

A Spanish account

The enemy opened heavy cannon fire on our flagship at seven o'clock in the morning, which carried on for nine hours. So tremendous was the fire that over 200 balls struck the sails and hull of the flagship on the starboard side, killing and wounding many men, disabling and dismounting guns and destroying much rigging. The holes made in the hull . . . caused such a great leak that two divers had as much as they could do to stop them with tar and lead plates, working all day. The galleon *San Felipe* of Portugal was surrounded by seventeen of the enemy's ships, which directed heavy fire on both sides and on her stern. The enemy approached so close that muskets and pistols on the galleon were brought into action, killing many enemy men on the enemy ships. The enemy did not dare, however, to come to close quarters, but kept up a hot cannon fire from a distance, smashing the rudder, breaking the foremast and killing over two hundred men in the galleon.

1 Does either account mention the use of fire ships? Why would both accounts stress other aspects of the battle? Do the accounts agree on any points? Or do they disagree?
2 What does the English account suggest about the English navy?
3 What explanation for the Spanish defeat is given by the Spanish account?
4 Of the following, which facts would you need to know to give a clearer picture of how the Spanish were defeated?
  a Who commanded the Spanish fleet.
  b Who commanded the English fleet.

214

c Whether the Dutch ships became involved in the battle.
d Where the Spanish ships sailed in retreat (precisely).
e How many Spanish ships were sunk.
f How many English ships were sunk.
g How long the battle lasted.
h How many ships were in the English fleet.
i The kind of weapons used by the English.
j The kind of weapons used by the Spanish.

Ancient Spanish wreck found

DUBLIN, Wednesday: The wreck of a ship from the Spanish Armada sent to invade England in 1588 has been found off the coast of Ireland, the Government said yesterday. A team of British divers found the wreck, thought to be that of the Juliana, over the weekend buried in sand off the coast of Sligo, north-west Ireland. The director of the expedition, Mr Colin Martin of St Andrews University in Scotland, said the find was one of the most important archaeological discoveries of the century. Three bronze cannon described as being in excellent condition and a cannonball have already been recovered from the wreck. — Reuter

Fig. 12.24 A newspaper report describing the discovery, in 1985, of one of the ships of the Spanish Armada.

13

Problems for the Stuarts

The reign of James I: the beginning of the problems

ELIZABETH I died on 24 March 1603. A messenger on horseback carried the news to Scotland. The heir to the throne was James Stuart, James VI of Scotland. He was the son of Mary, Queen of Scots. He became James I of England.

James I travelled south to England within a couple of weeks to take the throne. As he progressed south he was joined by men eager to find a place in the new court. Most towns held welcoming feasts in honour of the new king as he passed through.

James revelled in the celebrations. He felt that the people of England were pleased that he was their new king. He did not realise that the English would have given the same welcome to any king. By the time James was due to open parliament in March 1604, he had tired of the large crowds. James was not like the Tudor monarchs who had thought that being 'seen' by the people was necessary to keep the people's favour. Later in his reign, people said that James often 'dispersed them with frowns that we may not say with curses'.

During the reigns of the Tudors, parliament had been called when the monarch wanted to pass new laws or raise money through special taxes. The king or queen was supposed to govern using money gained from land he or she owned together with money gained from certain taxes on trade. James I found that this was not enough money. So he called a meeting of parliament and asked for more money.

Most of the members of parliament at this time were wealthy, influential members of English society. They felt that James I should listen to their views on matters such as foreign affairs, trade and religious questions. James felt that he did not have to listen to their views as he believed that God had given him the right to rule. This idea was known as the Divine Right of Kings. It meant that the king was 'accountable to none but God only'.

Parliament would not grant James I the money he wanted unless he agreed to listen to their views. This was the beginning of a long struggle between the Stuart kings and parliament. A civil war was eventually fought because of this struggle.

When James could not gain the money he wanted through parliament he sold monopolies on trade. A monopoly meant that one man was given the right to control trade of one article, for example silk or currants. The 'monopolist' could then sell the item for whatever price he wished, usually making a huge profit. Many people resented these monopolies because it made the prices of many different items much more expens-

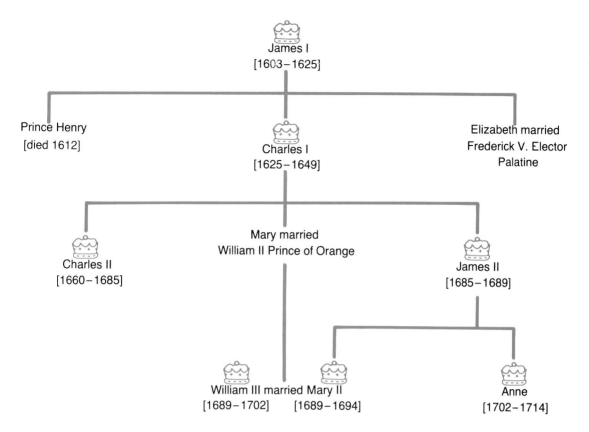

Fig. 13.1 The Stuart family tree.

ive. Parliament did not approve of monopolies either.

Another problem during James' reign was religion. Elizabeth I had made people attend the Church of England. When James I became king there were two religious groups who hoped that religious changes would be made. One group was the Roman Catholics, who hoped to be allowed to practise their religion openly. The other was the Puritans who wanted the services of the Church of England to be simpler and to abolish bishops because of the power they had.

James wanted to please the majority of his subjects, who attended the Church of England. Although a conference between important churchmen and James was held in 1604, no changes were made except a new translation of the Bible, called the Authorised Version.

A small group of Roman Catholics decided to blow up the king while he met with parliament. They succeeded in placing thirty-six barrels of gunpowder under the House of Lords where parliament met. But the plot was discovered, so many of the group fled from London. One of the plotters, Guy Fawkes, still tried to carry out the plan of exploding the gunpowder. He was discovered and arrested just in time. It became a tradition in England to celebrate the 'rescue' of James I with bonfires and fireworks on Guy Fawkes' Night (5 November).

The Puritans believed that people should lead simple and Christian lives. They were opposed to luxury and extravagance of any kind. When James I did not introduce the changes they hoped for in the Church of England many decided to leave England. Some of them went to Holland. Many others went to North America where they became some of the earliest English settlers.

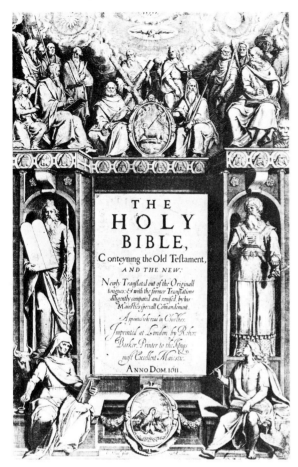

Fig. 13.2 The frontispiece of the Authorised Version of the Bible.

Time to understand

1 Look at the Tudor family tree in Fig. 12.1 (page 191). How many Tudor monarchs ruled England? What was the relationship between James VI of Scotland and Elizabeth I of England? Why had James VI's mother had a claim to the throne of England? Do you remember what happened to her?

2 Many traditional celebrations or festivals are based on events in the past, for example the celebration of the birth of Christ at Christmas. Often the festivities do not accurately reflect the event upon which they are based. Use an encyclopaedia to discover the traditional celebrations of Guy Fawkes' Night. Explain how these do or do not remind people of the time when a group of Roman Catholics tried to blow up the House of Lords, parliament and the king.

The reign of Charles I: the outbreak of the Civil War

Charles I came to the throne in 1625. He inherited not only his father's kingdom, but also the

Fig. 13.3 Guy Fawkes and other members of the 'gunpowder plot'.

many problems that went with it. Charles had the added problem of having an unpopular Catholic French wife, Henrietta Maria.

Charles has been described as 'a fairy prince in a fairy palace'. This was because he was not aware of the changes in the people's attitude towards their king. Not only members of parliament but also many others felt that the king did not have the right to rule as he pleased but should accept the resolutions passed by parliament.

Charles' main problem was with his parliament. During the early years of the reign parliament refused to grant him money he needed for a war against Spain, unless he increased its power to make laws. Charles tried to finance the wars by introducing special taxes. Some wealthy men simply refused to pay the taxes.

In 1628 parliament presented Charles with a Petition of Rights. This document was eventually accepted by Charles. It reduced the power of the king as it stated that taxes introduced without parliament's approval were illegal. It also stated that imprisonment without trial was illegal.

Parliament then began to criticise the king's religious policy which supported the Church of England. Charles believed in the Divine Right of Kings and so he felt that he was the guardian of the Church. He refused to listen to their religious views and dismissed parliament.

Charles ruled without a parliament for eleven years. To do this he had to rely on the advice of a few chosen ministers. He did not realise how much many people resented his ruling without a parliament. They felt it had taken away some of the freedom of England.

The Stuarts were also kings of Scotland. Charles felt that the Scots should practise the same religion as the English. In 1637 he tried to introduce the English Prayer Book into Scottish churches. The Scots, who were mostly Presby-

Fig. 13.4 Charles I (left) speaking to one of his generals during the Civil War.

terian, rebelled rather than accept the English Prayer Book.

In 1640 he summoned parliament once again, thinking that it would grant him money to put down the Scottish rebellion. Once again parliament refused to grant him money until he listened to its religious complaints. Charles dismissed parliament but found he was unable to deal with the Scottish rebellion without money.

Parliament met once again but its members were not interested in the Scottish rebellion. Two of the king's ministers who had helped him reign without parliament were imprisoned, tried and later executed.

In 1641 parliament presented Charles with another document called the Grand Remonstrance. It was longer and more demanding than the Petition of Rights. It proposed that the army and navy be controlled by parliament. It proposed religious reforms as well.

Charles felt that the Grand Remonstrance would take away his power as king. He tried to arrest the members of parliament responsible for the Grand Remonstrance but they escaped. In London itself, more and more people supported parliament.

Even before Charles declared war on parliament the population of England had begun to take sides. Those on the side of parliament were called 'Roundheads' by the king's supporters, as many were apprentices who had to wear their hair short. Many were also Puritans who wore their hair short to show they were not vain, as long hair was then the fashion. Those who supported the king were called 'Cavaliers' by their opponents. The word 'cavalier' means 'horseman' but at the time it referred to Spanish cavaliers who were notorious for their cruelty.

In August 1642, Charles I declared war on parliament and its supporters. This was the beginning of the Civil War in which Englishmen fought against Englishmen.

Time to understand

The city of London

London had become a city, the most important in England. (Now we call it the capital city.) The king and his court lived in London. Many thousands of people lived and worked there. By modern standards it was not a large city, even though some 500 000 people lived there in the mid-seventeenth century. Below are two descriptions of London at that time. Study them carefully before answering the questions.

Now at London the houses of the citizens (especially in the chief streets) are very narrow in the front towards the street, but are built five or six roofs high, commonly of timber and clay with plaster, and are very neat and commodious within: and the building of citizens' houses in other cities is not much unlike this. But withal understand, that in London many stately palaces, built by noblemen upon the river Thames, do make a very great shew to them that pass by water; and that there be many more like palaces, also built towards land, but scattered and great part of them in back lanes and streets . . .

The parish of St Margaret Lothbury complained in 1637 that Ralph Harrison, draper, was possessed of divers small tenements, five in number all in one passage called the Dark Entry . . . being so noisome and unhealthful a place as few the like in London, some . . . having been divided of late years and the rents of them much raised by the said Ralph Harrison all . . . being inhabited by poor and needy people which are a continual burden and charge to the said parish.

1 What materials were commonly used to construct buildings in London? What could be a reason for this?
2 How many storeys high were some houses? What possible reasons were there for this?
3 What other kind of building was found in London? What type of people owned these buildings?

4 What is a tenement? What kind of people lived in tenements? Can you suggest why?

From Civil War to the Restoration of Charles II

England was a divided nation even though most of the ordinary people would not have understood what the real causes of the war were. Most

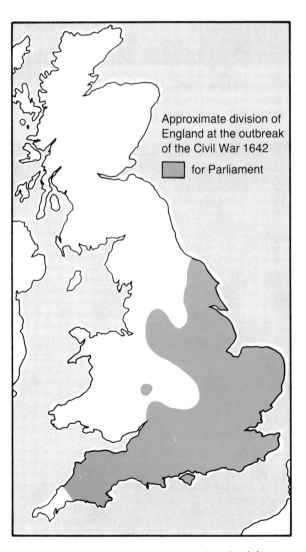

Fig. 13.5 England divided at the outbreak of the Civil War.

of the south and east of England, including London, sided with parliament. Most of the north and Wales remained loyal to the king. Each side felt that God was on its side. Each side felt confident of winning.

The Civil War

Charles I, having lost the support of most Londoners, had moved his capital to Oxford. This meant that many of the troops he had mustered were housed there, causing overcrowding of the town. The overcrowding sometimes led to the spread of infectious diseases.

At first both armies were inexperienced, but the king's army had a good cavalry. Both sides relied, to a large degree, on 'hirelings', men paid to fight. In the early stages the king's army had the advantage. Several minor battles were victories due to the leadership of Charles I's nephew, Prince Rupert, who had fought in wars in Europe.

Later, as the Roundheads gained more experience, the tide of war began to turn. The first major battle, at Edgehill in October 1642, was not decisive. Neither side could claim victory. The king's army lost the most men.

The second major battle, at Marston Moor in 1644, was a victory for the Roundheads. This was partly due to the entry of Scotland on the side of parliament. It was also due to two brilliant commanders who had emerged on the Roundheads' side, Oliver Cromwell and Sir Thomas Fairfax.

After the battle Cromwell organised the New Model Army which was well trained and strictly disciplined along Puritan guidelines. The soldiers sang hymns in camp before going into battle and listened to two sermons on Sundays. Punishments for small offences were severe. For example, a man caught swearing could be whipped.

The third and final major battle of the war, at Naseby in 1645, was a complete victory for the Roundheads' New Model Army. Charles I was forced to retreat. He later surrendered himself to the Scottish army. The Scots handed him over to Cromwell and parliament when he refused to help them establish a form of Presbyterianism in England.

Fig. 13.6 Oliver Cromwell.

Although Charles I was defeated, the struggle for power was not over. Members of parliament and army leaders argued over whether Charles should remain king with very little power or whether he should be executed. Charles tried to take advantage of this delay. He arranged with the Scottish army to introduce Presbyterianism into England for three years if they gave him military support. Unfortunately for Charles, the Scottish army was quickly defeated by the New Model Army.

Oliver Cromwell was the real leader of the parliamentary forces. He said that Charles' rule without parliament had caused the Civil War and because of this he must be executed. Many members of parliament still believed that Charles should be king, but only after parliament had been given more power. To overcome any opposition to his plans, Cromwell sent troops into parliament to 'purge' it. Presbyterians and those who did not want the king executed were expelled. Only sixty members, who were all loyal to the army, remained.

Charles was tried on a charge of being a tyrant who limited the freedom and rights of the English people. He was judged guilty and sentenced to death. Charles walked to the scaffold bravely on 30 January 1649. He claimed that he was innocent of the charges and that his trial was illegal.

Cromwell's England

After the death of Charles, England became a commonwealth, governed by Parliament without a king. The Puritan army, under the leadership of Oliver Cromwell, remained a strong force. There were many arguments between members of parliament and army leaders over how the country was to be governed and what laws should be made. In 1653 Oliver Cromwell was appointed Lord Protector so that the government could run more smoothly.

The position of Lord Protector was something like that of a king. The form of government was called a Protectorate. Cromwell lived in the royal palace and became more and more like a king. The first parliament called during the Protectorate was dismissed by Cromwell because its members would not co-operate. Other parliaments during the next seven years, until Cromwell's death, ended in the same way.

Cromwell divided England into eleven districts, each governed by a major-general. All of these major-generals were Puritans. Life under the major-generals was strict. Entertainment was almost completely abolished, swearing was punishable by fines and Christmas Day became a day of fasting rather than a day of feasting.

By the time Cromwell died in 1658 his rule had become extremely unpopular. Taxes had increased and Cromwell had dismissed any judge or official who disagreed with him. Many people secretly hoped that Charles I's son, who had fled to Holland, would return.

Cromwell's son Richard became Lord Protector in 1658. Richard had neither the ability nor the desire to govern England. He resigned after only a few months. The Puritan army and members of parliament began to quarrel again. During this time of confusion General Monk marched with an army from Scotland to England to challenge the Puritan army.

Fig. 13.7 The execution of Charles I.

When the Puritan army was defeated, parliament met and decided to invite Prince Charles to return from Holland to become king of England. The period following his return on 25 May 1660 is called the Restoration. This is because not only were the Stuarts returned to the throne of England but the old way of life was restored as well.

Time to understand

As you have read earlier in this chapter, Puritans were originally members of a religious group who wanted to 'purify' the Church. After the Civil War Puritan ideals affected the whole of society. Below is a list of fines paid for various offences committed in a small part of London during the Protectorate. All the fines are in shillings and pence.

		s	d
1644	Received of three poore men, for drinking on the Sabbath day at Tottenham Court	4	0
1645	Received of John Seagood, constable, which he had of a Frenchman for swearing three oathes	3	0
1645	Received of Mrs. Thunder, by the hands of Francis Potter for her being drunk and swearing seven oaths	12	0
1646	Received of Mr. Hooker for brewing on a Fast day	2	6
	Received of four men, travelling on the Fast day	1	0
1646	Received of Mr. Wetherill, Headboro', which he had of one for an oath	3	4

Fig. 13.8 Cromwell dismisses parliament.

1648	Received from the City Marshall, sent by the Lord Mayor, for one that was drunke at the Forts in our parish	5	0
	Received from Isabel Johnson at ye Coleyard for drinking on the Sabbath day	4	0
1652	Received of Mr. Huxley and Mr. Morris, who were riding out of town in sermon time on a Fast day	11	0
1654	Received of William Glover in Queen Street, and of Isaac Thomas a barber in Holborn, for trimming a beard on the Lord's day (sum omitted)		

1655	Received of Mayde taken in Mrs. Jackson's alehouse on the Sabbath day	5	0
1655	Received of a Scotchman drinking at Robert Owne's on the Sabbath	2	0
1658	Received of Joseph Piers for refusing to open his doores to have his house searched on the Lord's day	10	0

1 What were two of the most common offences? What does this tell us about Puritan ideals?
2 What were some of the offences committed on the Sabbath Day? What do you think Puritans believed should happen on the Sabbath Day?
3 How would you describe life during the Protectorate based on the evidence in this list?

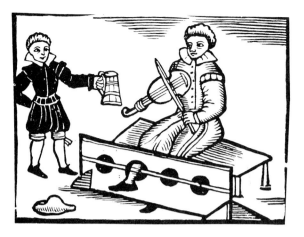

Fig. 13.9 A woman in the stocks during the Protectorate.

Two disasters in London: the Plague and the Fire

The Plague

The city of London had changed little in appearance since the time of Elizabeth I. Little had been done to improve sanitation or hygiene, despite a growth in population. Most people came to London to earn more money. If they were already reasonably well-off they often hoped to gain a position at court. If they were poor they sought employment in one of the trades or as a servant for the wealthy.

When the wealthy ventured onto the streets, they usually carried nosegays, which were small bunches of herbs and flowers designed to counteract the smell from the open drain running down the centre of each street. Into these drains were thrown all kinds of rubbish, excrement and water. When the stench became unbearable the refuse was taken away in carts to dumps outside the city limits. These dumps became a breeding ground for rats and other vermin.

Housing was overcrowded and unhygienic for the majority of people. Dilapidated wooden houses were packed along narrow streets. Clothing was heavy, cumbersome and rarely washed. The wealthy bathed only occasionally. The poor perhaps bathed once a year, if at all. Under these conditions it is not surprising that disease and sickness were common.

London had experienced outbreaks of bubonic plague on several occasions. During these times it was common for the court, and anyone else who could afford it, to leave the city. When the death rate began to drop, the court and the wealthy would return.

Accounts vary as to when the plague began during Charles II's reign. By the end of April 1665, the first deaths as a result of the plague had

Fig. 13.10 Leaving a plague-infected town.

been recorded in a poor, overcrowded part of the city. By the end of June many people were leaving the city, as the plague was spreading at an alarming rate.

Some villagers outside London tried to prevent those who had escaped from entering their villages. Nobody understood the cause of the plague, but all understood that it was highly contagious. Now it is known to have been carried by the fleas which lived on black rats.

Plague victims and their families were locked in their houses—from the outside! On the door of such a house was painted a large red cross and the words: 'Lord have mercy upon us'. Few people who contracted the plague survived. Often guards were posted outside the doors of infected houses to prevent the occupants escaping.

The once bustling streets of London became almost deserted as more shops, businesses and houses were closed. At night, carts were driven around the city while the drivers called, 'Bring out your dead!'. Huge pits were dug for mass burials as graveyards became full. At the height of the plague there were 5000 people dying each week. It is suspected, as well, that many deaths were unrecorded.

Doctors could do nothing to relieve the suffering, nor was there any known way of controlling the spread of the plague. Supplies of food and water in the city were low and many people died of starvation.

By November 1665, the number of deaths per week had decreased dramatically. It seemed as inexplicable as the outbreak itself. By January 1666, people were beginning to filter back into the city. The death toll in London was estimated at 100 000, which was about one-fifth of the population. The number of deaths outside London was possibly as great. Some people felt that it was a punishment sent by God and prayed, 'that God will never send the like, and that we nor our Posterity after us may never feel such another Judgement'.

Fig. 13.11 A 'plague pit' in London, 1665.

Time to understand

1 The scenes in Figs 13.10 and 13.11 show aspects of life during the time of the Plague. Write a short paragraph describing what is happening in each scene.
2 The following passages were written during the Plague. They tell us of the terrible effects the Plague had on everyday life. Read the passages carefully and then answer the questions.

For when the plague evidently spread itself, they soon began to see the folly of trusting to those unperforming creatures who had gulled them of their money; and then their fears worked another way, namely to amazement and stupidity, not knowing what course to take or what to do either to help or relieve themselves. But they ran about from one neighbour's house to another, and even in the streets, from one door to another, with repeated cries of 'Lord, have mercy upon us! What shall we do?'

No drop of water, perhaps, but what comes at the leisure of a drunken or careless halberd bearer at the door; no seasonable provision is theirs as a certainty for their support.

Not a friend to come nigh them in their many, many heart and house cares and complexities. They are compelled, though well, to lie by, to watch upon the death-bed of their dear relation, to see the corpse dragged away before their eyes. Affrighted children stand howling by their side. Thus they are fitted by fainting affliction to receive the impressions of a thousand fearful thoughts, in that long night they have to reckon with before release, as the family, so dismally exposed, sink one after another in the den of this dismal likeness of Hell, contrived by the advice of the English College of Doctors.

a Who were the 'unperforming creatures'?
b Why would people have trusted them?
c What happened to people who were locked in a house if they could not escape? Why?

The Great Fire of London

The summer of 1665 had been hot but the summer of 1666 was to be even hotter. People had returned to London and business had resumed. Warehouses near the Thames were packed with merchandise.

Fire was a constant threat in London, yet there was no adequate equipment for fighting large fires. Most streets were equipped with fire hooks to pull down straw thatching from roofs to stop a fire spreading. There were a few hand-operated watersquirts in the city as well.

Early in the morning of Sunday 2 September 1666, a fire started in a bakery. The baker and his family managed to escape, although the house and bakery were destroyed by the flames. The fire spread to the nearby Star Inn where the courtyard was filled with hay and straw. Before long the wind had spread the fire through streets leading down to the Thames and London Bridge itself was on fire.

At first, the Lord Mayor underestimated the strength of the fire and felt that it could be quenched with buckets of water passed along human chains. He was soon proved wrong. By

Fig. 13.12 A diorama of the Great Fire of London.

the afternoon many people were already beginning to pack up whatever goods they felt were worth saving. Carts and boats carried citizens and their possessions out of the city.

In an attempt to stop the spread of the fire, houses were pulled down but this proved futile. Charles II and his brother James moved among the chaos and confusion themselves, encouraging people to fight the fire, not simply run from it. Occasionally they joined in the fire-fighting by passing buckets of water along a chain of men.

By Monday the heat from the fire became so intense that it was almost impossible to walk on the cobblestones. For four days the fire burned, destroying over 13 000 houses, 87 churches and 44 public buildings. Over 200 000 homeless people were camped outside the city. Farmers and villages responded generously to the king's pleas for food for the homeless.

Most of the city was devastated. The wealthy had managed to save their most valuable pos-sessions by removing them to country houses. The poor were much less fortunate. Many tradesmen and shopkeepers were faced with complete ruin.

Charles II now undertook the task of rebuilding London. A number of plans were submitted, none of which was adopted. Most people wanted to rebuild their homes on the old foundations, so a number of building restrictions were introduced. Streets were made wider and overhanging upper storeys were forbidden. All new buildings had to be of brick and stone. New sewers and drains were built so that London was a fresher, healthier city in which to live.

The end of Stuart rule

During the reign of Charles II parliament gained more power. Charles did not intend to make the mistakes his father had made. He sometimes

Fig. 13.13 An early design for a fire engine.

Fig. 13.14 People fleeing London on the River Thames.

borrowed money from France instead of summoning parliament to raise taxes.

As king, Charles still had the final say in all matters of government and foreign policy. However, parliament now was strong enough to force the king to accept laws which it had passed. Some of these were designed to re-establish the position of the Church of England and to punish those who did not attend it.

When Charles II died in 1685 his Catholic brother James became King James II. He was not a popular monarch yet nobody wanted another civil war. His support of the Church of England and the freedom of parliament seemed secure. James was already fifty years old and would be succeeded by his daughter, Mary, who was married to William of Orange, the Protestant ruler of Holland.

In late 1685 there was a rebellion against James II by the Duke of Monmouth, a Protestant who tried to make himself king. This rebellion was easily crushed by James' large army. Monmouth and hundreds of his supporters were brutally executed. This event made James unpopular with the majority of the English people.

During 1686 and 1687 James became more unpopular. He dismissed parliament when he was unable to restrict its activities. He granted religious toleration to Catholics and Puritans. He appointed Catholics as his chief advisers. People began to feel that James intended to make England a Catholic country once again.

In 1688 a son was born to James and his second wife, who was also a Catholic. This meant that the throne would be passed on to James's son, James, instead of Mary. So a number of members of parliament decided to invite Mary

Fig. 13.15 Charles II.

Fig. 13.16 Queen Anne.

Fig. 13.17 William of Orange.

and her husband William to become joint rulers of England immediately.

William arrived with an army of 15 000 Dutch and English troops on 5 November 1688. James could offer no resistance, because much of his large army deserted to William's side. Fearing for his life, James II fled to France.

William and Mary signed a document called the Bill of Rights when they became king and queen. This had been drawn up by parliament and it gave parliament the right to debate freely, to pass laws and to raise taxes. It also stated that the monarch always had to be a member of the Church of England and that the monarch could only have an army if permitted to do so by parliament.

Fig. 13.18 A London coffee house.

Fig. 13.19 Samuel Pepys—his diary, which you can read about on page 233, is an important record of the Stuart Age.

The last of the Stuart monarchs was Anne, the second daughter of James II. She ruled with the help of advisers. None of her seventeen children survived her and so parliament decided that the throne should pass to the descendants of James I's daughter, Elizabeth. This was to exclude the line of Catholic descendants from James II's second marriage.

The Stuart age was marked by struggles between monarch and parliament. In the end parliament emerged with much greater powers and the monarch's control over government was greatly reduced. The powers won by parliament formed the basic model for our parliamentary system today.

Time to understand

Entertainment in Stuart England

All the Stuart monarchs found time for recreational sports. Because of this, sport and enter-

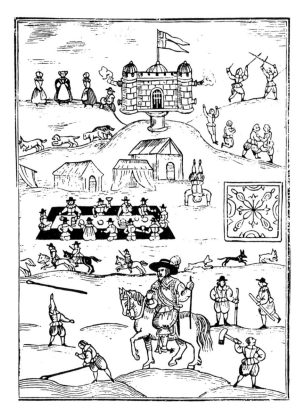

Fig. 13.20 A seventeenth century woodcut showing a number of sports and pastimes.

tainment were popular at all levels of society.

1 The description below comes from the reign of Charles II. Read it carefully before answering the questions.

> For variety of distractions, sports and recreations, no nation doth excel the English. The King hath abroad his Forests, Chases and Parks, full of variety of Game; for Hunting Red and Fallow Deer, Foxes, Otters; Hawking; his Paddock-courses, Horse-races, etc., and at home Tennis, Pelmel, Billiards, Comedies, Opera, Mascarades, etc. The Nobility and Gentry have their Parks, Warrens, Decoys, Paddock-Courses, Horse-races, Hunting, Fishing, Angling, Nets, Tennis, Bowling, Billiards, Tables, Chess, Draughts, Cards, Dice, etc. The citizens and peasants have Hand-Ball, Foot-Ball, Skittles or Nine Pins, Shovel-Board, Stow-Ball, Golfe, Cudgels, Bear-Baiting, Shuttlecock, Bowling, Leaping, Wrestling . . .

a Find five pastimes which are no longer popular. Can you think of possible reasons why?

b Which pastimes are still popular today? Can you also suggest reasons for this?

c Which of these pastimes were spectator sports? Are these still spectator sports today?

d Which of the pastimes involve participation rather than just spectating? How many of these are still played today?

e Write a list of the kinds of entertainment available today. How many of these require participation rather than just spectating?

f Compare the number of pastimes which required participation in Stuart times with the number today. Can you draw any conclusions from this comparison?

2 A popular form of entertainment during the Stuart age was visiting coffee houses. The first of these opened in about 1650 and by the time of Queen Anne there were approximately five hundred in London alone. Fig. 13.18 tells us much about London's coffee houses.

a What kind of people usually patronised coffee houses?

b What time of day was possibly the busiest in a coffee house?

c What normally happened at a coffee house?

d Coffee houses were a place to catch up on current news. Is there anything in this illustration which suggests that?

e How was coffee drunk at that time?

How do we know?

The diary of Samuel Pepys

A diary is a daily record of events. Often this record relates personal details but it may also contain accounts of contemporary current affairs, or things that happened while the writer was keeping the diary. Some diaries have been a great asset to historians trying to reconstruct the events of a particular period. The diary of Samuel Pepys is one of these.

Samuel Pepys was Clerk of the Acts to the Navy Board during the reign of Charles II. This was an important office in the government. Pepys had first-hand knowledge of happenings in parliament, at court and in London.

Pepys's account of the Great Fire is extremely vivid. It illustrates how valuable the diary has become to historians of the Stuart period.

2 September—Lords Day . . . Jane called us up, about three in the morning, to tell us of a great fire they saw in the City. So I rose, and slipped on my nightgown and went to her window, and thought it to be on the back side of Marketlane at the furthest; but being unused to such fires as fallowed, I thought it far enough off, and so went to bed again and to sleep. About seven I rose again to dress myself, and there looked out at the window and saw the fire not so much as it was, and further off. By and by Jane comes and tells me that she hears that above 300 houses have been burned down tonight by the fire we saw, and that it was now burning down all Fishstreet by London Bridge. So I made myself ready presently, and walked to the Tower . . . and there I did see the houses at that end of the bridge all on fire, and an infinite great fire on this and the other side the end of the bridge . . . So down, with my heart full of trouble, to the Lieutenant of the Tower, who tells me that it begun this morning in the King's bakers house in Pudding Lane, and that it hath burned down St Magnes Church and most part of Fishstreet already . . . Everybody endeavouring to remove their goods, and flinging into the river or bringing them into lighters that lay off. Poor people staying in their houses as long as till the very fire touched them, and then running into boats or

clambering from one pair of stair by the waterside to another.

Having stayed, and in an hour's time seen the fire rage every way, and nobody to my sight endeavouring to quench it, but to remove their goods and leave all to the fire; and having seen it get as far as the Steeleyard, and the wind mighty high and driving it into the city, and everything, after so long a drought, proving combustible, even the very stones of churches. I to Whitehall . . . and there up to the King's closet in the chapel . . . and word was carried in to the King, so I was called for and did tell the King and Duke of York what I saw, and that unless his Majesty did command houses to be pulled down, nothing could stop the fire. They seemed much troubled, and the King commanded me to go to my Lord Mayor from him and command him to spare no houses but to pull down before the fire every way. The Duke of York bid me tell him that if he would have any more soldiers, he shall . . . . At last met my Lord Mayor in Canning Streete, like a man spent, with a hankercher about his neck. To the King's message, he cried like a fainting woman, 'Lord, what can I do? I am spent! People will not obey me. I have been pull(ing) down houses. But the fire overtakes us faster then we can do it.' That he needed no more soldiers; and that for himself, he must go and refresh himself, having been up all night . . .

Having seen as much as I could now, I away to Whitehall by appointment, and there walked to St James's Park, and there met my wife and Creed and Wood and his wife and walked to my boat, and there upon the water again, and to the fire up and down, it still increasing and the wind great. So near the fire as we could for smoke; and all over the Thames, with one's face in the wind you were almost burned with a shower of firedrops . . . When we could endure no more upon the water, we to a little alehouse on the Bankside over against the Three Cranes, and there stayed till it was dark almost and saw the fire grow . . . in a most horrid malicious bloody flame, not like the fine flame of an ordinary fire, we saw the fire as only one entire arch of fire from this to the other side the bridge, and in a bow up the hill, for an arch of above a mile long.

1 According to Pepys, when did the Great Fire begin?
2 By the time Pepys saw the Lieutenant of the Tower, what were people doing?
3 What distressed Pepys most about the way people were behaving?
4 Whose advice did the king take about how to control the fire?
5 What had the Lord Mayor already tried to do?
6 How fiercely was the fire burning by nightfall?
7 How many of the answers to questions 1–6 would need to be checked with other historical sources? Why?
8 What other historical sources have been used in this chapter which could be compared with Pepys's account?

14

Colonisation of the New World

I N EARLIER CHAPTERS you learned how the Spanish and the Portuguese were leaders in world exploration. The Portuguese gained control of the spice trade with the East throughout the fifteenth and early sixteenth centuries by establishing trading bases and settlements along the coasts of East Africa and India. Once connections were firmly established they moved further to the East and set up bases in Malaysia. Sometimes they had to establish trading settlements by force, as Moslem merchants, who had been trading with the East for centuries, were reluctant to share their privileges with other traders.

The Spanish conquistadors in the New World were followed by friars and missionaries who wanted to educate and convert the conquered tribes. Spanish settlers in Mexico, South America and the West Indies exported gold and silver in order to pay for the imported goods they needed to survive. Much of the wealth which poured into Spain was spent on extravagant displays in the royal court and on payment of Spanish armies. After Magellan's voyage colonies were also established in the Philippines.

By 1600 other European countries had challenged the supremacy of Spain and Portugal. Holland decided to obtain spices directly from the East. England and France, as well as trading with the East, concentrated their efforts on settling North America. This chapter focuses on the life

of the early colonists in North America and the difficulties they faced and overcame.

England's first attempts

During the reign of Elizabeth I, England became prosperous. Trade with other countries had brought wealth to England. Industries such as the production of woollen cloth were flourishing. Since 1568, after the sinking of a English trading fleet off the coast of South America, English seadogs had been raiding Spanish ships returning from the New World. The final blow was the raid staged by Sir Francis Drake in 1577, after which he circumnavigated the world. As you read in Chapter Twelve, this was a cause of the famous sea battle between England and Spain in 1588, in which the Spanish Armada was defeated. For England, the defeat of the Armada meant that Spanish dominance of the New World could be challenged. The way to do this seemed to be by establishing colonies in North America.

Before the defeat of the Armada England had tried to establish settlements in the New World but all had failed. Colonists had taken all that they thought was necessary for survival, but the combination of a foreign climate, often hostile Indians and food shortages defeated them.

Sir Humphrey Gilbert had been given permission by Elizabeth I to found a colony in 1583 in

Newfoundland. Gilbert intended this colony to be a base for attacking the Spanish, but the venture failed.

Sir Walter Raleigh was the next Elizabethan courtier to attempt the founding of a colony. He decided to try further south, near the area he had named Virginia in honour of the unmarried Queen. The site eventually chosen was Roanoke Island, near the modern state of North Carolina in the USA. The first settlement in 1584 failed after a year when supplies ran out and the colonists returned to England.

A second attempt was made, again supported by Raleigh, in 1587. Greater efforts were made to organise the colony and each settler was given a large tract of land. The governor of the colony, John White, soon realised that the settlers did not have the right supplies and so returned to England. When he got there he was unable to return to the colony immediately because of the war with Spain. When he finally arrived with the supplies in 1590 he found the colony deserted and all the settlers gone. No trace was ever found of them.

Time to understand

The first attempts at colonisation failed but a detailed record of the 1587 attempt on Roanoke Island has been left by John White. The extract below gives some idea of what the difficulties were. In this case, it was hostile Indians.

> They conveied themselves secretly behind the trees, neere the houses, where our men carelesly lived: and having perceaved that of those 15, they could see but 11. Only two of those Savages appeared to the 11 Englishmen, calling to them by friendly signes, that but two of their chiefest men should come unarmed to speak with those two Savages, who seemed also to be unarmed. Wherefore two of the chiefest of our Englishmen went gladly to them: but whilst one of those Savages traitorously embraced one of our men, the other with his sword of wood, which he had secretly hidden under his mantell, stroke him on the head, and slewe him, and presently the other eight and twentie Savages shewed themselves: the other Englishman perceiving this, fled to his

companie, whom the Savages pursued with their bows and arrows, so fast, that the Englishmen were forced to take the house, wherein all their victuall and weapons were: but the Savages forthwith set the same on fire, by meanes whereof, our men were forced to take up such weapons as came first to hand, and without order to runforth among the Savages, with whom they skirmished above an houre. The place where they fought was of great advantage to the Savages, by means of the thick trees, behind which the Savages, through their nimblenes defended themselves, and so offended our men with their arrowes, that our men being some of them hurt, retired fighting to the water side, where their boate lay, with which they fled towards Hatorask . . . in the morning so early, that it was yet dark, we landed neere the dwelling place of our enemies, and very secretly conveyed ourselves through the woods, to that side, where we had their houses between us and the water: and having espied their fire, and some sitting about it we presently set on them: the miserable soules herewith amased, fledde into a place of thick reedes, growing fast by, where our men perceiving them, shotte one of them through the bodie with a bullet, and therewith wee entered the reedes, among which we hoped to acquite their evil doing towards us, but wee were deceaved, for those Savages were our friendes, and were come from Croatoan.

1 Why would the Englishmen have approached the Indians?
2 What advantages did the Indians have over the settlers?
3 How did the English retaliate?
4 Using this extract outline what you think may have been the main difficulty in dealing with the Indians.

The colony of Virginia

There were two main reasons for the founding of the early English colonies in America. One reason was for profit, the other to escape religious persecution. The colony of Virginia, founded in 1607 during the reign of James I, was founded by people who hoped to make money.

The experience gained from Sir Walter

Fig. 14.1 An Indian wearing ceremonial paint.

Raleigh's ventures showed that the money needed for establishing colonies was more than one or two individuals could provide. How was money raised to found a colony?

In England there had been an increase in the number of joint-stock companies. People who had a surplus amount of money would buy a share or a number of shares in a company for some purpose, such as trade, the retrieving of sunken treasure or the draining and reclaiming of land. The Virginia Company of London was given permission by James I to establish a colony in 1606.

Shares in the company were sold for £12 10s 0d, which was the estimated cost of establishing a settler. Most investors hoped that in return for their investment a profit would be made from the discovery of gold or silver. Each settler who went at his own expense was promised a share when it came to the return of profits.

An advance party was sent out to find a suitable place for settlement. The site chosen was a peninsula on the James River which was more accessible than Roanoke Island and also easily defended.

In May 1607 the first expedition, consisting of 144 colonists, arrived at Jamestown, as it was called. As well as being instructed to look for gold and silver, the settlers were also told to look for a river that flowed into the 'East India Sea', in the hope of finding the north-west passage to the East. James I also expected the settlers to 'civilise' the Indians and convert them to Christianity. The Indians would then need to buy English products, and this new market would earn more profits for England.

The voyage out took much longer than expected. As a result, there was little time to erect suitable shelters for the coming winter. Quarrels broke out among the settlers, as some looked for gold and others felt it necessary to secure their position from possible Indian attacks. Most settlers felt that their needs were going to be supplied by the Virginia Company and so did not think to plant corn for the next season.

Winter was disastrous for the colonists. More than half the colonists died due to diseases such as malaria, dysentery and typhoid. Some Indians were friendly, while others attacked the colony

Fig. 14.2 A model of the fort at Jamestown.

or killed men who went out exploring. The president of the colony at the time could do little to control the colonists, about whom Captain John Smith, who later became president, said that many 'would rather starve or rot with idleness, than be persuaded to do anything for their own relief'.

The search for gold and silver and for the passage to the East was fruitless. The settlers were forced to bargain with the friendly Indians for food.

The situation changed in late 1608 when John Smith was elected president of the colony. Under his leadership the colony became more organised and anybody who would not work was not allowed a share in the provisions. Smith also insisted that the colonists plant corn using Indian methods of cultivation. Smith was forced to return to England in 1609 for treatment of a wound. The next two years were the worst the colony had faced.

In 1609 the Virginia Company sent out a new fleet with more settlers and supplies. The ship carried a new governor, rather than an elected president. However, it disappeared off the coast of Bermuda on the way. The remaining settlers arrived at the end of the summer.

From 1609 to 1611 the settlers were reduced to eating cats, rats, dogs and even leather in an effort to stay alive. Over 400 died before 1611. When only sixty settlers remained they decided to return to England. The ships were ready to sail when the new governor, Lord Delaware, arrived from Bermuda, bringing new supplies and reinforcements.

The colony then progressed slowly, under a harsh system of laws. There was little to export, and many investors in the Virginia Company gave up hope of seeing a return for their investment.

By 1614 a suitable crop for export had been found—tobacco. It had become fashionable to smoke in London. The colony had made peace with the main Indian tribe in Virginia, the Powhatans. This was achieved by the marriage of Chief Powhatan's daughter, Pocahontas, to an English settler, John Rolfe.

It seemed that the most difficult years of the colony had passed, but there was still no return

Fig. 14.3 Smoking tobacco in 1625.

for investors. Private ownership of land had been introduced instead of communal use of land. This was an incentive for people to migrate and for settlers to work hard. By 1622 there were 4500 settlers in Virginia. Then disaster struck again.

In 1618 the Indian chief who had made peace with the Jamestown settlers died. The new chief, Opechancanough, wanted to drive the Jamestown settlers out of Virginia, but he allowed his people to continue mixing with the settlers for some years. Then, on Good Friday, 1622 the Powhatans struck Jamestown and outlying settlements with such force that over 300 men, women and children died in the massacre.

For two years the settlers and the Indians warred against each other. Finally, in 1624, the Indians were forced to ask for peace. The settlers had won due to their superior weapons. Plague had also broken out in the colony during the Indian war so that by 1623 there were only about 1200 settlers left.

The strain of supporting a colony with little return finally caused the Virginia Company to collapse in 1623. Virginia became a royal colony, with a governor appointed by the king. Virginia had passed through its darkest days. It then began to develop as a strong and more prosperous colony.

The Pilgrims

The second successful colony founded in North America by the English was established for religious reasons. Those who braved the risky sea voyage and an unknown future have been called the Pilgrims.

During the reign of Elizabeth I people who wanted to reform the Church of England were called Puritans. They felt that church services could be 'purified' and that the clergy had too much power. After the religious settlement, which you learned about in Chapter Twelve, Puritans began to hold their own services. In 1593 a law was passed to forbid this, but the services continued in secret.

When James I came to the throne in 1603 the Puritans tried once again to achieve religious reform. However, James wanted to please the majority of his subjects. He continued the religious policy of Elizabeth.

By 1607 Puritans were feeling the pressure of the laws passed against them. A group which had been meeting in the village of Scrooby in Nottinghamshire decided to leave England. They chose to go to Holland, where they felt they would be free to practise their own form of religion. They left in secret as they feared that James I would try to stop them.

After living in Amsterdam for a year the

Fig. 14.4 The manor house at Scrooby where Puritans met.

Puritans who had migrated from Scrooby found that they disagreed with other Puritans who had also migrated to Amsterdam. So in 1607 they moved to the city of Leyden.

Life in Leyden was more difficult than the Scrooby Puritans had imagined. Work was difficult to find and one complained: 'How like we were to lose our language, and our name, of English . . . How unable there, to give such education to our children as we ourselves have received.'

Some began to think that it would be better if they migrated to the New World. After much debate two of the Puritans were sent to London to ask the Virginia Company to finance their voyage. The Pilgrims were granted a patent, or right, to found a fishing and fur-trading settlement on the Hudson River. Only about forty of the Puritans at Leyden decided to go.

Two ships, the *Mayflower* and the *Speedwell* were fitted for the voyage. The small fleet picked up more crew and Pilgrims in Plymouth, England before sailing in late 1620. The *Speedwell* proved unseaworthy and so was forced to return to England. Some people decided to return to England with it.

Finally about one hundred Pilgrims, plus the crew, crowded aboard the *Mayflower* to make the hazardous voyage. One person died at sea, but a child was born, which kept the number of Pilgrims the same.

Fig. 14.5 Cape Cod, the landing place of the Pilgrims.

The *Mayflower* landed much further north of the Jamestown settlement than was planned. The colony, at Cape Cod, was called Plymouth. It was December, so the Pilgrims had no time to build the necessary houses to survive the winter. To add to their difficulties, the fishing equipment brought out from England proved inadequate.

During a long and difficult winter half the Pilgrims died from disease or malnutrition. The Pilgrims, however, still felt God was with them, and that they had come to the New World to do 'God's work'.

The Pilgrims had expected trouble from the Indians but found that the Indian population in the area had been largely wiped out by a smallpox epidemic. Some of the Indians who survived could speak English, which they had learned from fishermen who had fished off Cape Cod before the arrival of the Pilgrims.

These Indians taught inexperienced Pilgrims how to fish and hunt, and to cultivate corn, squash and beans. One Indian, Squanto, acted as an interpreter between the Pilgrims and the Indians. By autumn 1621, the Pilgrims were well established and they celebrated their first successful harvest with a feast. They called the feast Thanksgiving, during which they thanked God for helping them overcome their hardships. They invited Massasoit, the Indian chief, and ninety of his braves to the feast. Thanksgiving is still celebrated in North America today.

The Plymouth colony continued to develop and by 1627 good profits were being made from fishing and fur trading. The Pilgrims then began to pay off their debt to the 'adventurers' who had financed their original voyage. More Pilgrims had arrived in the colony, including some of the Puritans who had stayed behind in Leyden.

Fig. 14.6 The first Thanksgiving.

Time to understand

The passenger list of the Mayflower

*Denotes people who died during the first winter.

1 Alden, Mr. John (21)
2 Alderton, Mr. John (21)*
3 Alltterton, Master Bartholomew (8)
4 Allerton, Mr. Isaac (34)
5 Allerton, Miss Mary (4)
6 Allerton, Mrs. Mary Norris (32)*
7 Allerton, Miss Remember (6)
8 Billington, Mrs. Ellen/Eleanor/Helen (32)
9 Billington, Master Francis (14)
10 Billington, Mr. John (36)
11 Billington, Master John (8)
12 Bradford, Mrs. Dorothy May (23)*
13 Bradford, Elder William (31)
14 Brewster, Master Love (9)
15 Brewster, Mrs. Mary (52)
16 Brewster, Elder William (54)
17 Brewster, Master Wrestling (6)
18 Britteridge, Mr. Richard (21+)*
19 Browne, Mr. Peter (20)
20 Butten, Mr. William (died at sea) (22)
21 Carter, Mr. Robert*
22 Carver, Deacon John (54)*
23 Carver, Mrs. Catherine White Leggatt (40)*
24 Chilton, Mr. James (57)*
25 Chilton, Miss Mary (15)
26 Chilton, Mrs. Susanna*
27 Clarke, Mr. Richard*
28 Cooke, Mr. Francis (43)
29 Cooke, Master John (8)
30 Cooper, Miss Humility (8)
31 Crackston, Mr. John (35)*
32 Crackston, Master John
33 Dotey, Mr. Edward (27)
34 Eaton, Mr. Francis (25)
35 Eaton, Mrs. Sarah (30)*
36 Eaton, Master Samuel (infant)
37 Ely, Mr. (seaman)
38 English, Mr. Thomas (30 at least)*
39 Fletcher, Mr. Moses (38 at least)*
40 Fuller, Mrs. Ann*
41 Fuller, Mr. Edward (25? 45?)*
42 Fuller, Master Samuel (5)
43 Fuller, Dr. Samuel (35)
44 Gardiner, Mr. Richard (20)
45 Goodman, Mr. John (25)*
46 Holbeck, Mr. William*
47 Hooke, Master John (13–14)*
48 Hopkins, Miss Constanta (15)
49 Hopkins, Miss Damaris (3)
50 Hopkins, Mrs. Elizabeth (at least 20)
51 Hopkins, Master Giles (13)
52 Hopkins, Master Oceanus (born on voyage)*
53 Hopkins, Mr. Stephen (35)
54 Howland, Mr. John (28)
55 Langemore, Mr. John*
56 Latham, Mr William
57 Leister, Mr. Edward
58 Margerson, Mr. Edward*
59 Martin, Mr. Christopher (45)*
60 Martin, Mrs. Marie Prower (at least 40)*
61 Minter, Miss Desire (20)
62 More, Miss Ellen (8)*
63 More, Master Jasper (6)*
64 More, Master Richard (7)
65 More, Master (brother to Richard)*
66 Mullins, Mrs. Alice*
67 Mullins, Master Joseph (6)*
68 Mullins, Miss Priscilla (18)
69 Mullins, Mr. William (40)*
70 Priest, Mr. Digerie (40)*
71 Prower, Mr. Solomon*
72 Rigdale, Mrs. Alice*
73 Rigdale, Mr. John*
74 Rogers, Master Joseph (12)
75 Rogers, Mr. Thomas (30+)*
76 Sampson, Master Henry (6)
77 Sowle, Mr. George (21)
78 Standish, Captain Miles (36)
79 Standish, Mrs. Rose*
80 Story, Mr. Elias (42)*
81 Thomson, Mr. Edward*
82 Tilley, Mrs. Ann*
83 Tilley, Mrs. Bridget van der Velde*
84 Tilley, Mr. Edward (46)*
85 Tilley, Mr. John (49)*
86 Tilley, Miss Elizabeth (14)
87 Tinker, Mr. Thomas (39)*
88 Tinker, Mrs. Thomas*
89 Tinker, Master (son of above)*
90 Trevor, Mr. William (21 approx.)
91 Turner, Mrs. John (35)*
92 Turner, Master (elder son of above)*
93 Turner, Master (younger son of above)*
94 Warren, Mr. Richard (40)
95 White, Master Peregrine (born on arrival)

96 White, Master Resolved (5)
97 White, Mrs. Susanna Fuller (26)
98 White, Mr. William (28)*
99 Wilder, Mr. Roger*
100 Williams, Mr. Thomas*
101 Winslow, Mr. Edward (25)
102 Winslow, Mrs. Elizabeth Barker (23)*
103 Winslow, Mr. Gilbert (20)

a How many families were aboard the Mayflower? List them in order of size.

b How many children sailed to Plymouth on this voyage? How old was the youngest? the eldest? How many children died during the first winter?

c What was the proportion of adult males to adult females before arrival? What was the proportion after the first winter?

d Which Christian names seem unusual to you? Look up the meaning of these names in a dictionary or an encyclopaedia. Why would Pilgrims have given their children these names?

The growth of English colonies

By 1750 there were thirteen English colonies in North America. Four of these colonies formed a group called New England. The earliest of these, Massachusetts, was founded in 1629, not far from where the Pilgrims had settled at Plymouth.

The Massachusetts colony was organised by Puritan leaders. People who disagreed with the strict Puritan organisation broke away and formed the other New England colonies of Connecticut, Rhode Island and New Hampshire. All these colonies relied on fishing, whaling, fur trading and later, shipbuilding, for their incomes.

Another group of colonies was that formed by New York, New Jersey, Delaware and Pennsylvania. Of these, New York grew to be the most prosperous. The area was originally settled by the Dutch in 1623 and called New Amsterdam. The English took over the settlement in 1644, re-naming it New York. New York derived its wealth from the fur trade.

Pennsylvania was founded by another religious group seeking freedom, the Quakers. The founder, William Penn, named the main settlement Philadelphia, which means the city of brotherly love. He believed that all people could work and live as friends, no matter what their religious beliefs were. By 1775 Philadelphia was the second largest English city after London. Obviously other people were willing to try life in the city of brotherly love!

The colonies of Maryland, Virginia, North and South Carolina and Georgia formed the 'South'. The main products produced by the South were tobacco, rice and indigo, a plant which yielded a dark blue dye. Most farms, or plantations as they were called, were huge. Negro slaves were imported from Africa to work on the plantations. The colony of Georgia was founded in 1733 to prevent Spanish expansion from Florida.

If you look at Fig. 14.7 you will see that all the colonies were on the Atlantic or east coast of North America. Some attempts had been made to move further west but the Appalachian Mountains were almost impenetrable. Indian tribes were also a major problem. The opening up of the lands in the west of the continent required the conquest of strong tribes such as the Cherokees and the Iroquois.

The process of settlement was slow. The need for more land for new settlers was the main driving force in overcoming the obstacles. Many settlers made their profits from trapping and hunting animals for their furs, as farming was unpredictable. Crops or markets could fail, tools and seed needed to be bought. The movement west by English and European settlers has become legendary. The Hollywood 'western' has made names such as Daniel Boone, Buffalo Bill, Wild Bill Hickock, Jesse James, Wyatt Earp, Doc Holliday, Billy the Kid, Davey Crockett, Geronimo, Sitting Bull, Cochise and Cheyenne well known throughout the English-speaking world. These men were all part of the movement west, or, on the Indian side, the resistance to it.

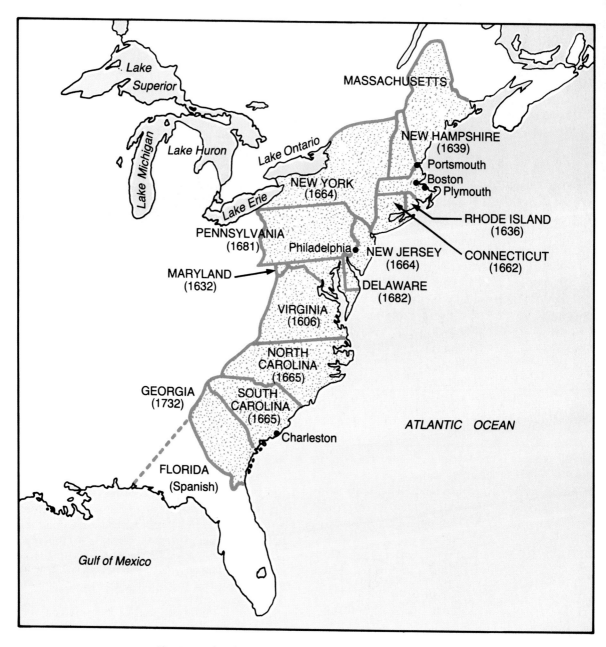

Fig. 14.7 The thirteen colonies in North America, 1750.

Fig. 14.8 William Penn buying land from Indians.

Time to understand

In 1631 Captain John Smith, the governor of Virginia, published advertisements designed to attract more settlers to New England. Fig. 14.10 shows the title page of one of these pamphlets.

The extract below is from Chapter Twelve of the pamphlet.

> For the building of houses, townes, and fortresses, where shall a man finde the like conveniency, as stones of most forts, as well lime stone, if I be not much deceived, as Iron stone, smooth stone, blue slate for covering houses, and great rockes we supposed Marble, so that one place is called the marble harbour. There is grasse plenty, though very long and thicke stalked, which being neither mowne nor eaten, is very ranke, yet all their cattell like and prosper well therewith, but indeed it is weeds, herbs, and grasse growing together, which although they be good and sweet in the Summer, they will deceive your cattell in winter; therefore be carefull in the Spring to mow the swamps, and the low lands of Auguan, where you may have harsh sheare-grasse enough to make hay of, till you can cleare ground to make pasture, which will beare as good grasse as can grow any where, as now it doth in Virginia; and unless you make this provision, if there come an extraordinary winter, you will lose many of them & hazard the rest ...
>
> The best way wee found in Virginia to spoile the woods, was first to cut a notch in the barke a hand broad round about the tree, which peel off and the tree will sprout no more, and all the small boughs in a year or two will decay, the greatest branches in the root they spoyle with fire, but you with more ease may cut them from the body and they will quickly rot: betwixt those trees they plant their corne, whose great bodies doe much defend it from extreme gusts, and heat

245

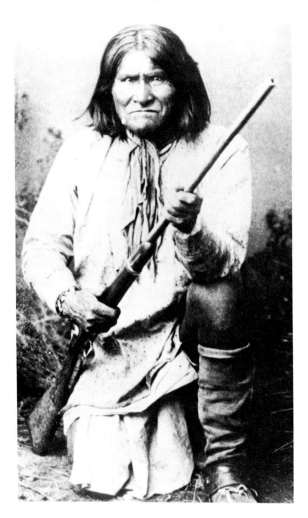

Fig. 14.9 Geronimo, leader of the Apache tribe, one of the last to resist the westward expansion of European settlement.

of the Sunne, where that in the plaines, where the trees by time they have consumed, is subject to both; and this is the most easie way to have pasture and cornefields, which is much more fertile than the other.

1. What building materials were available? Would settlers have used most of these? Why?
2. What advice does John Smith give settlers about the native grasses? Does it sound convincing? Why?
3. What does he mean by 'spoile the woods'? Why would this be necessary?

ADVERTISEMENTS
For the unexperienced Planters of
New-England, or any where.
OR,
The Path-way to experience to erect a
PLANTATION.

With the yearely proceedings of this Country in Fiſhing and Planting, ſince the yeare 1614. to the yeare 1630. and their preſent eſtate.

Alſo how to prevent the greateſt inconveniences, by their proceedings in Virginia, *and other Plantations, by approved examples.*

With the Countries Armes, a deſcription of the Coaſt, Harbours, Habitations, Land-markes, Latitude and Longitude: with the Map, allowed by our Royall King CHARLES.

By Captaine IOHN SMITH, ſometimes Governour of VIRGINIA, and Admirall of NEVV-ENGLAND.

LONDON,
Printed by IOHN HAVILAND, and are to be ſold by ROBERT MILBOVRNE, at the Grey-hound in *Pauls* Church-yard. 1631.

Fig. 14.10 An advertisement to attract new colonists.

French colonies in North America

The man considered the founder of French Canada is Jacques Cartier. In 1635 he explored the St Lawrence River as far as modern Montreal. He reported that the area abounded with fish and fur animals. The French government did nothing to follow up his exploration until 1604. Only a few French fishermen took advantage of his report by sailing annually to the Canadian coast to fish and trade furs with the Indians.

The small settlement founded in 1604 at the mouth of the St Croix river failed. Winters were long and bitterly cold. After three years the settlers gave up and returned to France.

In 1608 a second attempt was made at Quebec on the St Lawrence River. Although more than half the settlers died during the first winter, the leader of the settlement, Samuel de Champlain, explored the area during the summer with the help of Huron and Algonquin Indians.

The Hurons and Algonquins traded furs for iron axes, knives, woollen blankets, mirrors and trinkets. These Indians used the weapons provided by the French against the Iroquois Indians, who became the enemies of the French.

The settlement flourished and a second colony was established further upstream at Montreal. Even though the profits to be made from the fur trade were good, the settlements were very small. It was not until 1627 that a plan was adopted by the French to promote migration to 'New France'.

The French were more concerned with converting the Indians to Christianity than the English were. Jesuit priests arrived in New France in 1625. They often accompanied explorers on their expeditions.

French exploration extended the area of the fur trade further until the French controlled the Great Lakes area. In 1672 Louis Joliet and Father Jacques Marquette explored the Mississippi River as far as its junction with the Arkansas River. Their exploration was followed up in 1682 by Robert La Salle who explored the Ohio and Mississippi rivers, eventually reaching the Gulf of Mexico. He claimed the whole of this area for France, naming it Louisiana. Forts were built along the river system but it was not until 1700 that the French government founded a colony at New Orleans, near the mouth of Mississippi.

Fig. 14.11 The discovery of Niagara Falls by the French.

By 1750 the area controlled by France was much greater than that settled by the English, but the English population far exceeded the French. Louis XIV, king of France from 1661 to 1715, promoted migration to Canada by granting land to retired soldiers. Peasants were also sent out as small farmers. Even girls for the settlers to marry were regularly shipped across the Atlantic. Any single men who seemed to be avoiding marriage were fined and prevented from fur trading. No one was allowed to return to France without official permission. However, despite all these efforts, the French population was only 90 000 by 1750.

Rivalry between the French and the English in North America grew throughout the eighteenth century. The English were prevented from further expansion by the presence of the French. Finally war broke out in 1754, involving Indian tribes as well. In 1763, the English emerged victorious after a long struggle. England gained the territory of Canada and territory to the east of the Mississippi River. Spain, an ally of France, surrendered the colony of Florida to England. Spain, however, gained the territory west of the Mississippi River.

Time to understand

The extract below compares the English colonies with the French colonies in 1748, fifteen years before the French were defeated by the English.

> It is to be observed that each English colony in North America is independent of the other, and that each has its proper laws and coin, and may be looked upon in several lights, as a state by itself. From hence it happens, that in time of war, things go on very slowly and irregularly here: while the people are quarrelling about the best and cheapest manner of carrying on the war, an enemy has it in his power to take one place after another . . .
> The French in Canada, who are but an inconsiderable body in comparison with the English in America, have by this position of affairs been able to obtain great advantages in times of war; for it we judge from the number and power of the English, it would seem very

247

easy for them to get the better of the French in America . . .

For the English colonies in this part of the world have increased so much in their number of inhabitants, and in their riches, that they almost vie with Old England.

I have been told by Englishmen, and not only by such as were born in America, but even by such as came from Europe, that the English colonies in North America, in the space of thirty or fifty years, would be able to form a state by themselves, entirely independent [of] Old England. But as the whole country which lies along the sea shore, is unguarded, and on the land side is harassed by the French, in times of war these dangerous neighbours are sufficient to prevent the connection of the colonies with their mother country from being quite broken off. The English government has therefore sufficient reason to consider the French in North America as the best means of keeping the colonies in their due submission . . .

1 What did the writer mean when he said that each English colony was 'independent of the other'? How could he tell?
2 How was 'independence' a disadvantage to the English during times of war?
3 Why would it have been easy for the English 'to get the better of the French in America'?
4 Why does the writer feel that 'Old England' wanted to leave the French colonies in North America as they were?

The North American Indians

Before the arrival of the English and the French, North America was inhabited by approximately a million Indians. There were hundreds of different tribes, each with its own customs.

The Indians probably came to North America from Asia when the two continents were joined by land, between 20 000 and 50 000 years ago. By the time the English and the French arrived most tribes were leading settled lives in villages surrounded by fields in which they grew crops. They also collected berries and nuts, and hunted and fished.

Fig. 14.12 Inside a New England settler's house.

The differing customs of each tribe confused Europeans. Some tribes were friendly, others were hostile. The Indians were also confused by the behaviour of the Europeans, especially when they realised that they did not always agree. Some Europeans earned a reputation for fair dealing with the Indians, such as the Quakers of Pennsylvania, while others cruelly mistreated the Indians.

The Europeans saw the Indians as 'noble savages' at first. When artists drew Indians they simply made them look like Europeans without any clothes. An early settler of Roanoke Island describes them as 'very handsome and goodly people, and in their behavior as mannerly and civil as any of Europe'. Such reports were usually made by people who tried to encourage settlers to come to the New World. It was also suggested that Indians could be converted to Christianity, although few of the English colonists attempted to achieve this.

After the 1622 massacre at Jamestown the Indians were thought of more as 'brute beasts' and 'treacherous devils in human shape'. This view of the Indians made it easier for Europeans

Fig. 14.13 An Iroquois Indian scalping a victim.

to conquer the Indians without a guilty conscience.

Sometimes Europeans bribed the Indians to fight for them. In the Seven Years' War between the French and the English, Indians were used by both sides.

As the Europeans moved west, Indian tribes were forced off the land they inhabited. Often Europeans 'bought' the land from the Indians. However, as Indians did not feel they owned the land, they often did not realise what they were selling. Sometimes Indians continued to hunt on the land they had 'sold', angering the Europeans who thought they had bought it.

The Indians believed that all natural things, such as the land, water, wildlife, fruits and plants, were not owned by individuals. They thought that all the things of nature were gifts from the Great Spirit, or God, to be used by the whole tribe with gratitude and care. When Indians killed a buffalo they used the whole animal. After eating the meat, the hide could be used for clothing or for shelter. Even the bones were made into needles for sewing leather. Indians thought that everything in nature was interrelated. This is why they could not understand Europeans coming to America believing they had a 'right' to possess land. When asked to sell his land one Indian chief said: 'Sell the land? Why not sell the air, the clouds, the great sea?'

When Indians were forced off their land they often retreated to hunting grounds occupied by other tribes. This caused great tension, and often war between neighbouring tribes. Some tribes felt they had lost everything when they were forced to give up the land which they had inhabited all their lives. Some tribes are now extinct. Of the surviving Indians, some live on reservations which were eventually given to them, while others live in the cities, towns and the countryside of the USA.

Fig. 14.14 Pocahontas, a Powhatan Indian who married the Englishman John Rolfe, dressed in English clothes.

Fig. 14.15 Florida Indians hunting deer.

The Powhatans, who at first welcomed the Jamestown settlers, were typical of the eastern coastal tribes. The chief, Powhatan, guided his people with the aid of a council. Each clan, or family, within the tribe, had an elder.

Powhatan had conquered many villages in the area. He collected tribute from these villages and this had made him wealthy.

Clothes were made by the women, but these consisted of little more than a skin apron. Deer-skins were worn in the winter for warmth. Women wore their hair long, whilst men shaved the sides of their head leaving an upright crest down the centre. The crest was often decorated with feathers.

The Powhatans are well known because of the story about the chief's daughter Pocahontas.

When the Jamestown settlers first arrived the Powhatans were unsure about the Englishmen. Captain John Smith was captured and brought before Chief Powhatan. Some of the Indians wanted to execute Smith but his life was saved by Pocahontas who threw herself down to protect him from the axe. Later, as you learned, she married John Rolfe. She was taken to England where she died of smallpox, after only a couple of years.

When Pocahontas and her father Powhatan died the peace between the Powhatans and the English came to an abrupt halt. The 1622 massacre followed. Gradually the Europeans overcame the Powhatans so that by about 1650 the Powhatans had been totally conquered and forced off their land.

How do we know?

The extracts below are taken from a speech by Chief Seattle, chief of the Dwamish tribe, when he was forced to surrender land in 1854. It is a good record of Indian thought on land use and abuse.

The Great Chief in Washington sends word that he wishes to buy our land. The Great Chief also sends us words of friendship and goodwill. This is kind of him, since we know he has little need of our friendship in return. But we will consider your offer.

For we know that if we do not sell, the white man may come with guns and take our land. The idea is strange to us. If we do not own the freshness of the air and the sparkle of the water, how can you buy them? Every part of this earth is sacred to my people. Every shining pine needle, every sandy shore, every mist in the dark woods, every clearing and humming insect is holy in the memory and experience of my people. The sap which courses through the trees carries the memories of the red man . . .

The air is precious to the red man, for all things share the same breath—the beast, the tree, the man, they all share the same breath. The white man does not seem to notice the air he breathes. Like a man dying for many days, he is numb to the stench.

But if we sell you our land, you must remember that the air is precious to us, that the air shares its spirit with all the life it supports. The wind that gave our grandfather his first breath, also receives his last sigh, and the wind must also give our children the spirit of life.

This we know, the earth does not belong to man; man belongs to the earth. This we know, all things are connected, like the blood which unites one family. All things are connected. Whatever befalls the earth, befalls the sons of the earth.

Man did not weave the web of life; he is merely a strand in it. Whatever he does to the web, he does to himself . . .

Even the white man, whose God walks and talks with him as friend to friend, cannot be exempt from the common destiny. We may be brothers after all; we shall see. One thing we know, which the white man may one day discover—our God is the same God. You may think now that you own Him as you wish to own our land, but you cannot. He is the God of man, and His compassion is equal for the red man and the white. This earth is precious to Him, and to harm the earth is to heap contempt on its Creator. The whites too shall pass; perhaps sooner than all other tribes.

1 Why did American settlers offer to buy Indian land? Using extracts from Chief Seattle's speech, explain why Indians never understood why white men wanted to buy the land.
2 Explain why Indians regarded the earth as the 'mother of the red man'?
3 Why did Indians think the air was precious? Do modern people think air is precious? How can you tell?
4 Why does Chief Seattle say that 'whatever he does to the web, he does to himself'? Can you think of any examples which show that this is so today?
5 Why does Chief Seattle predict that 'The whites too shall pass; perhaps sooner than all other tribes'?
6 After reading the extract, would you say you understand the Indians' point of view? Why would Europeans of the seventeenth, eighteenth and nineteenth centuries not have understood this point of view?

Acknowledgements

For permission to reproduce photographs and illustrations we should like to thank the following: Aerofilms Limited, England, Figs. 3.21, 7.10; Archaelogical Survey of India, Fig. 1.16; Archives Publiques du Canada (Division de l'Iconographie, Direction des Archives), Ottawa, Ont. Canada, Fig. 14.9 (C4236); Archivio Fotografico dei Musei Vaticani, Vatican City, Figs. 8.12, 8.13; Ashmolean Museum, Oxford, England, Figs. 2.11, 12.11 (DB 4 Holbein: *A Young Englishwoman*), 13.7 (CIII 198 *The Execution of Charles I* [Bancket House]); Barnaby's Picture Library, London, Fig. 1.14; BBC Hulton Picture Library, London, Figs. 4.16, 5.6, 5.14–16, 6.2, 6.16–17, 7.2, 7.11, 7.14–15, 8.7–8, 11.7–8, 12.16, 13.2–3, 13.8, 14.4; The Bible Society, London, Fig. 11.4; Biblioteca Nazionale Centrale, Florence, Italy, Figs. 8.11, 10.5; Biblioteca Medicea Laurenziana, Florence, Fig. 10.3; Bibliotheque Nationale, Paris, France, Figs 7.8. (FR. 2630), 9.4 (FR. 2810); Bodleian Library, Oxford, Fig. 10.18 (MS Arch.Seld.A 1); The British Library, London, Figs. 2.15 (MS Cotton Nero D.IV, folio 139), 3.7 (Ada 10546), 6.12, 11.1 (Woodcut from Johann Litenburger's *Prenostication*, 1497); British Museum, London, Figs. 2.5 (PS063273), 2.13 (Sutton Hoo Collection, Neg. no K 3078), 2.14 (Sutton Hoo Collection, Neg. no. K200), 4.20, 13.18; B.V. Uitgeversmaatschappij Elsevier, Amsterdam, The Netherlands, Fig. 10.12; City of Bristol Museum & Art Gallery, England, Figs. 4.9, 9.18; Mr Simon Wingfield Digby, Sherborne Castle, Sherborne, Dorset, England, Fig. 12.4 (*Procession of Queen Elizabeth I*, attributed to Robert Peake the Elder); Edimedia, Paris, France, Fig. 6.15 (Guerrier Musulman. Neg. no. P. 5441); Foreign Language Press, Beijing 37, People's Republic of China, Fig. 4.10; John Freeman Group, London, Figs. 2.20–21 (The Fotomas Index ref. May 85241—Bayeux Tapestry); Historical Pictures Service, Inc., Chicago, USA, Fig. 9.5 (Neg. no. 3–20–31–25); Her Majesty The Queen of England, Fig. 12.3 (from the Royal Collection); Historiographical Institute, University of Tokyo, Japan, Fig. 5.11 ('Tōkaidō Takanawa ushigoya'); International Society for Educational Information, Inc. Tokyo, Fig. 5.3 (Haniwa-warrior with Sword and Armour) in Tokyo National Museum; Istanbul University, Istanbul, Turkey, Fig. 1.13 (by Matrakci Nasuh); Japanese Information Centre, Embassy of Japan, London, Figs. 5.9–10; Library of Congress, Washington DC, USA Figs. 14.8 (*Penn's Treaty with the Indians* Neg. no. LC–USZ62–3933), 14.13 (*Guerrier Iroquois*, plate 31, Rare Books GT70.G7), 14.15 (Florida Indians hunting deer, neg. no. C–USZ62–31871); Magdalene College, Cambridge, England, Fig. 13.13 (Keeling's Fire Engine) by permission of the Master and Fellows; The Mansell Collection, London, Figs. 3.5, 3.24, 6.11, 6.22, 7.1, 7.4, 7.9, 7.12, 7.16–17, 9.4, 11.5–6, 12.20, 12.23, 13.11, 14.2, 14.5; Merseyside County Museum, Liverpool, England, Figs. 10.4 (Neg. no. N64.996), 10.15 (Neg. no. CN67 (69).968), 10.16 (Neg. no. N68.1), 10.17 (Neg. no. N66.330.) all from Codex Fejervary–Mayer, accession no. 12014 Mayer; Musée National de Louvre, Paris, France, Figs. 8.2–3; Museum of London, England, Figs. 12.14 (Copperplate map of Moorfields in 1559), 13.12; National Portrait Gallery, London, Figs. 11.9, 12.2, 12.10, 13.4, 13.6, 13.15–16, 13.19; National Portrait Gallery, Smithsonian Institution, Washington, DC, Fig. 14.14 (Pocahontas, c. 1595–1617, unidentified artist, English school, after the 1616 engraving by Simon van de Passe. Oil on canvas. 77×64 cm. After 1616 NPG.65.61 [now believed to be 18C]; New York Public Library, New York, USA, Figs. 6.6–7, 6.10 (three illustrations from *Siyar-j Nabi* [MS3], Spencer Collection, Astor, Lenox and Tilden Foundations); Offentliche Kunstsammlung, Kunstmuseum Basel, Switzerland, Fig. 8.10 (*Ambrosius Holbein: Aushangeschild eines Schulmeisters. Ein Schulmeister und seine bringen drei Knaben und einem Madchen das Lesen bei. 1516.*); Peter Newark's Western Americana & Historical Pictures, Bath, England, Fig. 14.12; Photographies Giraudon, Paris, France, Fig. 11.3 (LA 98.474 Lucas Cranach dit l'Ancien; Portrait de Luther; Nuremburg, Germanisches Museum); Picturepoint Ltd London, Fig. 12.6 (Neg. no. 019228); The Pilgrim Society, Plymouth, Ma, USA, Fig. 14.6; SCALA, Florence, Italy, Fig. 8.4a (Neg. no. K 84223. S. Botticelli: *Adorazione dei magi.* (Firenze, Gall. degli Uffizi 13×18); Smithsonian Institution: National Anthropological Archives, Washington DC, USA, Fig. 14.9 *Geronimo* (Apache [Chiricahua]. Photograph by A. Frank Randall, 1886. Neg. no. 2508); Stadt-Und Universitatsbibliothek Bern, Switzerland, Fig. 11.2 (woodcut by Hans Rudolf Manuel, c. 1550); Topkapi Saray Museusi, Istanbul, Turkey, Figs. 6.3–6.5, 6.8–9, from *Siyar-i Nabi*, H 1221 f 214, H1222 f 30, H 1222 f 158, H 1223 f 409 (TSM Library); Victoria & Albert Museum, London, Figs. 1.17, 4.14 (lower right), 4.18–19, 5.8, 6.21, 12.7, 12.19, 12.21; The Walters Art Gallery, Baltimore, USA Fig. 1.12 (Eagle-shaped fibula; Visigothic, Spain; second half of the sixth century AD).

The following photographs were supplied by the authors: 1.4, 2.9, 2.10, 2.12, 3.12, 3.17, 3.20, 4.11, 6.18, 6.20, 7.13, 11.10, 12.12, 12.15.

Index

Aachen 40
Abbasid caliphs 105, 106–107
Abu Bakr 100, 104
Act of Supremacy 187, 188
Aidan, St 26, 28
Ajanta caves 15, 16
Akbar the Great 108, 207,
    210–213
Alaric 11
Alcuin 27, 39, 40–41
Alfred, King 21, 29, 32, 62
Alhambra 109
Allah 96–104, 114
Angles, Saxons and Jutes 19
An Lu Shan 66
Anne, Queen 230, 231
Anne of Cleves 190
Arabian Nights, The 110
Arabian peninsula 95–96, 100
Armada, Spanish 213–215,
    235
Arthur, King 20
Aryabhata 15
Ashikaga shoguns 87–88
Atahualpa 173, 174–175
Augustine, St 26, 27
Aztecs 162–170, 176–177

Baghdad 107, 108–109, 111
Balboa 154
barbarians 4–11, 17–18, 36
Barents, Willem 158–159
Basho 93
Bayeux Tapestry 35
Bede 27
Bedouins 95–96

Beowulf 27
Bernard of Clairvaux 123
Bill of Rights 230
Black Death 53–55
Black Stone 96
Boleyn, Anne 186, 188, 190
Book of Kells 31
Botticelli, Alessandro 133
Brunel, Oliver 158
Buddhism 80
Bushido 83
Byzantine empire 11–13, 108,
    114–115

Cabot, John 156
caliphs 104–108
Calvin, John 182
Canute, King 33
Cartier, Jacques 156, 246
castles 45, 46–47, 48–49,
    55–57, 122
Catherine of Aragon 186, 190
Cavaliers 220
Caxton, William 135
Cecil, William 197
Cellini, Benvenuto 137
Chancellor, Richard 158, 206
Chandragupta 13–14
Chandragupta II 14
Changan 64
Chao Kuang 67
Charlemagne 36–41, 62, 107,
    114, 144
Charles I, King 218–222, 223
Charles II, King 223, 228–229,
    230

Charles V, Emperor 182, 186
children's crusade 126
chinampas 169–170
chronicles 128
Church of the Holy
    Sepulchre 114, 119, 121
Chu Yuan Chang 75
Civil War, English 221–222
Clement VIII, Pope 186
Clermont 113, 115
Clovis 11, 36–37, 38
codices 176
Colet, John 137–138
Colomba, St 26
Columbus, Christopher 144,
    149–153
Confucius 63–64, 68
conquistadors 162
Constantine 4
Constantinople 4, 11–13, 104,
    108, 117, 118–119, 126, 127,
    146
Copernicus, Nicholas 139
Cortes, Hernando 164–169
Cosimo de Medici 132
counter-reformation 183–185
Cranmer, Thomas 186
Cromwell, Oliver 221–222,
    224
Cuzco 172

da Gama, Vasco 147–148
daimyo 81, 87
Damascus 104, 105, 124
Danelaw 32, 33
Dark Ages 36, 130

da Vinci, Leonardo 137
de Champlain, Samuel 246
Diamond Sutra 68
Diaz, Bartholomew 147, 150
Dona Marina 164–165
Drake, Francis 207–208, 235
Dudley, Robert 197, 209

East India Company 207
Edo 87
Edward (the Confessor),
    King 33
Edward VI, King 191, 192, 201
Elizabeth I, Queen 193,
    194–198, 200, 235

Fa Hsien 16–17
Fawkes, Guy 217
Ferdinand, King and Isabella,
    Queen 149, 183
feudal system
    in Europe 41–42;
    in Japan 81
Ficino, Marsilio 136–137
first crusade 118–122
Fitch, Ralph 207
Florence 130–134, 138,
    139–141
fourth crusade 126
Franks 36
Frobisher, Martin 156–157, 206
Fujiwara 84–85

Galilei, Galileo 139
Genghis Khan 72, 145
Germans 1–2, 5–6
Geronimo 246
Gilbert, Sir Humphrey 235
Globe theatre 209
Go-Daigo 87
Grand Canal 61
Grand Remonstrance 220
Great Fire 27–228, 233
Gupta empire 1, 13–17, 65
Gutenberg, Johann 135
Guthrum 32

Hadrian's Wall 3
Harun Al Rashid 107, 114
Hegira 100
Henry VIII, King 186–188,
    190, 192, 193

Henry the Navigator,
    Prince 147
Holy Land 114, 119
Huayna Ccapac 173
Hudson, Henry 157
Huguenots 183
Hung Wu 75
Huns 1, 2, 5, 10, 13, 17–18

illuminated manuscripts 30,
    135
Incas 162–163, 170–175
Indians, American 237,
    238–239, 241, 243, 245,
    248–251
indulgences 178–179
Inquisition 184
Islam 101–111, 114, 212

James I, King 216–217, 236
James II, King 229
Jamestown 237–239, 248
Jerusalem 114, 117, 119, 124
Jesuits 185–186
Justinian 11–12

Kaaba 96, 97, 100, 102
Kaifeng 68
Kalidasa 15
Kin Tartars 68
knights 117–118, 128
Knights Hospitaller 121, 122
Knights Templar 121, 122
Knox, John 182
Koran 101, 102, 106, 110
Krak des Chevaliers 122, 123,
    127
Kublai Khan 72, 75, 85, 86
Kumaragupta 16

Lindisfarne 26, 28, 29, 30
Li Po 65, 66
Li Shih Min 61
London 203–204, 220,
    225–228, 233
Lorenzo the Magnificent 134
Loyola, Ignatius 185
Luther, Martin 180–183, 189

Machu Picchu 175
mandarins 60
Manutius, Aldus 135

Marco Polo 73, 145, 146
Martel, Charles 38, 105
Mary, Queen 191–194
Mary, Queen of Scots 197,
    202, 216
Maximian 4
Mayflower 240–243
Mecca 95, 97–103
Medici familiy 130, 132–134
Medina 100
Michelangelo 141
Ming dynasty 74–75
Mohammed 97–101, 114
Mona Lisa 132
monasteries 26–28, 50, 187–189
Mongols 1, 13, 60, 71–73, 85
Mongol Scroll 85
Montezuma 164–169
mosques 101–103, 110, 114
Muawiya 104
muezzin 101
Mughal dynasty 210–213
Muromachi period 87–88

ninety-five theses 181, 182–183
Northumberland, Duke of 191

Ostrogoths 11
Ottoman Turks 108, 146
Outremer 120, 124

Palestine 114, 119
Parr, Catherine 191
Patrick, St 26
Paul III, Pope 183
Penn, William 243
Pennsylvania 243
Pepys, Samuel 231
Perry, Matthew 92
Peter the Hermit 117
Petition of Rights 219
Phillip II, King 213
Pilgrim Fathers 239–243
Pilgrims 50, 114, 178
Pillow Sketches 94
Pizarro, Francisco 170–175
Plague 225–226
Pocohontas 238, 249, 250
Prester John 147
printing 68, 69, 134–135
Puritans 202, 209, 217,
    224–224, 239

Quakers   243
Quetzalcoatl   165–166
quipu   173
Quryash   99

Raleigh, Sir Walter   236, 237
Ramadan   102
Razi   110–111
Restoration   223
Richard I, King   124–126
Rolfe, John   238, 249, 250
Roman empire   1–4
Roundheads   220, 221

Saladin   124–126
Samudragupta   14
samurai   81–83, 90, 91
Santa Sophia   12, 13, 127
Saracens   114, 128, 129
Savonarola   139–140
second crusade   122–124
Seljuk Turks   108, 114–115,
   144
Seneca   4
Seymour, Jane   190
Shakespeare, William   209
Shinto   79
shoguns   85
Shotoku, Prince   80, 81
Skandagupta   16

Smith, Captain John   238, 245,
   250
Somerset, Duke of   191
Stephen of Cloyes   126
Sui dynasty   61
Sung dynasty   67–71

Tacitus   5
Tai Tsung   64
Taj Mahal   108
Tang dynasty   62–67
Tenochtitlan   165, 166–170
Tetzel   181
Texcoco, Lake   171
Tezcatlipoca   165–166, 169
Theodore of Tarsus   27
third crusade   124–126
Tokugawa Ieyasu   91
Tokugawa shoguns   91
Toltecs   165
Tower of London   194, 196
*Travels of Marco Polo,
   The*   73, 75, 145, 149
Tudor dynasty   190–210
Tu Fu   65, 66

uji   78
Umayyad caliphs   104–106
Urban II, Pope   113, 115

Vandals   10
Verranzano, Giovanni   156
Vespucci, Amerigo   151
Vikings   31–32
Virginia   236–239, 245
Vortigern   20

Wars of the Roses   190
William and Mary, King and
   Queen   229–230
William of Normandy   34–35
Willoughby, Sir Hugh   158, 206
Witan   23
Witches   202–203
Woden   22
Wolsey, Cardinal   186
Wu Chao   65

Xavier, Francis   91

Yamato   78, 79
Yang Chien   61
Yang Ti   61
Yathrib   100
Yoritomo   86

Zenghi   122–123, 124